Survival Communications
in Rhode Island

John E. Parnell, KK4HWK

ISBN978-1475191288

Cover design by:
Lynda Colón
FREELANCE GRAPHIC DESIGN &
MARKETING COMMUNICATIONS
www.hirelynda.webs.com

Titles available in this series:

Survival Communications in Alabama
Survival Communications in Alaska
Survival Communications in Arizona
Survival Communications in Arkansas
Survival Communications in California
Survival Communications in Colorado
Survival Communications in Connecticut
Survival Communications in Delaware
Survival Communications in Florida
Survival Communications in Georgia
Survival Communications in Hawaii
Survival Communications in Idaho
Survival Communications in Illinois
Survival Communications in Indiana
Survival Communications in Iowa
Survival Communications in Kansas
Survival Communications in Kentucky
Survival Communications in Louisiana
Survival Communications in Maine
Survival Communications in Maryland
Survival Communications in Massachusetts
Survival Communications in Michigan
Survival Communications in Minnesota
Survival Communications in Mississippi
Survival Communications in Missouri

Survival Communications in Montana
Survival Communications in Nebraska
Survival Communications in Nevada
Survival Communications in New Hampshire
Survival Communications in New Jersey
Survival Communications in New Mexico
Survival Communications in New York
Survival Communications in North Carolina
Survival Communications in North Dakota
Survival Communications in Ohio
Survival Communications in Oklahoma
Survival Communications in Oregon
Survival Communications in Pennsylvania
Survival Communications in Rhode Island
Survival Communications in South Carolina
Survival Communications in South Dakota
Survival Communications in Tennessee
Survival Communications in Texas
Survival Communications in Utah
Survival Communications in Vermont
Survival Communications in Virginia
Survival Communications in Washington
Survival Communications in West Virginia
Survival Communications in Wisconsin
Survival Communications in Wyoming

The above titles are available from your favorite online or brick-and-mortar bookstore or directly from the publisher at Tutor Turtle Press LLC, 1027 S. Pendleton St. – Suite B-10, Easley, SC 29642.

TABLE OF CONTENTS

Appendix A – Rhode Island Ham Radio Clubs

ARRL Affiliated Amateur and Ham Radio Clubs – By City

Appendix B – Rhode Island Ham Licensees by City

Survival Communications in Rhode Island

Perhaps you have prepared for WTSHTF or TEOTWAWKI with respect to food, water, self-defense and shelter. But what about communication?

Whenever there is a disaster (hurricane, earthquake, economic collapse, nuclear war, EMF, solar eruption, etc.), the normal means of communication that we're all reliant upon (cell phone, land line phone, the Internet, etc.) will probably be, at best, sporadic and at worst, non-existent.

As this author sees it, short of smoke signals and mirrors, there are three options for communication in "trying times": (1) GMRS or FRS radios; (2) CB radios; and (3) ham or amateur radio. Let's consider each of these options to come up with the most acceptable one.

GMRS (General Mobile Radio Service) / FRS (Family Radio Service)

GMRS (General Mobile Radio Service) / FRS (Family Radio Service) radios work optimally over short distances where there is minimal interference. Originally designed to be used as pagers, particularly inside a building or other such confined area, these radios are low-cost and convenient to carry. Unfortunately their small size and light weight comes with a trade-off – short range and short battery life. These radios are supposed to be able to communicate for up to 25-30 miles. Right. That's on level terrain, without buildings or trees getting in the way. While battery life technology is constantly improving, you will need spare batteries to keep communicating or someway of recharging the ones in the radio. In this author's opinion, GMRS/FRS radios are not first choice when concerned with medium or long range communication.

CB (Citizens Band)

CB (Citizens Band) radios operate in a frequency range originally reserved for ham or amateur radio operation. Because of the overwhelming number of people wishing quick, low-cost, regulation-free communication, the FCC (Federal Communication Commission) split off a portion of the frequency spectrum and allowed anyone to purchase a CB radio and start communicating. No test. No license. Just personal/business communication. Today, CB radios are readily available in such outlets as eBay and Craigslist. This author has seen them at yard/garage/tag sales and at flea markets.

CB radios come in a variety of "flavors." Fixed units, sometimes referred to as base units are intended for home use. For the most part, they derive their power from the utility company. In the event of loss of electricity, most base units can also be connected to a 12-volt battery, like that in your car/truck. If you choose to obtain a fixed unit, make sure you know how to connect the unit to the battery – ahead of time. Trying to figure this out when you're under extra stress is not a good situation.

A second type of CB radio is designed to be mobile, that is, installed in your car/truck. It gets its power from the vehicle's battery. You can either attach an antenna permanently to the vehicle or have a removable, magnetic type antenna.

The third type of CB radio is designed for handheld use. They are small and light. Most weigh less than a pound and operate on batteries. Yes, using batteries in a CB poses the same limitations as those by the GMRS/FRS radios, but have the added advantage that most handheld units come with a cigarette lighter adapter. Comes in handy when you are on the move and wish to be able to communicate both from a vehicle and also when you have to abandon it.

While they have a greater range than GMRS/FRS radios, CB radios are, legally, limited to operate on 40 channels, with a power rating of four (4) watts or less. Yes, it is possible to alter CB radios to get around these limitations, but not legally,

Ham/Amateur Radio

Ham/Amateur radio is very appealing. With a ham radio, you are not limited to less than 50 miles, but can communicate with anyone in the world (who also has access to a ham radio, of course).

Standardized Amateur Radio Prepper Communications Plan

In the event of a nationwide catastrophic disaster, the nationwide network of Amateur Radio licensed preppers will need a set of standardized meeting frequencies to share information and coordinate activities between various prepper groups. This Standardized Amateur Radio Communications Plan establishes a set of frequencies on the 80 meter, 40 meter, 20 meter, and 2 meter Amateur Radio bands for use during these types of catastrophic disasters.

Routine nets will not be held on all of these frequencies, but preppers are encouraged to use them when coordinating with other preppers on a routine basis. Routine nets may be conducted by The American Preparedness Radio Net (TAPRN) on these or other frequencies as they see fit. However, TAPRN will promote the use of these standardized frequencies by all Amateur Radio licensed preppers during times of catastrophic disaster. The promotion of this Standardized Amateur Radio Communications Plan is encouraged by all means within the prepper community, including via Amateur Radio, Twitter, Facebook, and various blogs.

Standardized Frequencies and Modes
80 Meters – 3.818 MHz LSB (TAPRN Net: Sundays at 9 PM ET) 40 Meters – 7.242 MHz LSB 40 Meters Morse Code / Digital – 7.073 MHz USB (TAPRN: Sundays at 7:30 PM ET on CONTESTIA 4/250) 20 Meters – 14.242 MHz USB 2 Meters – 146.420 MHz FM

Nets and Network Etiquette

In times of nationwide catastrophic disaster, the ability of any one prepper to initiate and sustain themselves as a net control may be limited by the availability of power and other resource shortages. However, all licensed preppers are encouraged to maintain a listening watch on these frequencies as often as possible during a catastrophic disaster. Preppers may routinely announce themselves in the following manner:

• This is [Your Callsign Phonetically] in [Your State], maintaining a listening watch on [Standard Frequency] for any preppers on frequency seeking information or looking to provide information. Please call [Your Callsign Phonetically]. Preppers exchanging information that may require follow up should agree upon a designated time to return to the frequency and provide further information. If other stations are utilizing the frequency at the designated time you return, maintain watch and proceed with your communications when those stations are finished. If your communications are urgent and the stations on frequency are not passing information of a critical nature, interrupt with the word "Break" and request use of the frequency.

For More Information

Catastrophe Network: http://www.catastrophenetwork.org or @CatastropheNet on Twitter The American Preparedness Radio Network: http://www.taprn.com or @TAPRN on Twitter

© 2011 Catastrophe Network, Please Distribute Freely

In order to use a ham radio, legally, one must be licensed to do so by the FCC (other countries have analogous governmental bodies to regulate ham radio). To obtain a license is quite easy – take a test and pay your license fee. There are currently three classes of license – Technician, General, and Amateur Extra. With each of these licenses come specific abilities.

Technician class is the beginning level. The exam consists of 35 multiple choice questions randomly drawn from a pool of 395 questions. The question pool is readily available online for free downloading (http://www.ncvec.org/downloads/Revised%20Element%202.Pdf) or in such publications at *Ham Radio License Manual Revised 2nd Edition* (ISBN 978-0-87259-097-7). The current Technician pool of questions is to be used from July 1, 2010 to June 30, 2014. Be sure the question pool you are studying from is current. You will need to score at least 26 correct to pass. (Do not worry, Morse Code is no longer on the test, although many ham operators use it anyway.) You do not need to take a formal class in order to qualify to take the exam. You can learn the material on your own. Most people spend 10-15 hours studying and then successfully take the exam. The cost of taking the exam is under $20. The exam is given in MANY locations throughout the US. Usually the exam is given by area ham clubs. You do not have to belong to the club to take the exam. Check Appendix A for a listing of clubs in Rhode Island.

Topics for the Technician License in Amateur Radio

The Technician license exam covers such topics as basic regulations, operating practices, and electronic theory, with a focus on VHF and UHF applications. Below is the syllabus for the Technician Class.

Subelement T1 – FCC Rules, descriptions and definitions for the amateur radio service, operator and station license responsibilities

[6 Exam Questions – 6 Groups]

T1A – Amateur Radio services; purpose of the amateur service, amateur-satellite service, operator/primary station license grant, where FCC rules are codified, basis and purpose of FCC rules, meanings of basic terms used in FCC rules

T1B – Authorized frequencies; frequency allocations, ITU regions, emission type, restricted sub-bands, spectrum sharing, transmissions near band edges

T1C – Operator classes and station call signs; operator classes, sequential, special event, and vanity call sign systems, international communications, reciprocal operation, station license licensee, places where the amateur service is regulated by the FCC, name and address on ULS, license term, renewal, grace period

T1D – Authorized and prohibited transmissions

T1E – Control operator and control types; control operator required, eligibility, designation of control operator, privileges and duties, control point, local, automatic and remote control, location of control operator

T1F – Station identification and operation standards; special operations for repeaters and auxiliary stations, third party communications, club stations, station security, FCC inspection

---

Subelement T2 – Operating Procedures

[3 Exam Questions – 3 Groups]

T2A – Station operation; choosing an operating frequency, calling another station, test transmissions, use of minimum power, frequency use, band plans

T2B – VHF/UHF operating practices; SSB phone, FM repeater, simplex, frequency offsets, splits and shifts, CTCSS, DTMF, tone squelch, carrier squelch, phonetics

T2C – Public service; emergency and non-emergency operations, message traffic handling

---

Subelement T3 – Radio wave characteristics, radio and electromagnetic properties, propagation modes

[3 Exam Questions – 3 Groups]

T3A – Radio wave characteristics; how a radio signal travels; distinctions of HF, VHF and UHF; fading, multipath; wavelength vs. penetration; antenna orientation

T3B – Radio and electromagnetic wave properties; the electromagnetic spectrum, wavelength vs. frequency, velocity of electromagnetic waves

T3C – Propagation modes; line of sight, sporadic E, meteor, aurora scatter, tropospheric ducting, F layer skip, radio horizon

Subelement T4 - Amateur radio practices and station setup

[2 Exam Questions – 2 Groups]

T4A – Station setup; microphone, speaker, headphones, filters, power source, connecting a computer, RF grounding

T4B – Operating controls; tuning, use of filters, squelch, AGC, repeater offset, memory channels

Subelement T5 – Electrical principles, math for electronics, electronic principles, Ohm's Law

[4 Exam Questions – 4 Groups]

T5A – Electrical principles; current and voltage, conductors and insulators, alternating and direct current

T5B – Math for electronics; decibels, electronic units and the metric system

T5C – Electronic principles; capacitance, inductance, current flow in circuits, alternating current, definition of RF, power calculations

T5D – Ohm's Law

Subelement T6 – Electrical components, semiconductors, circuit diagrams, component functions

[4 Exam Groups – 4 Questions]

T6A – Electrical components; fixed and variable resistors, capacitors, and inductors; fuses, switches, batteries

T6B – Semiconductors; basic principles of diodes and transistors

T6C – Circuit diagrams; schematic symbols

T6D – Component functions

Subelement T7 – Station equipment, common transmitter and receiver problems, antenna measurements and troubleshooting, basic repair and testing

[4 Exam Questions – 4 Groups]

T7A – Station radios; receivers, transmitters, transceivers

T7B – Common transmitter and receiver problems; symptoms of overload and overdrive, distortion, interference, over and under modulation, RF feedback, off frequency signals; fading and noise; problems with digital communications interfaces

T7C – Antenna measurements and troubleshooting; measuring SWR, dummy loads, feedline failure modes

T7D – Basic repair and testing; soldering, use of a voltmeter, ammeter, and ohmmeter

Subelement T8 – Modulation modes, amateur satellite operation, operating activities, non-voice communications

[4 Exam Questions – 4 Groups]

T8A – Modulation modes; bandwidth of various signals

T8B – Amateur satellite operation; Doppler shift, basic orbits, operating protocols

T8C – Operating activities; radio direction finding, radio control, contests, special event stations, basic linking over Internet

T8D – Non-voice communications; image data, digital modes, CW, packet, PSK31

Subelement T9 – Antennas, feedlines

[2 Exam Groups – 2 Questions]

T9A – Antennas; vertical and horizontal, concept of gain, common portable and mobile antennas, relationships between antenna length and frequency

T9B – Feedlines; types, losses vs. frequency, SWR concepts, matching, weather protection, connectors

Subelement T0 – AC power circuits, antenna installation, RF hazards

[3 Exam Questions – 3 Groups]

T0A – AC power circuits; hazardous voltages, fuses and circuit breakers, grounding, lightning protection, battery safety, electrical code compliance

T0B – Antenna installation; tower safety, overhead power lines

T0C – RF hazards; radiation exposure, proximity to antennas, recognized safe power levels, exposure to others

Once your name and call sign are available in the FCC database, you have the privilege of operating on all VHF (2 m) and UHF (70 cm) frequencies above 30 megahertz (MHz) and HF frequencies 80, 40, and 15 meter, and on the 10 meter band using Morse code (CW), voice, and digital mode. For a Technician license in Rhode Island, your call sign will consist of a two-letter prefix beginning with K or W, the number one (1), and a three-letter suffix. The single digit number in the call sign is determined according to which area of the US you obtain your first license. Even though you may move to another state, you keep this number in your call sign. This is also true should you upgrade to a higher license and get a new call sign. The numeral portion of your call sign stays the same.

Call Sign Numbers

Below is a chart showing the various numbers and the state(s) in which you would obtain the number.

Call Sign Number	State(s)
0	CO, IA, KS, MN, MO, NE, ND, SD
1	CT, ME, MA, NH, RI, VT
2	NJ, NY
3	DE, DC, MD, PA
4	AL, FL, GA, KY, NC, SC, TN, VA
5	AR, LA, MS, NM, OK, TX
6	CA
7	AZ, ID, MT, NV, OR, WA, UT, WY
8	MI, OH, WV
9	IL, IN, WI

Residents of Alaska may have any of the following call sign prefixes assigned to them: AL0-7, KL0-7, NL0-7, or WL0-7. Likewise, residents of Hawaii may have the prefix AH6-7, KH6-7, NH6-7, or WH6-7 assigned.

Once you obtain your Technician license, do not stop there. Go and get your General license.

General is the second of three ham license classes. Like the Technician license, to get a General license, you merely have to take a 35-question multiple choice exam and pay your license fee. Passing is still at least 26 correct answers and the fee is the same (less than $20). Again the question pool is available for free online (http://www.ncvec.org/page.php?id=358). It is also available in such print publications as *The ARRL General Class License Manual 7th Edition* (ISBN 978-0-87259-811-9). The current General pool of questions is to be used from July 1, 2011 to June 30, 2015. Be sure the question pool you are using is current. Being a bit more comprehensive than the Technician license, the General license usually requires 15-20 hours of study to learn the material. Check Appendix A for a listing of clubs in Rhode Island where you might take your exam. Once your name and NEW call sign is listed in the FCC database, you're good to go. For a General license in Rhode Island, your call sign will consist of a one-letter prefix beginning with K, N or W, the number one (1), and a three-letter suffix.

Topics for the General License in Amateur Radio

The General license exam covers regulations, operating practices and electronic theory. Below is the syllabus for the General Class.

Subelement G1 – Commission's Rules

(5 Exam Questions – 5 Groups)
G1A – General Class control operator frequency privileges; primary and secondary allocations
G1B – Antenna structure limitations; good engineering and good amateur practice, beacon operation; restricted operation; retransmitting radio signals
G1C – Transmitter power regulations; data emission standards
G1D – Volunteer Examiners and Volunteer Examiner Coordinators; temporary identification
G1E – Control categories; repeater regulations; harmful interference; third party rules; ITU regions

---

Subelement G2 – Operating procedures

(5 Exam Questions – 5 Groups)
G2A – Phone operating procedures; USB/LSB utilization conventions; procedural signals; breaking into a OSO in progress; VOX operation
G2B – Operating courtesy; band plans, emergencies, including drills and emergency communications
G2C – CW operating procedures and procedural signals; Q signals and common abbreviations; full break in

G2D – Amateur Auxiliary; minimizing interference; HF operations

G2E – Digital operating; procedures, procedural signals and common abbreviations

Subelement G3 – Radio wave propagation

(3 Exam Questions – 3 Groups)

G3A – Sunspots and solar radiation; ionospheric disturbances; propagation forecasting and indices

G3B – Maximum Usable Frequency; Lowest Usable Frequency; propagation

G3C – Ionospheric layers; critical angle and frequency; HF scatter; Near Vertical Incidence Sky waves

Subelement G4 – Amateur radio practices

(5 Exam Questions – 5 Groups)

G4A – Station Operation and setup

G4B – Test and monitoring equipment; two-tone test

G4C – Interference with consumer electronics; grounding; DSP

G4D – Speech processors; S meters; sideband operation near band edges

G4E – HF mobile radio installations; emergency and battery powered operation

Subelement G5 – Electrical principles

(3 Exam Questions – 3 Groups)

G5A – Reactance; inductance; capacitance; impedance; impedance matching

G5B – The Decibel; current and voltage dividers; electrical power calculations; sine wave root-mean-square (RMS) values; PEP calculations

G5C – Resistors; capacitors and inductors in series and parallel; transformers

Subelement G6 – Circuit components

(3 Exam Questions – 3 Groups)

G6A – Resistors; capacitors; inductors

G6B – Rectifiers; solid state diodes and transistors; vacuum tubes; batteries

G6C – Analog and digital integrated circuits (ICs); microprocessors; memory; I/O devices; microwave ICs (MMICs); display devices

Subelement G7 – Practical circuits

(3 Exam Questions – 3 Groups)

G7A – Power supplies; schematic symbols

G7B – Digital circuits; amplifiers and oscillators

G7C – Receivers and transmitters; filters, oscillators

Subelement G8 – Signals and emissions

(2 Exam Questions – 2 Groups)

> G8A – Carriers and modulation; AM; FM; single and double sideband; modulation envelope; overmodulation
>
> G8B – Frequency mixing; multiplication; HF data communications; bandwidths of various modes; deviation

Subelement G9 – Antennas and feed lines

(4 Exam Questions – 4 Groups)

G9A – Antenna feed lines; characteristic impedance and attenuation; SWR calculation, measurement and effects; matching networks

G9B – Basic antennas

G9C – Directional antennas

G9D – Specialized antennas

Subelement G0 – Electrical and RF safety

(2 Exam Questions – 2 Groups)

G0A – RF safety principles, rules and guidelines; routine station elevation

G0B – Safety in the ham shack; electrical shock and treatment, safety grounding, fusing, interlocks, wiring, antenna and tower safety

With a General license, you can use all VHF and UHF frequencies and most of the HF frequencies. You would have access to the 160, 30, 17, 12, and 10 meter bands and access to major parts of the 80, 40, 20, and 15 meter bands. Of course, this is in addition to all bands available to Technician license holders.

Amateur Extra is the third of three ham license classes. Like the Technician and General classes, you merely have to pass a test and pay your fee to get your Amateur Extra license. This class of license is more comprehensive than the lower license classes. The exam is longer – 50 questions – and the minimum passing score is higher – 37. However, once you get your Amateur Extra license, all ham frequencies, VHF, UHF and HF are available for your enjoyment. The Extra exam covers regulations, specialized operating practices, advanced electronics theory, and radio equipment design.

Like for the other license classes, the question pool for the Amateur Extra license is available online for downloading (http://www.ncvec.org/downloads/REVISED%202012-2016%20Extra%20Class%20Pool.doc). It is also available in print form in such publications as *The ARRL Extra Class License Manual Revised 9th Edition* (ISBN 978-0-87259-887-4).

Topics for the Extra License in Amateur Radio

Below is the syllabus for the Amateur Extra Class for July 1, 2012 to June 30, 2016.

Subelement E1 – Commission's Rules

[6 Exam Questions – 6 Groups]

E1A – Operating Standards: frequency privileges; emission standards; automatic message forwarding; frequency sharing; stations aboard ships or aircraft

E1B – Station restrictions and special operations: restrictions on station location; general operating restrictions, spurious emissions, control operator reimbursement; antenna structure restrictions; RACES operations

E1C – Station control: definitions and restrictions pertaining to local, automatic and remote control operation; control operator responsibilities for remote and automatically controlled stations

E1D – Amateur Satellite service: definitions and purpose; license requirements for space stations; available frequencies and bands; telecommand and telemetry operations; restrictions, and special provisions; notification requirements

E1E – Volunteer examiner program: definitions, qualifications, preparation and administration of exams; accreditation; question pools; documentation requirements

E1F – Miscellaneous rules: external RF power amplifiers; national quiet zone; business communications; compensated communications; spread spectrum; auxiliary stations; reciprocal operating privileges; IARP and CEPT licenses; third party communications with foreign countries; special temporary authority

Subelement E2 – Operating procedures

[5 Exam Questions – 5 Groups]

E2A – Amateur radio in space: amateur satellites; orbital mechanics; frequencies and modes; satellite hardware; satellite operations

E2B – Television practices: fast scan television standards and techniques; slow scan television standards and techniques

E2C – Operating methods: contest and DX operating; spread-spectrum transmissions; selecting an operating frequency

E2D – Operating methods: VHF and UHF digital modes; APRS

E2E – Operating methods: operating HF digital modes; error correction

Subelement E3 – Radio wave propagation

[3 Exam Questions – 3 Groups]

E3A – Propagation and technique, Earth-Moon-Earth communications; meteor scatter

E3B – Propagation and technique, trans-equatorial; long path; gray-line; multi-path propagation

E3C – Propagation and technique, Aurora propagation; selective fading; radio-path horizon; take-off angle over flat or sloping terrain; effects of ground on propagation; less common propagation modes

Subelement E4 – Amateur practices

[5 Exam Questions – 5 Groups]

E4A – Test equipment: analog and digital instruments; spectrum and network analyzers, antenna analyzers; oscilloscopes; testing transistors; RF measurements

E4B – Measurement technique and limitations: instrument accuracy and performance limitations; probes; techniques to minimize errors; measurement of "Q"; instrument calibration

E4C – Receiver performance characteristics, phase noise, capture effect, noise floor, image rejection, MDS, signal-to-noise-ratio; selectivity

E4D – Receiver performance characteristics, blocking dynamic range, intermodulation and cross-modulation interference; 3rd order intercept; desensitization; preselection

E4E – Noise suppression: system noise; electrical appliance noise; line noise; locating noise sources; DSP noise reduction; noise blankers

Subelement E5 – Electrical principles

[4 Exam Questions – 4 Groups]

E5A – Resonance and Q: characteristics of resonant circuits: series and parallel resonance; Q; half-power bandwidth; phase relationships in reactive circuits

E5B – Time constants and phase relationships: RLC time constants: definition; time constants in RL and RC circuits; phase angle between voltage and current; phase angles of series and parallel circuits

E5C – Impedance plots and coordinate systems: plotting impedances in polar coordinates; rectangular coordinates

E5D – AC and RF energy in real circuits: skin effect; electrostatic and electromagnetic fields; reactive power; power factor; coordinate systems

Subelement E6 – Circuit components

[6 Exam Questions – 6 Groups]

E6A – Semiconductor materials and devices: semiconductor materials germanium, silicon, P-type, N-type; transistor types: NPN, PNP, junction, field-effect transistors: enhancement mode; depletion mode; MOS; CMOS; N-channel; P-channel

E6B – Semiconductor diodes

E6C – Integrated circuits: TTL digital integrated circuits; CMOS digital integrated circuits; gates

E6D – Optical devices and toroids: cathode-ray tube devices; charge-coupled devices (CCDs); liquid crystal displays (LCDs); toroids: permeability, core material, selecting, winding

E6E – Piezoelectric crystals and MMICs: quartz crystals; crystal oscillators and filters; monolithic amplifiers

E6F – Optical components and power systems: photoconductive principles and effects, photovoltaic systems, optical couplers, optical sensors, and optoisolators

Subelement E7 – Practical circuits

[8 Exam Questions – 8 Groups]

E7A – Digital circuits: digital circuit principles and logic circuits: classes of logic elements; positive and negative logic; frequency dividers; truth tables

E7B – Amplifiers: Class of operation; vacuum tube and solid-state circuits; distortion and intermodulation; spurious and parasitic suppression; microwave amplifiers

E7C – Filters and matching networks: filters and impedance matching networks: types of networks; types of filters; filter applications; filter characteristics; impedance matching; DSP filtering

E7D – Power supplies and voltage regulators

E7E – Modulation and demodulation: reactance, phase and balanced modulators; detectors; mixer stages; DSP modulation and demodulation; software defined radio systems

E7F – Frequency markers and counters: frequency divider circuits; frequency marker generators; frequency counters

E7G – Active filters and op-amps: active audio filters; characteristics; basic circuit design; operational amplifiers

E7H – Oscillators and signal sources: types of oscillators; synthesizers and phase-locked loops; direct digital synthesizers

Subelement E8 – Signals and emissions

[4 Exam Questions – 4 Groups]

E8A – AC waveforms: sine, square, sawtooth and irregular waveforms; AC measurements; average and PEP of RF signals; pulse and digital signal waveforms

E8B – Modulation and demodulation: modulation methods; modulation index and deviation ratio; pulse modulation; frequency and time division multiplexing

E8C – Digital signals: digital communications modes; CW; information rate vs. bandwidth; spread-spectrum communications; modulation methods

E8D – Waves, measurements, and RF grounding: peak-to-peak values, polarization; RF grounding

Subelement E9 – Antennas and transmission lines

[8 Exam Questions – 8 Groups]

E9A – Isotropic and gain antennas: definition; used as a standard for comparison; radiation pattern; basic antenna parameters: radiation resistance and reactance, gain, beamwidth, efficiency

E9B – Antenna patterns: E and H plane patterns; gain as a function of pattern; antenna design; Yagi antennas

E9C – Wire and phased vertical antennas: beverage antennas; terminated and resonant rhombic antennas; elevation above real ground; ground effects as related to polarization; take-off angles

E9D – Directional antennas: gain; satellite antennas; antenna beamwidth; losses; SWR bandwidth; antenna efficiency; shortened and mobile antennas; grounding

E9E – Matching: matching antennas to feed lines; power dividers

E9F – Transmission lines: characteristics of open and shorted feed lines: 1/8 wavelength; 1/4 wavelength; 1/2 wavelength; feed lines: coax versus open-wire; velocity factor; electrical length; transformation characteristics of line terminated in impedance not equal to characteristic impedance

E9G – The Smith chart

E9H – Effective radiated power; system gains and losses; radio direction finding antennas

Subelement E0 – Safety

[1 exam question – 1 group]

E0A – Safety: amateur radio safety practices; RF radiation hazards; hazardous materials

Once your new call sign is listed in the FCC database, you are good to go. For an Amateur Extra license in Rhode Island, your call sign will consist of a prefix of K, N or W, the number one (1), and a two-letter suffix, or a two-letter prefix beginning with A, N, K or W, the number one (1), and a one-letter suffix, or a two-letter prefix beginning with A, the number one (1), and a two-letter suffix.

Ham radio equipment can be expensive or you can do it "on the cheap." The cost will run from a couple hundred dollars to well in the thousands, depending on what you have available. eBay, and Craigslist are good places to start looking. Most ham clubs do some sort of hamfest annually wherein club members or others are willing to part with older equipment. See Appendix A for a list of clubs in Rhode Island.

Another excellent source of equipment, as well as advice on setting the equipment up and how to use it properly, is current ham operators. In Appendix B, the author has listed all the FCC licensed ham operators in Rhode Island, listed by city, and then sorted by street and house number on the street. Who knows, maybe someone who lives close to you is a ham operator. Be a good neighbor, stop by and have a chat with him/her.

Like CB radios, ham radios come in three formats – base, mobile, and handheld. They can use the electric company for power, or operate off a car battery. In the opinion of this author, in spite of the slightly higher cost of the equipment and having to take a test to legally use the equipment, ham radio is the way to go when concerned about communication during times of crisis.

Canadian Call Sign Prefixes

Because of our proximity to Canada, many times ham contact is made with our northern neighbors. Below is a chart showing the origin of Canadian call sign prefixes.

Call Sign Prefix	Provence or Territory
CY0	Sable Island
CY9	St. Paul Island
VA1, VE1	New Brunswick, Nova Scotia
VA2, VE2	Quebec
VA3, VE3	Ontario
VA4, VE4	Manitoba
VA5, VE5	Saskatchewan
VA6, VE6	Alberta
VA7, VE7	British Columbia
VE8	North West Territories
VE9	New Brunswick
VO1	Newfoundland
VO2	Labrador
VY0	Nunavut
VY1	Yukon
VY2	Prince Edward Island

Common Radio Bands in the United States

Certain radio bands are more popular with ham radio enthusiasts than others. Below is a chart showing these bands and when they are most popular.

	Band (meter)	Frequency (MHz)	Use
HF	160	1.8 – 2.0	Night
	80	3.5 – 4.0	Night and Local Day
	40	7.0 – 7.3	Night and Local Day
	30	10.1 – 10.15	CW and Digital
	20	14.0 – 14.350	World Wide Day and Night
	17	18.068 – 18.168	World Wide Day and Night
	15	21.0 – 21.450	Primarily Daytime
	12	24.890 – 24.990	Primarily Daytime
	10	28.0 – 29.70	Daytime during Sunspot highs
VHF	6	50 – 54	Local to World Wide
	2	144 – 148	Local to Medium Distance
UHF	70 cm	430 – 440	Local

Common Amateur Radio Bands in Canada

160 Meter Band - Maximum bandwidth 6 kHz
1.800 - 1.820 MHz - CW
1.820 - 1.830 MHz - Digital Modes
1 830 - 1.840 MHz - DX Window
1.840 - 2.000 MHz - SSB and other wide band modes

80 Meter Band - Maximum bandwidth 6 kHz
3.500 - 3.580 MHz - CW
3.580 - 3.620 MHz - Digital Modes
3.620 - 3.635 MHz - Packet/Digital Secondary
3.635 - 3.725 MHz - CW
3.725 - 3.790 MHz - SSB and other side band modes*
3.790 - 3.800 MHz - SSB DX Window
3.800 - 4.000 MHz - SSB and other wide band modes

40 Meter Band - Maximum bandwidth 6 kHz
7.000 - 7.035 MHz - CW
7.035 - 7.050 MHz - Digital Modes
7.040 - 7.050 MHz - International packet
7.050 - 7.100 MHz - SSB
7.100 - 7.120 MHz - Packet within Region 2
7.120 - 7.150 MHz - CW
7.150 - 7.300 MHz - SSB and other wide band modes

30 Meter Band - Maximum bandwidth 1 kHz

10.100 - 10.130 MHz - CW only
10.130 - 10.140 MHz - Digital Modes
10.140 - 10.150 MHz - Packet

20 Meter Band - Maximum bandwidth 6 kHz

14.000 - 14.070 MHz - CW only
14.070 - 14.095 MHz - Digital Mode
14.095 - 14.099 MHz - Packet
14.100 MHz - Beacons
14.101 - 14.112 MHz - CW, SSB, packet shared
14.112 - 14.350 MHz - SSB
14.225 - 14.235 MHz - SSTV

17 Meter Band - Maximum bandwidth 6 kHz

18.068 - 18.100 MHz - CW
18.100 - 18.105 MHz - Digital Modes
18.105 - 18.110 MHz - Packet
18.110 - 18.168 MHz - SSB and other wide band modes

15 Meter Band - maximum bandwidth 6 kHz

21.000 - 21.070 MHz - CW
21.070 - 21.090 MHz - Digital Modes
21.090 - 21.125 MHz - Packet
21.100 - 21.150 MHz - CW and SSB
21.150 - 21.335 MHz - SSB and other wide band modes
21.335 - 21.345 MHz - SSTV
21.345 - 21.450 MHz - SSB and other wide band modes

12 Meter Band - Maximum bandwidth 6 kHz

24.890 - 24.930 MHz - CW
24.920 - 24.925 MHz - Digital Modes
24.925 - 24.930 MHz - Packet
24.930 - 24.990 MHz - SSB and other wide band modes

10 Meter Band - Maximum band width 20 kHz

28.000 - 28.200 MHz - CW
28.070 - 28.120 MHz - Digital Modes
28.120 - 28.190 MHz - Packet
28.190 - 28.200 MHz - Beacons
28.200 - 29.300 MHz - SSB and other wide band modes
29.300 - 29.510 MHz - Satellite
29.510 - 29.700 MHz - SSB, FM and repeaters

160 Meters (1.8-2.0 MHz)

1.800 - 2.000 CW
1.800 - 1.810 Digital Modes
1.810 CW QRP
1.843-2.000 SSB, SSTV and other wideband modes
1.910 SSB QRP
1.995 - 2.000 Experimental
1.999 - 2.000 Beacons

80 Meters (3.5-4.0 MHz)

3.590 RTTY/Data DX
3.570-3.600 RTTY/Data
3.790-3.800 DX window
3.845 SSTV
3.885 AM calling frequency

40 Meters (7.0-7.3 MHz)

7.040 RTTY/Data DX
7.080-7.125 RTTY/Data
7.171 SSTV
7.290 AM calling frequency

30 Meters (10.1-10.15 MHz)

10.130-10.140 RTTY
10.140-10.150 Packet

20 Meters (14.0-14.35 MHz)

14.070-14.095 RTTY
14.095-14.0995 Packet
14.100 NCDXF Beacons
14.1005-14.112 Packet
14.230 SSTV
14.286 AM calling frequency

17 Meters (18.068-18.168 MHz)

18.100-18.105 RTTY
18.105-18.110 Packet

15 Meters (21.0-21.45 MHz)

21.070-21.110 RTTY/Data
21.340 SSTV

12 Meters (24.89-24.99 MHz)

24.920-24.925 RTTY
24.925-24.930 Packet

10 Meters (28-29.7 MHz)

28.000-28.070 CW
28.070-28.150 RTTY
28.150-28.190 CW
28.200-28.300 Beacons
28.300-29.300 Phone
28.680 SSTV
29.000-29.200 AM
29.300-29.510 Satellite Downlinks
29.520-29.590 Repeater Inputs
29.600 FM Simplex
29.610-29.700 Repeater Outputs

6 Meters (50-54 MHz)

50.0-50.1 CW, beacons
50.060-50.080 beacon subband
50.1-50.3 SSB, CW
50.10-50.125 DX window
50.125 SSB calling
50.3-50.6 All modes
50.6-50.8 Nonvoice communications
50.62 Digital (packet) calling
50.8-51.0 Radio remote control (20-kHz channels)
51.0-51.1 Pacific DX window
51.12-51.48 Repeater inputs (19 channels)
51.12-51.18 Digital repeater inputs
51.5-51.6 Simplex (six channels)
51.62-51.98 Repeater outputs (19 channels)
51.62-51.68 Digital repeater outputs
52.0-52.48 Repeater inputs (except as noted; 23 channels)
52.02, 52.04 FM simplex
52.2 TEST PAIR (input)
52.5-52.98 Repeater output (except as noted; 23 channels)
52.525 Primary FM simplex
52.54 Secondary FM simplex
52.7 TEST PAIR (output)
53.0-53.48 Repeater inputs (except as noted; 19 channels)
53.0 Remote base FM simplex
53.02 Simplex
53.1, 53.2, 53.3, 53.4 Radio remote control
53.5-53.98 Repeater outputs (except as noted; 19 channels)
53.5, 53.6, 53.7, 53.8 Radio remote control
53.52, 53.9 Simplex

2 Meters (144-148 MHz)

144.00-144.05 EME (CW)
144.05-144.10 General CW and weak signals
144.10-144.20 EME and weak-signal SSB
144.200 National calling frequency
144.200-144.275 General SSB operation
144.275-144.300 Propagation beacons
144.30-144.50 New OSCAR subband
144.50-144.60 Linear translator inputs
144.60-144.90 FM repeater inputs
144.90-145.10 Weak signal and FM simplex (145.01,03,05,07,09 are widely used for packet)
145.10-145.20 Linear translator outputs
145.20-145.50 FM repeater outputs
145.50-145.80 Miscellaneous and experimental modes
145.80-146.00 OSCAR subband
146.01-146.37 Repeater inputs
146.40-146.58 Simplex
146.52 National Simplex Calling Frequency
146.61-146.97 Repeater outputs
147.00-147.39 Repeater outputs
147.42-147.57 Simplex
147.60-147.99 Repeater inputs

1.25 Meters (222-225 MHz)

222.0-222.150 Weak-signal modes
222.0-222.025 EME
222.05-222.06 Propagation beacons
222.1 SSB & CW calling frequency
222.10-222.15 Weak-signal CW & SSB
222.15-222.25 Local coordinator's option; weak signal, ACSB, repeater inputs, control
222.25-223.38 FM repeater inputs only
223.40-223.52 FM simplex
223.52-223.64 Digital, packet
223.64-223.70 Links, control
223.71-223.85 Local coordinator's option; FM simplex, packet, repeater outputs
223.85-224.98 Repeater outputs only

70 Centimeters (420-450 MHz)

420.00-426.00 ATV repeater or simplex with 421.25 MHz video carrier control links and experimental
426.00-432.00 ATV simplex with 427.250-MHz video carrier frequency
432.00-432.07 EME (Earth-Moon-Earth)
432.07-432.10 Weak-signal CW
432.10 70-cm calling frequency

432.10-432.30 Mixed-mode and weak-signal work
432.30-432.40 Propagation beacons
432.40-433.00 Mixed-mode and weak-signal work
433.00-435.00 Auxiliary/repeater links
435.00-438.00 Satellite only (internationally)
438.00-444.00 ATV repeater input with 439.250-MHz video carrier frequency and re-
    peater links
442.00-445.00 Repeater inputs and outputs (local option)
445.00-447.00 Shared by auxiliary and control links, repeaters and simplex (local option)
446.00 National simplex frequency
447.00-450.00 Repeater inputs and outputs (local option)

33 Centimeters (902-928 MHz)

902.0-903.0 Narrow-bandwidth, weak-signal communications
902.0-902.8 SSTV, FAX, ACSSB, experimental
902.1 Weak-signal calling frequency
902.8-903.0 Reserved for EME, CW expansion
903.1 Alternate calling frequency
903.0-906.0 Digital communications
906-909 FM repeater inputs
909-915 ATV
915-918 Digital communications
918-921 FM repeater outputs
921-927 ATV
927-928 FM simplex and links

23 Centimeters (1240-1300 MHz)

1240-1246 ATV #1
1246-1248 Narrow-bandwidth FM point-to-point links and digital, duplex with 1258-
    1260.
1248-1258 Digital Communications
1252-1258 ATV #2
1258-1260 Narrow-bandwidth FM point-to-point links digital, duplexed with 1246-1252
1260-1270 Satellite uplinks, reference WARC '79
1260-1270 Wide-bandwidth experimental, simplex ATV
1270-1276 Repeater inputs, FM and linear, paired with 1282-1288, 239 pairs every 25
    kHz, e.g. 1270.025, .050, etc.
1271-1283 Non-coordinated test pair
1276-1282 ATV #3
1282-1288 Repeater outputs, paired with 1270-1276
1288-1294 Wide-bandwidth experimental, simplex ATV
1294-1295 Narrow-bandwidth FM simplex services, 25-kHz channels
1294.5 National FM simplex calling frequency
1295-1297 Narrow bandwidth weak-signal communications (no FM)
1295.0-1295.8 SSTV, FAX, ACSSB, experimental
1295.8-1296.0 Reserved for EME, CW expansion

1296.00-1296.05 EME-exclusive
1296.07-1296.08 CW beacons
1296.1 CW, SSB calling frequency
1296.4-1296.6 Crossband linear translator input
1296.6-1296.8 Crossband linear translator output
1296.8-1297.0 Experimental beacons (exclusive)
1297-1300 Digital Communications

2300-2310 and 2390-2450 MHz

2300.0-2303.0 High-rate data
2303.0-2303.5 Packet
2303.5-2303.8 TTY packet
2303.9-2303.9 Packet, TTY, CW, EME
2303.9-2304.1 CW, EME
2304.1 Calling frequency
2304.1-2304.2 CW, EME, SSB
2304.2-2304.3 SSB, SSTV, FAX, Packet AM, Amtor
2304.30-2304.32 Propagation beacon network
2304.32-2304.40 General propagation beacons
2304.4-2304.5 SSB, SSTV, ACSSB, FAX, Packet AM, Amtor experimental
2304.5-2304.7 Crossband linear translator input
2304.7-2304.9 Crossband linear translator output
2304.9-2305.0 Experimental beacons
2305.0-2305.2 FM simplex (25 kHz spacing)
2305.20 FM simplex calling frequency
2305.2-2306.0 FM simplex (25 kHz spacing)
2306.0-2309.0 FM Repeaters (25 kHz) input
2309.0-2310.0 Control and auxiliary links
2390.0-2396.0 Fast-scan TV
2396.0-2399.0 High-rate data
2399.0-2399.5 Packet
2399.5-2400.0 Control and auxiliary links
2400.0-2403.0 Satellite
2403.0-2408.0 Satellite high-rate data
2408.0-2410.0 Satellite
2410.0-2413.0 FM repeaters (25 kHz) output
2413.0-2418.0 High-rate data
2418.0-2430.0 Fast-scan TV
2430.0-2433.0 Satellite
2433.0-2438.0 Satellite high-rate data
2438.0-2450.0 WB FM, FSTV, FMTV, SS experimental

3300-3500 MHz

3456.3-3456.4 Propagation beacons

5650-5925 MHz
5760.3-5760.4 Propagation beacons

10.00-10.50 GHz
10.368 Narrow band calling frequency 10.3683-10.3684 Propagation beacons
10.3640 Calling frequency

Now that you have your license (you do, don't you?), and your equipment, you are ready to go live. Below is a suggested start.

1) Assuming you have the HT set up to the appropriate frequency, and offset, press the mic button on the HT and say, "KK4HWX listening." Replace the KK4HWX with your own call sign, the one assigned to you by the FCC (it's the law). If no one responds to your call, you may wish to try again. Hopefully someone will respond to your call.

2) Once you get a response, it will be in the form of something like, "KK4HWX this is ??1??? in Eastport returning. My name is Florence. Back to you. ??1???" then a tone. Let us examine the response more closely. She first acknowledged your call sign (KK4HWX), then identified hers (??1???). From the 1 in her call sign, you know that she first got her license in Region 1, meaning she got it while a resident of CT, ME, MA, NH, RI, or VT. She then told you where she's transmitting from (Eastport). The term "returning" means that she is returning your call. Her name is Florence. The phrase, "Back to you" indicates that she is turning over the conversation to you. She then repeats her call sign. The tone indicates to you that it is okay to proceed with your response. BTW if she had used the term "Over" instead of "Back to you," it would mean the same thing, just fewer words.

3) At this point, press the mic button and continue with the conversation. You should restate your call sign often during the conversation (perhaps every 10 minutes or less and whenever you begin transmitting). Don't forget to say, "Over" or "Back to you" whenever you are giving Florence control of the conversation again.

4) When you are ready to stop the conversation, you should say goodbye or use the phrase "73", meaning "best wishes." Your conversation would end something like, "??1??? 73, this is KK4HWX clear and monitoring." The "clear and monitoring" indicates that you are going to continue to monitor the frequency. If you are not going to continue monitoring, you may wish to end the conversation with Florence with, "clear and QRT" instead. The QRT means that you are stopping transmissions.

Call Sign Phonics

Because of different accents of various people, sometimes it is difficult to understand call sign letters when spoken. For this reason, most ham operators verbalize their call sign using phonics. Below is a table listing the accepted phonics for letters and numbers.

A = ALFA
B = BRAVO
C = CHARLIE
D = DELTA
E = ECHO
F = FOXTROT
G = GOLF
H = HOTEL
I = INDIA
J = JULIETT
K = KILO
L = LIMA
M = MIKE
N = NOVEMBER
O = OSCAR
P = PAPA (PA-PA')
Q = QUEBEC (KAY-BEK')
R = ROMEO

S = SIERRA
T = TANGO
U = UNIFORM
V = VICTOR
W = WHISKEY
X = X-RAY
Y = YANKEE
Z = ZULU (ZED)
1 = ONE
2 = TWO
3 = THREE (TREE)
4 = FOUR
5 = FIVE (FIFE)
6 = SIX
7 = SEVEN
8 = EIGHT
9 = NINE (NINER)
0 = ZERO

The words in parentheses are the pronunciation or the alternate pronunciations for the words or numbers, but you will hear both used. With the letter Z, (ZED) is by far the most commonly used. With the number 9, NINER is the most common and easiest to understand ON THE AIR.

If you wish to use Morse code (CW) instead of voice communication, the "conversation" would follow the same steps, with a few modifications. To type out each word would require a lot of typing and translating. If you are like this author, more means more, i.e., more typing means more typos are likely. To help with this situation, CW enthusiasts have developed a language all their own – they use abbreviations for common phrases. Below is a chart showing some of these abbreviations.

Abbreviation	Use
AR	Over
de	From or "this is"
ES	And
GM	Good Morning
K	Go
KN	Go only
NM	Name
QTH	Location
RPT	Report
R	Roger
SK	Clear
tnx	Thanks
UR	Your, you are
73	Best Wishes

Morse Code and Amateur Radio

If you wish to use CW, but are concerned about accuracy, you might consider purchasing a Morse code translator. This is an electronic device that you place in front of your speakers. It takes the CW sounds and translates them into English and displays the transmission on an LCD display. For the reverse, you can pick up a CW keyboard. With the keyboard, you type in your message and it converts the text to Morse code. The translator does not need to be attached to your ham equipment, whereas the keyboard would.

For your convenience, below is a table showing the Morse code signals and their meaning.

Character	Code
A	· —
B	— · · ·
C	— · — ·
D	— · ·
E	·
F	· · — ·
G	— — ·
H	· · · ·
I	· ·
J	· — — —
K	— · —
L	· — · ·
M	— —
N	— ·
O	— — —
P	· — — ·
Q	— — · —
R	· — ·
S	· · ·
T	—
U	· · —
V	· · · —
W	· — —
X	— · · —
Y	— · — —
Z	— — · ·
0	— — — — —
1	· — — — —
2	· · — — —
3	· · · — —
4	· · · · —
5	· · · · ·

6	— · · · ·
7	— — · · ·
8	— — — · ·
9	— — — — ·
Ampersand [&], Wait	· — · · ·
Apostrophe [']	· — — — — ·
At sign [@]	· — — · — ·
Colon [:]	— — — · · ·
Comma [,]	— — · · — —
Dollar sign [$]	· · · — · · —
Double dash [=]	— · · · —
Exclamation mark [!]	— · — · — —
Hyphen, Minus [-]	— · · · · —
Parenthesis closed [)]	— · — — · —
Parenthesis open [(]	— · — — ·
Period [.]	· — · — · —
Plus [+]	· — · — ·
Question mark [?]	· · — — · ·
Quotation mark ["]	· — · · — ·
Semicolon [;]	— · — · — ·
Slash [/], Fraction bar	— · · — ·
Underscore [_]	· · — — · —

An advantage of using Morse Code is that when broadcasting CW, you are using reduced power, thereby saving your battery. Your battery is used only while actually transmitting or receiving.

International Call Sign Prefixes

As was stated earlier, all ham radio call signs begin with letters (or numbers) taken from blocks assigned to each country of the world by the *ITU - International Telecommunications Union,* a body controlled by the United Nations. The following chart indicates which call sign series are allocated to which countries.

Call Sign Series	Allocated to
AAA-ALZ	**United States of America**
AMA-AOZ	Spain
APA-ASZ	Pakistan (Islamic Republic of)
ATA-AWZ	India (Republic of)
AXA-AXZ	Australia
AYA-AZZ	Argentine Republic
A2A-A2Z	Botswana (Republic of)
A3A-A3Z	Tonga (Kingdom of)
A4A-A4Z	Oman (Sultanate of)
A5A-A5Z	Bhutan (Kingdom of)

A6A-A6Z	United Arab Emirates
A7A-A7Z	Qatar (State of)
A8A-A8Z	Liberia (Republic of)
A9A-A9Z	Bahrain (State of)
BAA-BZZ	China (People's Republic of)
CAA-CEZ	Chile
CFA-CKZ	Canada
CLA-CMZ	Cuba
CNA-CNZ	Morocco (Kingdom of)
COA-COZ	Cuba
CPA-CPZ	Bolivia (Republic of)
CQA-CUZ	Portugal
CVA-CXZ	Uruguay (Eastern Republic of)
CYA-CZZ	Canada
C2A-C2Z	Nauru (Republic of)
C3A-C3Z	Andorra (Principality of)
C4A-C4Z	Cyprus (Republic of)
C5A-C5Z	Gambia (Republic of the)
C6A-C6Z	Bahamas (Commonwealth of the)
C7A-C7Z	World Meteorological Organization
C8A-C9Z	Mozambique (Republic of)
DAA-DRZ	Germany (Federal Republic of)
DSA-DTZ	Korea (Republic of)
DUA-DZZ	Philippines (Republic of the)
D2A-D3Z	Angola (Republic of)
D4A-D4Z	Cape Verde (Republic of)
D5A-D5Z	Liberia (Republic of)
D6A-D6Z	Comoros (Islamic Federal Republic of the)
D7A-D9Z	Korea (Republic of)
EAA-EHZ	Spain
EIA-EJZ	Ireland
EKA-EKZ	Armenia (Republic of)
ELA-ELZ	Liberia (Republic of)
EMA-EOZ	Ukraine
EPA-EQZ	Iran (Islamic Republic of)
ERA-ERZ	Moldova (Republic of)
ESA-ESZ	Estonia (Republic of)
ETA-ETZ	Ethiopia (Federal Democratic Republic of)
EUA-EWZ	Belarus (Republic of)
EXA-EXZ	Kyrgyz Republic
EYA-EYZ	Tajikistan (Republic of)
EZA-EZZ	Turkmenistan
E2A-E2Z	Thailand
E3A-E3Z	Eritrea
E4A-E4Z	Palestinian Authority

E5A-E5Z	New Zealand - Cook Islands (WRC-07)
E7A-E7Z	Bosnia and Herzegovina (Republic of) (WRC-07)
FAA-FZZ	France
GAA-GZZ	United Kingdom of Great Britain and Northern Ireland
HAA-HAZ	Hungary (Republic of)
HBA-HBZ	Switzerland (Confederation of)
HCA-HDZ	Ecuador
HEA-HEZ	Switzerland (Confederation of)
HFA-HFZ	Poland (Republic of)
HGA-HGZ	Hungary (Republic of)
HHA-HHZ	Haiti (Republic of)
HIA-HIZ	Dominican Republic
HJA-HKZ	Colombia (Republic of)
HLA-HLZ	Korea (Republic of)
HMA-HMZ	Democratic People's Republic of Korea
HNA-HNZ	Iraq (Republic of)
HOA-HPZ	Panama (Republic of)
HQA-HRZ	Honduras (Republic of)
HSA-HSZ	Thailand
HTA-HTZ	Nicaragua
HUA-HUZ	El Salvador (Republic of)
HVA-HVZ	Vatican City State
HWA-HYZ	France
HZA-HZZ	Saudi Arabia (Kingdom of)
H2A-H2Z	Cyprus (Republic of)
H3A-H3Z	Panama (Republic of)
H4A-H4Z	Solomon Islands
H6A-H7Z	Nicaragua
H8A-H9Z	Panama (Republic of)
IAA-IZZ	Italy
JAA-JSZ	Japan
JTA-JVZ	Mongolia
JWA-JXZ	Norway
JYA-JYZ	Jordan (Hashemite Kingdom of)
JZA-JZZ	Indonesia (Republic of)
J2A-J2Z	Djibouti (Republic of)
J3A-J3Z	Grenada
J4A-J4Z	Greece
J5A-J5Z	Guinea-Bissau (Republic of)
J6A-J6Z	Saint Lucia
J7A-J7Z	Dominica (Commonwealth of)
J8A-J8Z	Saint Vincent and the Grenadines
KAA-KZZ	**United States of America**
LAA-LNZ	Norway
LOA-LWZ	Argentine Republic

LXA-LXZ	Luxembourg
LYA-LYZ	Lithuania (Republic of)
LZA-LZZ	Bulgaria (Republic of)
L2A-L9Z	Argentine Republic
MAA-MZZ	United Kingdom of Great Britain and Northern Ireland
NAA-NZZ	**United States of America**
OAA-OCZ	Peru
ODA-ODZ	Lebanon
OEA-OEZ	Austria
OFA-OJZ	Finland
OKA-OLZ	Czech Republic
OMA-OMZ	Slovak Republic
ONA-OTZ	Belgium
OUA-OZZ	Denmark
PAA-PIZ	Netherlands (Kingdom of the)
PJA-PJZ	Netherlands (Kingdom of the) - Netherlands Antilles
PKA-POZ	Indonesia (Republic of)
PPA-PYZ	Brazil (Federative Republic of)
PZA-PZZ	Suriname (Republic of)
P2A-P2Z	Papua New Guinea
P3A-P3Z	Cyprus (Republic of)
P4A-P4Z	Netherlands (Kingdom of the) - Aruba
P5A-P9Z	Democratic People's Republic of Korea
RAA-RZZ	Russian Federation
SAA-SMZ	Sweden
SNA-SRZ	Poland (Republic of)
SSA-SSM	Egypt (Arab Republic of)
SSN-STZ	Sudan (Republic of the)
SUA-SUZ	Egypt (Arab Republic of)
SVA-SZZ	Greece
S2A-S3Z	Bangladesh (People's Republic of)
S5A-S5Z	Slovenia (Republic of)
S6A-S6Z	Singapore (Republic of)
S7A-S7Z	Seychelles (Republic of)
S8A-S8Z	South Africa (Republic of)
S9A-S9Z	Sao Tome and Principe (Democratic Republic of)
TAA-TCZ	Turkey
TDA-TDZ	Guatemala (Republic of)
TEA-TEZ	Costa Rica
TFA-TFZ	Iceland
TGA-TGZ	Guatemala (Republic of)
THA-THZ	France
TIA-TIZ	Costa Rica
TJA-TJZ	Cameroon (Republic of)
TKA-TKZ	France

TLA-TLZ	Central African Republic
TMA-TMZ	France
TNA-TNZ	Congo (Republic of the)
TOA-TQZ	France
TRA-TRZ	Gabonese Republic
TSA-TSZ	Tunisia
TTA-TTZ	Chad (Republic of)
TUA-TUZ	Côte d'Ivoire (Republic of)
TVA-TXZ	France
TYA-TYZ	Benin (Republic of)
TZA-TZZ	Mali (Republic of)
T2A-T2Z	Tuvalu
T3A-T3Z	Kiribati (Republic of)
T4A-T4Z	Cuba
T5A-T5Z	Somali Democratic Republic
T6A-T6Z	Afghanistan (Islamic State of)
T7A-T7Z	San Marino (Republic of)
T8A-T8Z	Palau (Republic of)
UAA-UIZ	Russian Federation
UJA-UMZ	Uzbekistan (Republic of)
UNA-UQZ	Kazakhstan (Republic of)
URA-UZZ	Ukraine
VAA-VGZ	Canada
VHA-VNZ	Australia
VOA-VOZ	Canada
VPA-VQZ	United Kingdom of Great Britain and Northern Ireland
VRA-VRZ	China (People's Republic of) - Hong Kong
VSA-VSZ	United Kingdom of Great Britain and Northern Ireland
VTA-VWZ	India (Republic of)
VXA-VYZ	Canada
VZA-VZZ	Australia
V2A-V2Z	Antigua and Barbuda
V3A-V3Z	Belize
V4A-V4Z	Saint Kitts and Nevis
V5A-V5Z	Namibia (Republic of)
V6A-V6Z	Micronesia (Federated States of)
V7A-V7Z	Marshall Islands (Republic of the)
V8A-V8Z	Brunei Darussalam
WAA-WZZ	**United States of America**
XAA-XIZ	Mexico
XJA-XOZ	Canada
XPA-XPZ	Denmark
XQA-XRZ	Chile
XSA-XSZ	China (People's Republic of)
XTA-XTZ	Burkina Faso

XUA-XUZ	Cambodia (Kingdom of)
XVA-XVZ	Viet Nam (Socialist Republic of)
XWA-XWZ	Lao People's Democratic Republic
XXA-XXZ	China (People's Republic of) - Macao (WRC-07)
XYA-XZZ	Myanmar (Union of)
YAA-YAZ	Afghanistan (Islamic State of)
YBA-YHZ	Indonesia (Republic of)
YIA-YIZ	Iraq (Republic of)
YJA-YJZ	Vanuatu (Republic of)
YKA-YKZ	Syrian Arab Republic
YLA-YLZ	Latvia (Republic of)
YMA-YMZ	Turkey
YNA-YNZ	Nicaragua
YOA-YRZ	Romania
YSA-YSZ	El Salvador (Republic of)
YTA-YUZ	Serbia (Republic of) (WRC-07)
YVA-YYZ	Venezuela (Republic of)
Y2A-Y9Z	Germany (Federal Republic of)
ZAA-ZAZ	Albania (Republic of)
ZBA-ZJZ	United Kingdom of Great Britain and Northern Ireland
ZKA-ZMZ	New Zealand
ZNA-ZOZ	United Kingdom of Great Britain and Northern Ireland
ZPA-ZPZ	Paraguay (Republic of)
ZQA-ZQZ	United Kingdom of Great Britain and Northern Ireland
ZRA-ZUZ	South Africa (Republic of)
ZVA-ZZZ	Brazil (Federative Republic of)
Z2A-Z2Z	Zimbabwe (Republic of)
Z3A-Z3Z	The Former Yugoslav Republic of Macedonia
2AA-2ZZ	United Kingdom of Great Britain and Northern Ireland
3AA-3AZ	Monaco (Principality of)
3BA-3BZ	Mauritius (Republic of)
3CA-3CZ	Equatorial Guinea (Republic of)
3DA-3DM	Swaziland (Kingdom of)
3DN-3DZ	Fiji (Republic of)
3EA-3FZ	Panama (Republic of)
3GA-3GZ	Chile
3HA-3UZ	China (People's Republic of)
3VA-3VZ	Tunisia
3WA-3WZ	Viet Nam (Socialist Republic of)
3XA-3XZ	Guinea (Republic of)
3YA-3YZ	Norway
3ZA-3ZZ	Poland (Republic of)
4AA-4CZ	Mexico
4DA-4IZ	Philippines (Republic of the)
4JA-4KZ	Azerbaijani Republic

4LA-4LZ	Georgia (Republic of)
4MA-4MZ	Venezuela (Republic of)
4OA-4OZ	Montenegro (Republic of) (WRC-07)
4PA-4SZ	Sri Lanka (Democratic Socialist Republic of)
4TA-4TZ	Peru
4UA-4UZ	United Nations
4VA-4VZ	Haiti (Republic of)
4WA-4WZ	Democratic Republic of Timor-Leste (WRC-03)
4XA-4XZ	Israel (State of)
4YA-4YZ	International Civil Aviation Organization
4ZA-4ZZ	Israel (State of)
5AA-5AZ	Libya (Socialist People's Libyan Arab Jamahiriya)
5BA-5BZ	Cyprus (Republic of)
5CA-5GZ	Morocco (Kingdom of)
5HA-5IZ	Tanzania (United Republic of)
5JA-5KZ	Colombia (Republic of)
5LA-5MZ	Liberia (Republic of)
5NA-5OZ	Nigeria (Federal Republic of)
5PA-5QZ	Denmark
5RA-5SZ	Madagascar (Republic of)
5TA-5TZ	Mauritania (Islamic Republic of)
5UA-5UZ	Niger (Republic of the)
5VA-5VZ	Togolese Republic
5WA-5WZ	Samoa (Independent State of)
5XA-5XZ	Uganda (Republic of)
5YA-5ZZ	Kenya (Republic of)
6AA-6BZ	Egypt (Arab Republic of)
6CA-6CZ	Syrian Arab Republic
6DA-6JZ	Mexico
6KA-6NZ	Korea (Republic of)
6OA-6OZ	Somali Democratic Republic
6PA-6SZ	Pakistan (Islamic Republic of)
6TA-6UZ	Sudan (Republic of the)
6VA-6WZ	Senegal (Republic of)
6XA-6XZ	Madagascar (Republic of)
6YA-6YZ	Jamaica
6ZA-6ZZ	Liberia (Republic of)
7AA-7IZ	Indonesia (Republic of)
7JA-7NZ	Japan
7OA-7OZ	Yemen (Republic of)
7PA-7PZ	Lesotho (Kingdom of)
7QA-7QZ	Malawi
7RA-7RZ	Algeria (People's Democratic Republic of)
7SA-7SZ	Sweden
7TA-7YZ	Algeria (People's Democratic Republic of)

7ZA-7ZZ	Saudi Arabia (Kingdom of)
8AA-8IZ	Indonesia (Republic of)
8JA-8NZ	Japan
8OA-8OZ	Botswana (Republic of)
8PA-8PZ	Barbados
8QA-8QZ	Maldives (Republic of)
8RA-8RZ	Guyana
8SA-8SZ	Sweden
8TA-8YZ	India (Republic of)
8ZA-8ZZ	Saudi Arabia (Kingdom of)
9AA-9AZ	Croatia (Republic of)
9BA-9DZ	Iran (Islamic Republic of)
9EA-9FZ	Ethiopia (Federal Democratic Republic of)
9GA-9GZ	Ghana
9HA-9HZ	Malta
9IA-9JZ	Zambia (Republic of)
9KA-9KZ	Kuwait (State of)
9LA-9LZ	Sierra Leone
9MA-9MZ	Malaysia
9NA-9NZ	Nepal
9OA-9TZ	Democratic Republic of the Congo
9UA-9UZ	Burundi (Republic of)
9VA-9VZ	Singapore (Republic of)
9WA-9WZ	Malaysia
9XA-9XZ	Rwandese Republic
9YA-9ZZ	Trinidad and Tobago

Third-Party Communications and Amateur Radio

If all of this information about ham radios is somewhat intimidating, do not despair. "You" can still use ham radios for communications without being a licensed operator. Yes, you do have to have a ham license in order to legally transmit by ham equipment (or be under the direct supervision of someone else who is licensed), but there is an alternative – third-party communication.

Third-party communications occur when a licensed operator sends either written or verbal messages on behalf of unlicensed persons or organizations. There are two "controls" on third-party communication.

First, the communication must be noncommercial and of a personal nature. Asking a ham operator to contact another ham operator located in an area just hit by tornados and, because of being without power, phones do not work in Grandma Sally's city so you can check up on her, is okay. Asking a ham to send a message out that you have an old Chevy for sale would not be okay.

Second, the message must be going to a permitted area. Transmitting from a US location to another US location is okay, but transmitting from the US to another country may not. Because third-party communications bypass a country's normal telephone and postal systems, many foreign governments forbid such communications. In order to transmit from one country to another, the other country must have signed a third-party agreement with the US. What follows is a list of those countries that do have third-party a communications agreement with the US.

V2	Antigua / Barbuda
LU	Argentina
VK	Australia
V3	Belize
CP	Bolivia
T9	Bosnia-Herzegovina
PY	Brazil
VE	Canada
CE	Chile
HK	Colombia
D6	Comoros (Federal Islamic Republic of)
TI	Costa Rica
CO	Cuba
HI	Dominican Republic
J7	Dominica
HC	Ecuador
YS	El Salvador
C5	Gambia, The
9G	Ghana
J3	Grenada
TG	Guatemala
8R	Guyana
HH	Haiti
HR	Honduras
4X	Israel
6Y	Jamaica
JY	Jordan
EL	Liberia
V7	Marshall Islands
XE	Mexico
V6	Micronesia, Federated States of
YN	Nicaragua
HP	Panama
ZP	Paraguay
OA	Peru
DU	Philippines
VR6	Pitcairn Island

V4	St. Christopher / Nevis
J6	St. Lucia
J8	St. Vincent and the Grenadines
9L	Sierra Leone
ZS	South Africa
3DA	Swaziland
9Y	Trinidad / Tobago
TA	Turkey
GB	United Kingdom
CX	Uruguay
YV	Venezuela
4U1ITUITU	Geneva
4U1VICVIC	Vienna

Remember, before TSHTF, keep your pantry well stocked, your powder dry, and your batteries fully charged. 73

APPENDIX A

American Radio Relay League

Affiliated Amateur Radio Clubs in

Rhode Island

ARRL Affiliated Club:	**Ocean State Amateur Radio Group Inc**
City:	Cranston, RI
Call Sign:	K1OS
Section:	RI

ARRL Affiliated Club:	**Association Radio Amateurs of Southern NE**
City:	East Providence, RI
Call Sign:	W1AQ
Section:	RI
Links:	http://www.w1aq.com/

ARRL Affiliated Club:	**The Providence Radio Association, Inc.**
City:	Johnston, RI
Call Sign:	W1OP
Section:	RI
Links:	www.w1op.org

ARRL Affiliated Club:	**CTRI Contest Group Club**
City:	Johnston, RI
Call Sign:	WA1RR
Section:	RI
Links:	http://members.cox.net/wa1rr

ARRL Affiliated Club:	**Narragansett Bay Amateur Radio Club NBARC**
City:	Lincoln, RI
Call Sign:	NB1RI
Section:	RI
Links:	http://saltyhams.org/

ARRL Affiliated Club:	**Newport County Radio Club**
City:	Newport, RI
Call Sign:	W1SYE
Section:	RI
Links:	http://www.w1sye.org

ARRL Affiliated Club:	**Fidelity Amateur Radio Club**
City:	West Greenwich, RI
Call Sign:	K1NQG
Section:	RI
Links:	http://www.k1nqg.org

ARRL Affiliated Club:	**Kent County Amateur Radio Group, Inc**
City:	West Warwick, RI
Call Sign:	W1KCG
Section:	RI
Links:	http://www.geocities.com/kb1awv/arc.html

ARRL Affiliated Club: **Blackstone Valley Amateur Radio Club**
City: Woonsocket, RI
Call Sign: W1DDD
Section: RI
Links: http://www.w1ddd.org

APPENDIX B

Amateur Radio License Holders

in

Rhode Island
(by City)

FCC Amateur Radio Licenses in Adamsville

Call Sign: KA1QCQ
Daniel A Curran
Box 432
Adamsville RI 02801

Call Sign: KB1NWY
Gabriel J Farias
62 Crandall Rd
Adamsville RI 02801

Call Sign: W1CCA
Thomas Clarke Jr
Adamsville RI 02801

FCC Amateur Radio Licenses in Albion

Call Sign: N1FGA
Kenneth J Tremblay
Albion RI 028020641

FCC Amateur Radio Licenses in Ashaway

Call Sign: KB1TFG
Owen E Bostrom
99 Chase Hill Rd
Ashaway RI 02804

Call Sign: AB1TT
Owen E Bostrom
99 Chase Hill Rd
Ashaway RI 02804

Call Sign: W4OYB
Charles Tobias
19 Church St
Ashaway RI 02804

Call Sign: N1XHT
Linda J Chaffee
10 Colonial Village Rd

Ashaway RI 028040004

Call Sign: WA1YEN
Dunns Corners School
Amateur Radio Club
10 Colonial Village Rd
Ashaway RI 028040004

Call Sign: WA1GEC
William D Crandall Sr
62 Egypt St
Ashaway RI 02804

Call Sign: N1HRA
William R Champagne
105 Main St
Ashaway RI 02804

Call Sign: WA1RR
Connecticut Rhode Island
Contest Group
105 Main St
Ashaway RI 02804

Call Sign: KB1KGM
Southern Rhode Island
Contest Group
105 Main St
Ashaway RI 02804

Call Sign: NY1Q
Southern Rhode Island
Contest Group
105 Main St
Ashaway RI 02804

Call Sign: KB1KIA
John S Syren
194 Main St
Ashaway RI 02804

Call Sign: WA1YFJ
Edwin G Hoffman
10 Ridgewood Ave
Ashaway RI 02804

Call Sign: KA1PJF
Raymond T Tella
10 Valley Dr
Ashaway RI 02804

Call Sign: AA1SS
Howard R Johnson
11 Valley Dr
Ashaway RI 028041310

Call Sign: KB1AUS
Maurice M Young
19 Williams St
Ashaway RI 02804

Call Sign: WA1QXR
Kenneth F Chaffee
Ashaway RI 028040004

FCC Amateur Radio Licenses in Barrington

Call Sign: N1XW
Sosio A Andreozzi Jr
1 Andreozzi Dr
Barrington RI 02806

Call Sign: KA1PBD
John H Stiness
40 Appian Way
Barrington RI 02806

Call Sign: KB1QCY
Anthony J Raimondi
38 Blanding Ave
Barrington RI 02806

Call Sign: N1WQW
M Kay Chapin
10 Blount Circle
Barrington RI 02806

Call Sign: WA1KAW
Richard A Fontaine

10 Columbus Ave
Barrington RI 02806

21 Heritage Rd
Barrington RI 02806

8 Knapton St
Barrington RI 02806

Call Sign: W1UKD
Edward L Holley
15 Columbus Ave
Barrington RI 028063909

Call Sign: K1BIL
William M Whelihan
21 Heritage Rd
Barrington RI 02806

Call Sign: KB1QIP
Bradford V Ellsworth
64 Lake Ave
Barrington RI 02806

Call Sign: KB1JBB
Kevin N Raponi
58 County Rd
Barrington RI 02806

Call Sign: N1DXO
David W Young
31 Houghton St
Barrington RI 02806

Call Sign: N1OTF
Joseph G Vargas
19 Leslie Ave
Barrington RI 02806

Call Sign: N1CED
James T Olive
9 Ernest St
Barrington RI 02806

Call Sign: W1MEK
David W Young
31 Houghton St
Barrington RI 02806

Call Sign: KA1CTN
John W Boutcher
53 Lincoln Ave
Barrington RI 02806

Call Sign: KD1WE
Richard T Tjader
15 Eton Rd
Barrington RI 02806

Call Sign: N1DXW
John S Seavor
33 Houghton St
Barrington RI 02806

Call Sign: N1GQM
George W Gallipeau Iii
76 Lincoln Ave
Barrington RI 02806

Call Sign: KA1VUH
Michael Romano Iii
91 Fales Avenue
Barrington RI 02806

Call Sign: N1GXT
Eric J Hecker
8 Humphreys Rd
Barrington RI 02806

Call Sign: KA1EHS
Frank J Cummings
14 Manor Rd
Barrington RI 02806

Call Sign: KA1GVI
Michael Romano Iii
91 Fales Avenue
Barrington RI 02806

Call Sign: KB1SDP
Tim E Hecker
8 Humphreys Rd
Barrington RI 02806

Call Sign: N1PFU
Thomas J Ferreira
124 Maple Ave
Barrington RI 02806

Call Sign: KA1TBJ
Alexander Natale
8 Greene Ave
Barrington RI 02806

Call Sign: KA1WRU
Byron F Kahr
6 Karen Dr
Barrington RI 02806

Call Sign: KB1NMH
Thomas J Ferreira Jr
124 Maple Ave
Barrington RI 02806

Call Sign: KB1AWW
Peter D Pockel
1 Grove St
Barrington RI 02806

Call Sign: KA1WRV
Frank M Kahr
6 Karen Dr
Barrington RI 02806

Call Sign: AA1HC
Richard J Carroll Jr
77 Maple Ave 2
Barrington RI 02806

Call Sign: KB1JQF
William M Whelihan

Call Sign: WB1HIJ
John W Wheeler

Call Sign: WA1IAF
Thomas R Williams

38 Massasoit Ave
Barrington RI 02806

Call Sign: W1BIS
Charles J Ashworth Jr
35 Mathewson Rd
Barrington RI 02806

Call Sign: N1ELG
Shalom Wertsberger
1 Mathewson Road
Barrington RI 02806

Call Sign: WB1EIE
Joseph C Silvia
7 Miller St
Barrington RI 02806

Call Sign: W1YDH
John R Woodhouse
8 New Hampshire Ave
Barrington RI 02806

Call Sign: K1FT
Charles L Lightfoot Iii
324 New Meadow Rd
Barrington RI 02806

Call Sign: KB1ELX
Will L Lightfoot
324 New Meadow Rd
Barrington RI 02806

Call Sign: W2KAE
Charles L Lightfoot Iii
324 New Meadow Rd
Barrington RI 02806

Call Sign: K1FT
Charles L Lightfoot Iii
324 New Meadow Rd
Barrington RI 02806

Call Sign: KA1PL
John T Kroenert

349 New Meadow Rd
Barrington RI 02806

Call Sign: N1PQW
Austin G Lightfoot
324 New Meadow Road
Barrington RI 02806

Call Sign: KA1NOG
Raymond W Stone
12 Northwest Passage
Barrington RI 028062342

Call Sign: N1DVM
Donald J Mara
5 Old Chimney Rd
Barrington RI 02806

Call Sign: N6JHM
Shawn T Hulsebos
22 Old Chimney Rd
Barrington RI 02806

Call Sign: N1VFX
Joseph A Miranda
9 Palisade Ln
Barrington RI 02806

Call Sign: W1TW
Jefferson Borden Iv
16 Peck Ave
Barrington RI 02806

Call Sign: KB1KYX
Jared B Marshall
13 Plymouth Dr
Barrington RI 02806

Call Sign: WA1A
East Bay Amateur Wireless
Association
101 Promenade St
Barrington RI 02806

Call Sign: WB1DEZ

Carl F Furtado
101 Promenade St
Barrington RI 02806

Call Sign: N1DXV
Joseph J Sears
68 Prospect
Barrington RI 02806

Call Sign: N1WGF
Jeffrey S Gordon
71 Rumstick Rd
Barrington RI 02806

Call Sign: N1JBC
Edwin S Barton Iv
306 Rumstick Rd
Barrington RI 02806

Call Sign: KI4FME
Susan M Zoll
369 Sowams Rd
Barrington RI 02806

Call Sign: KI4FMS
Sierra F Zoll
369 Sowams Rd
Barrington RI 02806

Call Sign: N1TOQ
Barry Y Zoll
369 Sowams Rd.
Barrington RI 02806

Call Sign: K1POM
Robert Warren
17 Stacy St
Barrington RI 02806

Call Sign: KA1OIA
William T Mc Innis
19 Surrey Rd
Barrington RI 02806

Call Sign: K1LHA

John H Heim
11 Telford Rd
Barrington RI 02806

Call Sign: KB1CRL
Raymond F Bourassa
54 Third St
Barrington RI 02806

Call Sign: W1VEF
Alfred F Duarte
10 Valentine Cir
Barrington RI 02806

Call Sign: KS1J
James P Bowman
50 Walnut Rd
Barrington RI 02806

Call Sign: KB1PJP
George C Neubauer
75 Walnut Rd
Barrington RI 028062110

Call Sign: N1TIS
Gregory C Sanborn
7 Winsor Dr
Barrington RI 028062413

Call Sign: W1OOV
Frank A Carter Jr
24 Winsor Dr
Barrington RI 02806

Call Sign: KA1YLM
Kelly L West
18 Woodland Rd
Barrington RI 02806

Call Sign: KA2HXS
Ralph M Greenlee
Coast Guard Rd

Block Island RI 02807

Call Sign: WW1K
William G Bendokas
High St
Block Island RI 02807

Call Sign: KB1ENH
Mary C Clow
One Jobs Hill Road
Block Island RI 02807

Call Sign: K2YIZ
Lewis S Fitzgerald
430 Payne Rd
Block Island RI 02807

Call Sign: WA1RJS
Stanley N Smith
858 West Side Rd Box 31
Block Island RI 02807

Call Sign: W1FVY
Carl T Milner
Block Island RI 02807

Call Sign: KB1ENO
Richard J Clow Sr
Block Island RI 02807

Call Sign: K2LCA
Lyle C Anderson
Block Island RI 02807

Call Sign: W1LSX
Dwight C Brown Jr
174 Ashaway Rd
Bradford RI 02808

Call Sign: KB1AVI
Joseph G Burns
177 Ashaway Rd

Bradford RI 02808

Call Sign: KA1FFY
Ronald J Adriano
303 Bradford Rd
Bradford RI 02808

Call Sign: N1XCT
Robert E Reightler
6 Canton St
Bradford RI 02808

Call Sign: N1HFG
David A Cowley
5 Gurnsey Ave
Bradford RI 02808

Call Sign: K1MDR
James J Augeri
14 N Capalbo Dr
Bradford RI 02808

Call Sign: N1OBW
George H Marsh Jr
10 Red Barn Dr
Bradford RI 02808

Call Sign: WA1ZBI
Marilyn L Almy
Rfd 1
Bradford RI 02808

Call Sign: WA1GED
John H Christie Sr
1 Riverside Dr
Bradford RI 02808

Call Sign: KB1ONI
Kathleen D Crider
12 Wayland St
Bradford RI 02808

Call Sign: N1VXG
Charles E Taylor
Bradford RI 02808

Call Sign: W1FEO
A Walter Gardner
Bradford RI 028080377

FCC Amateur Radio Licenses in Bristol

Call Sign: WA1WVI
David L Bidwell
45 Aaron Ave
Bristol RI 02809

Call Sign: W1CG
Charles R Greene
115 Aaron Ave
Bristol RI 02809

Call Sign: KA1YXJ
George E Schmitt
42 Addy Dr
Bristol RI 02809

Call Sign: N1MOA
George L Schmitt
42 Addy Dr
Bristol RI 02809

Call Sign: KB1RDW
Kenneth J Machado Jr
3 Alves St
Bristol RI 02809

Call Sign: W1PRD
Roy C Moore
5 Ambrose Dr
Bristol RI 02809

Call Sign: KA1KKA
William H Shaw
220 Arboretum Ln
Bristol RI 02809

Call Sign: K1MCT
Bernard E Ebbitt

82 Beach Rd
Bristol RI 02809

Call Sign: N1RAK
Ralph R Trotter Jr
103 Beach Rd
Bristol RI 02809

Call Sign: K1WK
Walter L Klimasewski
19 Belvedere Dr
Bristol RI 02809

Call Sign: N1RCN
Dwight P Fletcher
78 Berry Ln
Bristol RI 02809

Call Sign: N2AQK
John D Flanders
9 Betsy Dr
Bristol RI 02809

Call Sign: KA1VOC
Jason B La Porte
Bristol Harbor
Bristol RI 02809

Call Sign: K1BZA
John J Salinger
15 Burton Street
Bristol RI 02809

Call Sign: KA1SHW
Richard F Amaral
101 Charles St
Bristol RI 02809

Call Sign: KA1ZQE
Charles E Fortin Jr
114 Constitution St
Bristol RI 02809

Call Sign: WD4EUQ
Larry P Di Sano

19 Dolly Dr
Bristol RI 02809

Call Sign: W1GXW
Robert R Dennis
8 Everett Ave
Bristol RI 028091419

Call Sign: N1IUO
Kenneth E Duckworth
55 Fales Rd
Bristol RI 02809

Call Sign: KB1BLX
Philip J Da Ponte
141 Fales Rd
Bristol RI 02809

Call Sign: N1IKB
Albert E Proffitt Jr
10 Fort Hill Rd
Bristol RI 02809

Call Sign: KB7RNH
Keith D Farney
16 Franca Drive
Bristol RI 02809

Call Sign: KB1VKT
Noah J Bedford
111 Franklin St
Bristol RI 02809

Call Sign: AA1AY
Virginio C Franco
239 Franklin St
Bristol RI 02809

Call Sign: KB1BWT
Portuguese Amateur Radio
Association
239 Franklin St
Bristol RI 02809

Call Sign: KA1RYW

David B Yutzy Sr
24 Fried Ave
Bristol RI 02809

Call Sign: KB1KNZ
Marie L Knapman
14 Goulart Ave
Bristol RI 02809

Call Sign: WA1GJF
Leeds Mitchell Iii
14 Griswold Avenue
Bristol RI 02906

Call Sign: KB1AKN
Serafin Pimentel
4 Harker Ave
Bristol RI 02809

Call Sign: KB1PDY
Wayne D Wilbur
36 Harrison St
Bristol RI 02809

Call Sign: N1GEE
Wayne D Wilbur
36 Harrison St
Bristol RI 028094402

Call Sign: N1MMU
David A Sylvestre
39 Harrison Street
Bristol RI 02809

Call Sign: N1MMV
Martha B Sylvestre
39 Harrison Street
Bristol RI 02809

Call Sign: W1ERV
William V Barlow
140 Hope St
Bristol RI 02809

Call Sign: WA1POX

Stephen B Anthony
240 Hope St
Bristol RI 02809

Call Sign: W1SJL
Emilio D Iannuccillo
1350 Hope St
Bristol RI 02809

Call Sign: W1IJM
Lewis P Ketchie
1014 Hope St Apt B2
Bristol RI 02809

Call Sign: KC2DNZ
Kevin P Moynahan
700 Hope Street Apt 2
Bristol RI 02809

Call Sign: KB1DGT
Paul Leite
29 Hopeworth Ave
Bristol RI 02809

Call Sign: KB1DGU
Antonio C Leite
29 Hopeworth Ave
Bristol RI 02809

Call Sign: K1LQH
Joseph E Darling
34 King Philip Ave
Bristol RI 02809

Call Sign: KB1VBQ
Darwin E Clemens
11 Lea Dr
Bristol RI 02809

Call Sign: W1DWZ
David E Roscoe
12 Lea Drive
Bristol RI 02809

Call Sign: W1WRC

Francisco T Canario
457 Metacom Ave
Bristol RI 02809

Call Sign: WN1S
Vincent J Santo Jr
506 Metacom Ave
Bristol RI 028095145

Call Sign: KA1AZ
John F Sardinha
711 Metacom Ave
Bristol RI 02809

Call Sign: WA1VAL
Edward A Calkins Jr
Metacom Ave
Bristol RI 02809

Call Sign: KB1LGN
James A Porth
5 Mount Ave
Bristol RI 02809

Call Sign: W1JAP
James A Porth
5 Mount Ave
Bristol RI 02809

Call Sign: N2PGD
Mark K Dieterich
23 Naomi St
Bristol RI 02809

Call Sign: K1STW
C A Peter Lynch
Poppasquash Rd
Bristol RI 02809

Call Sign: W4DCT
Domingo Camara
27 Primrose Road
Bristol RI 02809

Call Sign: KB1KOA

Terri Anne Moreira
4 Proto Ln
Bristol RI 02809

Call Sign: KB1KOB
James J Moreira
4 Proto Ln
Bristol RI 02809

Call Sign: KB1GGY
William J Kehoe
8 Reilly Lane
Bristol RI 028094015

Call Sign: WA1KFL
William J Kehoe
8 Reilly Lane
Bristol RI 028094015

Call Sign: KA1FQI
Matthew J Salcone
25 Roma St
Bristol RI 02809

Call Sign: KB1SLA
Daniel Vieira
23 Roosevelt Dr
Bristol RI 02809

Call Sign: W1HTO
Richard K Heitzenrater
57 Roosevelt Dr
Bristol RI 02809

Call Sign: N1RHH
Octavio M Vieira
23 Roosevelt Dr.
Bristol RI 02809

Call Sign: KD1VU
Antonio S Ferreira
34 San Jose Dr
Bristol RI 02809

Call Sign: KA1TM

Lawrence J Pietrzyk
23 Sandra Dr
Bristol RI 02809

Call Sign: KB1KNY
Diane Sousa
24 Sandy Ln
Bristol RI 02809

Call Sign: WE3V
John C Ufford
350 Spinnaker Lane
Bristol RI 02809

Call Sign: W1MZB
Frederick J Coyle
45 Sunset Rd
Bristol RI 02809

Call Sign: KA1ZKT
Sharon F Bennett
13 Sweeney Ln
Bristol RI 02809

Call Sign: K1DRM
David R Mcdonald
23 Tobin Lane
Bristol RI 02809

Call Sign: KB1NYM
Butch Balzano
24 Vernon Avenue
Bristol RI 02809

Call Sign: N1GTR
Kenneth J Machado Jr
14 Violet Ct.
Bristol RI 02809

Call Sign: N1TLE
Sean E Squire
49 Wapping Drive
Bristol RI 02809

Call Sign: N1VOP

Donajene D Rice
49 Wapping Drive
Bristol RI 02809

Call Sign: N1XRA
Walter J Machado
14 Washington St
Bristol RI 02809

Call Sign: KE1CB
Timothy M H Charles
1 Weetamoe Farm Drive
Bristol RI 02809

Call Sign: KB1IIO
Bristol Yacht Club Radio
143 Windward Lane
Bristol RI 02809

Call Sign: W1BYC
Bristol Yacht Club Radio
143 Windward Lane
Bristol RI 02809

Call Sign: KB1HPH
David R Mcdonald
143 Windward Ln
Bristol RI 02809

Call Sign: KB1LQJ
Hilary C Williams
116 Wood St
Bristol RI 028093116

Call Sign: N1CAW
Stanley Livingston Jr
Bristol RI 02809

Call Sign: N1WQD
Kenneth J Catalano
Bristol RI 02809

Call Sign: KB1HVB
Paul M Sanroma
Bristol RI 02809

Call Sign: KB1RAP
Linda M Knowles
Bristol RI 02809

Call Sign: KB1UZE
Cody Bryan
Bristol RI 02809

FCC Amateur Radio Licenses in Carolina

Call Sign: N1XXT
Linda L Markhart
One Pinecrest Road
Carolina RI 02812

Call Sign: W1RZQ
Edwin I Saunders
7 Pine Hill Rd
Carolina RI 02812

Call Sign: WB1FDP
Carmine Lapati Jr
Pine Hill Rd
Carolina RI 02812

Call Sign: WA1UWH
Wayne De Forest
170 Richmond Townhouse
Road
Carolina RI 028121037

Call Sign: K1QMO
Martha S Arsics
Shannock Hill Rd
Carolina RI 02812

Call Sign: KA1TPO
Joseph A Dargie
24 Small Pond Rd
Carolina RI 02812

Call Sign: W2MCF
George F Arsics

Carolina RI 02812

FCC Amateur Radio Licenses in Centerdale

Call Sign: K1JHH
Cecil E Mc Intosh
90 Angell Ave
Centerdale RI 02911

Call Sign: KA1PID
Elaine B Vota
41 Brookside Ave
Centerdale RI 02911

Call Sign: WB1FDY
John R Vota
41 Brookside Ave
Centerdale RI 02911

Call Sign: N1KBG
Mary Anne Ferreira
91 Jacksonia Dr
Centerdale RI 02911

Call Sign: N1KF
Kenneth M Ferreira
91 Jacksonia Dr
Centerdale RI 02911

Call Sign: KF1DX
Kenneth M Ferreira
91 Jacksonia Dr
Centerdale RI 02911

FCC Amateur Radio Licenses in Central Falls

Call Sign: KB1BDM
Todd A Wallace
53 Butler Ave
Central Falls RI 02863

Call Sign: KB1SML
Robert T Falkowski

292 Central St
Central Falls RI 02863

Call Sign: KB1SVE
Susan E Nadeau
294 Central St
Central Falls RI 02863

Call Sign: WA1BMF
Susan E Nadeau
294 Central St
Central Falls RI 02863

Call Sign: K1MZN
Owen L Boland
83 Darling St
Central Falls RI 02863

Call Sign: WA1AIX
Charles E Himeon
12 George Street
Central Falls RI 028632323

Call Sign: KB1KQA
Dinsey Doumbia
645 High St
Central Falls RI 02863

Call Sign: KC2GAN
Joaquim F Miranda
318 Hunt St
Central Falls RI 02863

Call Sign: KB1IKB
Jonathan D Issa
1011 Lonsdale Ave
Central Falls RI 02863

Call Sign: KA1UYL
Thomas N Paquette
109 Sacred Heart Ave
Central Falls RI 02863

Call Sign: W1VRM
Leonard J Nadeau

115 Shawmut Ave
Central Falls RI 02863

Call Sign: K1CZD
Charles A Pare
149 Tremont
Central Falls RI 02863

Call Sign: KB1IEZ
Joao D Rodrigues
Central Falls RI 02863

Call Sign: KB1MZI
Michael Nerney
16 Redfern St
Centredale RI 02911

FCC Amateur Radio Licenses in Charlestown

Call Sign: N1WXT
Robert E Monaco
99 Arbutus Trl
Charlestown RI 02813

Call Sign: NS1K
Richard C De Bari
209 Biscuit City Rd
Charlestown RI 02813

Call Sign: KB1MWJ
Ronald J Anderson
2 Botka Dr
Charlestown RI 028133739

Call Sign: KB1ASF
Billie B Mc Intire
Box 194
Charlestown RI 02813

Call Sign: W1GJO
William J Reeves Jr
Box 22
Charlestown RI 02813

Call Sign: AF4UT
Anthony P Marchetti
18 Breton Dr
Charlestown RI 02813

Call Sign: KA1GEU
Christopher T Seeber
255 Carolina Back Rd
Charlestown RI 02813

Call Sign: KA1OYJ
Joseph H Deslaurier
24 Cayuga Rd
Charlestown RI 02813

Call Sign: KB1QBT
Andrew P Checchia
73 Cherokee Bend Way
Charlestown RI 02813

Call Sign: N3RRC
Robert W Klein
143 Clearview Rd
Charlestown RI 02813

Call Sign: W1HF
Robert P White
83 Columbia Heights Rd
Charlestown RI 02813

Call Sign: KD1KN
Joseph J Maher
5 Crystal Ct
Charlestown RI 02813

Call Sign: NO1JM
Joseph J Maher
5 Crystal Ct
Charlestown RI 02813

Call Sign: KB1WRL
Jordan M Dolock
38 East Quail Run
Charlestown RI 02813

Call Sign: K1RKJ
Frederick G Cooney
49 King Tom Dr
Charlestown RI 02813

Call Sign: K1TDE
William C King
120 Land Harbor Dr
Charlestown RI 02813

Call Sign: N1AKU
Joseph A Massini
20 Oak Ridge Rd
Charlestown RI 02813

Call Sign: W1KUI
Guy W Badger
31 Prosser Trail
Charlestown RI 02813

Call Sign: KB1BSL
South Coast Wireless
Society Arc
79 Prosser Trail
Charlestown RI 02813

Call Sign: N1NE
Rhode Island Radio Arc
79 Prosser Trail
Charlestown RI 02813

Call Sign: W1RAF
Ryan A Fenick
79 Prosser Trail
Charlestown RI 02813

Call Sign: WA1UBG
Francis M Fabian
106 Prosser Trail
Charlestown RI 02813

Call Sign: K1WI
Andrew L Fenick
79 Prosser Trl
Charlestown RI 02813

Call Sign: N1WGZ
August A Maserati
54 Ram Island Rd
Charlestown RI 02813

Call Sign: N1CAG
Neal A Fiorio
114 Ross Hill Road
Charlestown RI 02813

Call Sign: N1XKV
Andrew B Barrows
4115 S County Tr
Charlestown RI 02813

Call Sign: KB1PFP
Elizabeth A Bray
129 Sand Plain Rd
Charlestown RI 02813

Call Sign: KB1RDE
Charlestown EOC ARES
4540 South County Trail
Charlestown RI 02813

Call Sign: W1JPZ
John P Zabriskie Sr
23 Unkuri Dr
Charlestown RI 02813

Call Sign: KB1QBR
Diana C Welch
179 W Beach Rd
Charlestown RI 02813

Call Sign: KB1NTE
Charlestown Rhode Island
Eoc Amateur Radio
Association
179 W Branch Rd
Charlestown RI 02813

Call Sign: WA1ANB
William M Welch Jr

179 West Beach Rd
Charlestown RI 02813

Call Sign: KB1QWU
Jennifer L Welch
179 West Beach Rd
Charlestown RI 02813

Call Sign: KB1IUX
Abba's House Amateur
Radio Club
179 West Beach Road
Charlestown RI 02813

Call Sign: W1AHP
Abba's House Amateur
Radio Club
179 West Beach Road
Charlestown RI 02813

Call Sign: KB1AXC
Donna E Delorey
Charlestown RI 02813

Call Sign: KB1KNS
Mary A Grimley
Charlestown RI 02813

Call Sign: KB1NJG
Gregory Crawford
Charlestown RI 02813

**FCC Amateur Radio
Licenses in Chepachet**

Call Sign: KA1RLG
Marion M Howard
Box 105
Chepachet RI 02814

Call Sign: N1MIV
Bruce A Wattendorf
341 Chestnut Hill Rd
Chepachet RI 02814

Call Sign: K1HZF
Harry A Wolstenholme
64 Chestnut Hill Rd D2
Chepachet RI 02814

Call Sign: N1QBD
Sandra K Greene
29 Diamond Hill Rd
Chepachet RI 02814

Call Sign: KC1FJ
Ernest A La Fazia
51 Evelyn Way
Chepachet RI 028142091

Call Sign: KD1DI
Frank J Moon
70 Farnum Rd
Chepachet RI 02814

Call Sign: KB1CCE
Rf Commandos Rhode
Island Chapter
156 Gazza Road
Chepachet RI 02814

Call Sign: WH6DCX
Michael P Deignan Amateur
Radio Association
156 Gazza Road
Chepachet RI 02814

Call Sign: WH6DCY
Closed Repeater
Coordination Society
156 Gazza Road
Chepachet RI 02814

Call Sign: WH6DDM
Greater Honolulu Qrp
Society
156 Gazza Road
Chepachet RI 02814

Call Sign: WH6DDP

Rf Commandos Hawaii
Chapter
156 Gazza Road
Chepachet RI 02814

Call Sign: WH6DDR
Waikiki Wireless
Association
156 Gazza Road
Chepachet RI 02814

Call Sign: N1JXF
Allen Zatonsky
12 Goldie Rd
Chepachet RI 02814

Call Sign: W1SNE
Allen Zatonsky
12 Goldie Rd
Chepachet RI 02814

Call Sign: N1RWK
Alfred J Cortis Jr
201 Indian Trail Rd.
Chepachet RI 02814

Call Sign: KA1FRF
Eric L Croft Jr
75 Keach Dam Rd
Chepachet RI 02814

Call Sign: W1CPC
Albert P Van Herpe
18 Lake View Dr
Chepachet RI 02814

Call Sign: N1BU
Robert T Alberg
30 Lakeview Dr
Chepachet RI 02814

Call Sign: N1QBE
Louise A Alberg
30 Lakeview Dr
Chepachet RI 02814

Call Sign: N1OPX
Eric P Cote
133 Long Entry Rd
Chepachet RI 02814

Call Sign: KB1MTM
William J Flynn
156 Old Snake Hill Rd
Chepachet RI 02864

Call Sign: KB0O
William J Flynn
156 Old Snake Hill Rd
Chepachet RI 02864

Call Sign: KA1SQU
Thomas A Leech
38 Parker St
Chepachet RI 02918

Call Sign: N1KK
Kenneth Klimasewski
64 Pray Hill Rd
Chepachet RI 02814

Call Sign: KB1MRY
Robert L Van Herpe
146 Pray Hill Rd
Chepachet RI 02814

Call Sign: W1OSP
Robert L Van Herpe
146 Pray Hill Rd
Chepachet RI 02814

Call Sign: KB1TNF
Lawrence F Pesce
190 Sawmill Rd
Chepachet RI 02814

Call Sign: KE4PBD
Jeffery S Blackmon
48 Teaberry Dr
Chepachet RI 02814

Call Sign: K4GSU
Jeffery S Blackmon
48 Teaberry Dr
Chepachet RI 02814

Call Sign: WB1EUY
Roger D Hamm
6 Tucker St
Chepachet RI 02814

Call Sign: KA1CSR
Lester J Phillips
56 Victory Highway Apt C7
Chepachet RI 02814

Call Sign: KA1NJX
Elton A Greene
Victory Hwy
Chepachet RI 02814

Call Sign: KB1QIJ
Edward J Ross
64 Whipple Rd
Chepachet RI 02814

Call Sign: KA1GAH
Roland W Gingell Jr
Chepachet RI 02814

Call Sign: N1ADO
Emilio W Ambrosino
Chepachet RI 02814

Call Sign: N1VDV
Anthony F Ciarlo
Chepachet RI 02814

**FCC Amateur Radio
Licenses in Conventry**

Call Sign: KB1QVH
Lawrence M Celani
198 Colvintown Rd
Conventry RI 02816

Call Sign: WA1LMC
Lawrence M Celani
198 Colvintown Rd
Conventry RI 02816

Call Sign: N1JL
JOSEPH P Mcallister
98 Bates Avenue
Coventry RI 02816

Call Sign: KC1CE
Gregory J Iannucelli
8 Canyon Drive
Coventry RI 02816

Call Sign: N1QHJ
Terry L Upton
7 Acorn St
Coventry RI 02816

Call Sign: N1WGG
John N Bedford
18 Beach St
Coventry RI 028165664

Call Sign: KB1LOM
James M Tarro
5 Catalpa Way
Coventry RI 02816

Call Sign: N1ZBB
Linda C Palmquist
16 Airport Rd
Coventry RI 02816

Call Sign: N1QMJ
Richard R Gamelin
28 Black Rock Rd
Coventry RI 02816

Call Sign: N1PQN
Joseph B Hanrahan
8 Chandler Dr
Coventry RI 02816

Call Sign: KA1YYW
Joseph A Kress
24 Airport Rd
Coventry RI 02816

Call Sign: N1QHK
Frederick E Pendlebury
144 Blackrock Rd
Coventry RI 02816

Call Sign: N1VHE
Daniel J Field
8 Chopin St
Coventry RI 02816

Call Sign: N1ZXF
Raymond J Leduc
43 Angus St
Coventry RI 02816

Call Sign: KB1CJQ
Roger E Caine
8 Bonney St
Coventry RI 02816

Call Sign: K1UAM
Charles E Jalbert
15 Chopin St
Coventry RI 02816

Call Sign: KC1XO
Peter J Simeone
5 Archer Way
Coventry RI 02816

Call Sign: KB1PUH
Max D Reynolds
10 Bostonian Drive
Coventry RI 02816

Call Sign: K1LR
Leroy W Ratliff
43 Clubhouse Road
Coventry RI 028166518

Call Sign: KA1JSM
Normand R Martin
208 Arnold Rd
Coventry RI 02816

Call Sign: K1GJ
Max D Reynolds
10 Bostonian Drive
Coventry RI 02816

Call Sign: KB1BCT
Dennis S Arcaro
3 Collier Way
Coventry RI 02816

Call Sign: N1JKM
Steven C Demers Sr
59 Bates Ave
Coventry RI 02816

Call Sign: KB1EHG
Normand O Houle
5 Bow St
Coventry RI 02816

Call Sign: KB1BCU
Regina M Arcaro
3 Collier Way
Coventry RI 02816

Call Sign: KB1HQX
Joseph R Demers
59 Bates Ave
Coventry RI 02816

Call Sign: KB1ERM
Helen R Andrade
53 Breezy Lake Dr
Coventry RI 02816

Call Sign: KA1WOW
Laurie J Clark
14 Columbia Ave
Coventry RI 02816

Call Sign: KA1JGB
Suzanne R Ortgiesen
35 Colvintown Rd
Coventry RI 02816

Call Sign: WF1B
Raymond R Ortgiesen Iv
35 Colvintown Rd
Coventry RI 02816

Call Sign: KB1SUH
Dawn Lewis
84 Colvintown Rd
Coventry RI 02816

Call Sign: KA1NMT
Raymond D Patten
9 Cove Road
Coventry RI 02816

Call Sign: K1RDP
Raymond D Patten
9 Cove Road
Coventry RI 02816

Call Sign: N1OPJ
James H Morton
87 Coventry Dr
Coventry RI 02816

Call Sign: K1ADK
Francis W Morton
7 Deborah Ave
Coventry RI 02816

Call Sign: KA1YOM
Thomas J Danusis
24 Diane Dr
Coventry RI 02816

Call Sign: KA1ZHO
Dolores F Danusis
24 Diane Dr
Coventry RI 02816

Call Sign: KB1QBU
John A Leonelli
86 East Shore Drive
Coventry RI 02816

Call Sign: WA1CJT
Robert C Lindsay
6 Edna
Coventry RI 02816

Call Sign: WA1USA
Michael R Tracz
8 Edward St
Coventry RI 02816

Call Sign: KB1GVF
Kenneth L Averill Jr
50 Edward St
Coventry RI 02816

Call Sign: K2KLA
Kenneth L Averill Jr
50 Edward St
Coventry RI 02816

Call Sign: KB1EXS
B Charles Sutton
10 Eleanor Dr
Coventry RI 02816

Call Sign: W1MCP
B Charles Sutton
10 Eleanor Dr
Coventry RI 02816

Call Sign: W1JDA
P Anthony Salvati
18 Enzo Dr
Coventry RI 02816

Call Sign: KB1UDS
Michael J Lyman
49 Fieldstone Dr
Coventry RI 02816

Call Sign: K1CZG
Eugene B Perkins
122 Five Elms Cir Box
4050
Coventry RI 02816

Call Sign: KB1EGS
John A Buco
3672 Flat River Rd
Coventry RI 02816

Call Sign: N1EGS
John A Buco
3694 Flat River Rd
Coventry RI 02816

Call Sign: KA1OCH
Stephen D Balme
610 Franklin Rd
Coventry RI 02816

Call Sign: KB1CJR
Robert S Beaudreau
10 Gilles St
Coventry RI 02816

Call Sign: KB1RWN
James E Grant
22 Glenwood Dr
Coventry RI 02816

Call Sign: KB1SHX
James E Grant
22 Glenwood Dr
Coventry RI 02816

Call Sign: KB1AKE
Rebecca M Hunt
21 Grant Dr
Coventry RI 02816

Call Sign: N1YZN
Sharon L Daniels
490 Hammet Rd

Coventry RI 02816

Call Sign: KA1POT
Karen M Tracz
50 Hammett Rd
Coventry RI 02816

Call Sign: W1CCU
Andrew L Boucher
359 Harkney Hill Rd
Coventry RI 02816

Call Sign: KE1GL
Ralph K Nahigian
1556 Harkney Hill Rd
Coventry RI 02816

Call Sign: WA1OFT
Thomas J Barbish
1564 Harkney Hill Rd
Coventry RI 02816

Call Sign: K1TVS
Edward H Cayer Jr
2290 Harkney Hill Rd
Coventry RI 02816

Call Sign: KB1HQW
Edward H Cayer Jr
2290 Harkwey Hill Rd
Coventry RI 02816

Call Sign: W1NNU
Frederick L Fenton Sr
15 Hickory Rd
Coventry RI 02810

Call Sign: KE1BY
Herbert R Knott
62 Highwood Dr
Coventry RI 02816

Call Sign: N1WUP
Donna A Knott
62 Highwood Dr

Coventry RI 02816

Call Sign: K1FEY
Ruth M Hopkins
13 Hill Farm Camp Rd
Coventry RI 02816

Call Sign: K1VZU
Harold C Hopkins
13 Hill Farm Camp Rd
Coventry RI 02816

Call Sign: WA1PXX
Joseph R Muzzy Jr
201 Hill Farm Rd
Coventry RI 02816

Call Sign: KA1BLD
Robert H Lodge Sr
1025 Hill Farm Rd
Coventry RI 02816

Call Sign: W1FMO
Robert H Lodge Sr
1025 Hill Farm Rd
Coventry RI 02816

Call Sign: K1BDN
Drusilla J Muzzy
Hill Farm Rd
Coventry RI 02816

Call Sign: KA1WNI
Steven R Clark
40 Holden St Apt F
Coventry RI 02816

Call Sign: W6NJH
Gerald W Sylvester
67 Island Dr
Coventry RI 02816

Call Sign: N1MXP
Robert R Page
14 Jade Rd

Coventry RI 02816

Call Sign: KA1ZHB
Lori J Forget
17 Jade Rd
Coventry RI 02816

Call Sign: N1YNI
Alfred G Folco
18 Jennifer Lane
Coventry RI 02816

Call Sign: AA1N
Philip E Palmquist Jr
26 Kelly Ln
Coventry RI 02816

Call Sign: K1LCP
Linda C Palmquist
26 Kelly Ln
Coventry RI 02816

Call Sign: KB1KOM
Denise S Brophy
18 Kiley Way
Coventry RI 02816

Call Sign: KB1AXA
Daniel J Belanger
10 Knotty Oak Ln
Coventry RI 02816

Call Sign: KE1CC
Lonnie R St Jean
64 Knotty Oak Rd
Coventry RI 02816

Call Sign: WG1A
Raymond A Clark
184 Knotty Oak Rd
Coventry RI 02816

Call Sign: N1PDT
Raymond Straight Jr
992 Knotty Oak Rd

Coventry RI 02816

Call Sign: KB1MRJ
Adam G Caldow
62 Lakeside Dr
Coventry RI 02816

Call Sign: K1TBD
Walter W Stewart
Lane F
Coventry RI 02816

Call Sign: KE1EH
Freeman B Knowlton Jr
3 Laurie Ave
Coventry RI 02816

Call Sign: WF1Z
Freeman B Knowlton Jr
3 Laurie Ave
Coventry RI 02816

Call Sign: W1DAA
Douglas A Aldrich
42 Ledge Road
Coventry RI 028164924

Call Sign: N1ULJ
Gerald T May
301 Log Bridge Rd
Coventry RI 02816

Call Sign: KB1TYC
Todd R Matheny
18 Long Pond Rd
Coventry RI 02816

Call Sign: KB1TYE
Lori A Noonan
18 Long Pond Rd
Coventry RI 02816

Call Sign: W5ESW
Herman L Ware
12 Lydia Rd

Coventry RI 02816

Call Sign: WA1WSM
Wayne A Simoneau
40 Lydia Rd
Coventry RI 02816

Call Sign: KB1UIT
John J Botello Jr
40 Lydia Rd
Coventry RI 02816

Call Sign: KA1RXK
Gerard Rochefort
115 Mac Arthur Blvd
Coventry RI 02816

Call Sign: W1WFZ
Fred T Perry
34 Maple Root Rd
Coventry RI 02816

Call Sign: KB1KFC
James M Perry
34 Maple Root Rd
Coventry RI 02816

Call Sign: KB1RIS
Carol L Perry
34 Maple Root Rd
Coventry RI 02816

Call Sign: K1FTA
Carol L Perry
34 Maple Root Rd
Coventry RI 02816

Call Sign: N1YNM
Antonio F Rosa
450 Maple Valley Road
Coventry RI 02816

Call Sign: K1OZM
Milton F Pierce
156 Mapleroot Village 53

Coventry RI 02816

Call Sign: KA1SLQ
Charles L Hughes
24 Matteson St
Coventry RI 02816

Call Sign: KA1SID
Michelle L Burnham
55 Meredith Dr
Coventry RI 02816

Call Sign: KB1PTD
Kenneth A Chapman
3 Milton Lane
Coventry RI 02816

Call Sign: N1CLG
Kenneth A Chapman
3 Milton Lane
Coventry RI 02816

Call Sign: WA1WM
William H May
20 Montana Ave
Coventry RI 02816

Call Sign: WA1RJY
Joseph Rogowski
5 Nancy St
Coventry RI 02816

Call Sign: AG1L
Marvin G Weinman
One Red Coach Dr
Coventry RI 02816

Call Sign: W1KPH
Kevin P Harris
22 Park Ave
Coventry RI 02816

Call Sign: N1VVR
Michael Therrien
56 Pembroke Ln

Coventry RI 02816   Coventry RI 02816   Coventry RI 02816

Call Sign: N1KEP   Call Sign: KE1GM   Call Sign: W1SCW
Paul E Catalani   Leo Noiseux   Shawn C Whitmore
33 Pettine St   109 Princeton Ave   1 Rosewood Ct
Coventry RI 02816   Coventry RI 02816   Coventry RI 02816

Call Sign: KB1JDB   Call Sign: KB1CWE   Call Sign: K1JEU
Hui Seamans   William J Bezak   Charles P Earley
31 Phillips Hill Rd   1 Puritan Ave   46 S Main St
Coventry RI 02816   Coventry RI 02816   Coventry RI 02816

Call Sign: WB2PLS   Call Sign: K1YOA   Call Sign: KA1QHO
Herbert L Paul Jr   Roy L Sassi   Doreen A Sadowski
101 Pilgrim Ave   34 Rawlinson Dr   452 Shady Valley Rd
Coventry RI 02816   Coventry RI 02816   Coventry RI 028166811

Call Sign: WA1MVI   Call Sign: N1JVJ   Call Sign: W1BF
Frank P Soito   Rene J Chaput   Edward J Sadowski Jr
137 Pilgrim Ave Apt 44   155 Read Ave   452 Shady Valley Rd
Coventry RI 02816   Coventry RI 02816   Coventry RI 028166811

Call Sign: KB1JCS   Call Sign: KB1JED   Call Sign: WA1ULJ
Raymond F Skorski   Cory M Therrien   Raymond F Cain
10 Pine Acres Blvd   56 Rembroke Ln   89 Sherwood Valley Ln
Coventry RI 02816   Coventry RI 02816   Coventry RI 02816

Call Sign: KB1KFA   Call Sign: KB1GLE   Call Sign: KA1ZSL
Dorothea F Skorski   Andrew J Bent   Donald P Briggs
10 Pine Acres Blvd   32 Reservoir Rd   177 South Main Street
Coventry RI 02816   Coventry RI 02816   Coventry RI 02616

Call Sign: N1LYB   Call Sign: N1APD   Call Sign: KB1QIL
Richard A Houle Sr   Anthony C Gudeczauskas   Jared M Plante
26 Pine Grove Ave   21 Robbins Dr   10 Spencer St
Coventry RI 02816   Coventry RI 028166129   Coventry RI 02816

Call Sign: KB1JEA   Call Sign: KA1BQP   Call Sign: KA1YYX
Timothy A Jackson   Matthew R White   Robert A Despres Sr
5 Pine Ln   27 Rosemary St   166 Station St
Coventry RI 02816   Coventry RI 028166046   Coventry RI 02816

Call Sign: N1MIS   Call Sign: N1VRA   Call Sign: KB1SJU
Jerry Shepherd   Susanne D Stearns   Karen A Capotosto
82 Princeton Ave   27 Rosemary Street   16 Stephanie Dr

Coventry RI 02816

Call Sign: N1TKC
Kevin J Green
1 Stoney Hill Cr.
Coventry RI 02816

Call Sign: N1YDQ
Scott W Bentley
978 Tiogue Ave Apt 55
Coventry RI 02816

Call Sign: KA1HIR
Alfred L Snape Jr
345 Townfarm Road
Coventry RI 02816

Call Sign: W1PX
Allen E Bestwick Sr
44 Valley Crest Rd
Coventry RI 02816

Call Sign: KB1HES
Beavertail ARC
44 Valley Crest Rd
Coventry RI 02816

Call Sign: K1BTL
Beavertail ARC
44 Valley Crest Rd
Coventry RI 028168834

Call Sign: K1HNA
Joseph M Mattias
57 Valley Crest Rd
Coventry RI 02816

Call Sign: AG1J
Peter W Harris
18 Vera Rd
Coventry RI 02816

Call Sign: KA1BLE
Bridie B Harris
18 Vera Rd

Coventry RI 02816

Call Sign: N1EZN
Kevin P Harris
18 Vera Rd
Coventry RI 02816

Call Sign: W1PWH
Peter W Harris
18 Vera Rd
Coventry RI 02816

Call Sign: W1BBH
Bridie B Harris
18 Vera Rd
Coventry RI 02816

Call Sign: K1PH
Peter W Harris
18 Vera Rd
Coventry RI 02816

Call Sign: N1OTG
Randy T Parrott
10 Walker Lane
Coventry RI 02816

Call Sign: KA1ARX
Peter P Golomb
601 Washington St
Coventry RI 02816

Call Sign: KC1VL
Barnes K Scarlett
439 Weaver Hill Rd
Coventry RI 02816

Call Sign: KB1CXM
Scott T Marcotte
630 Weaver Hill Rd
Coventry RI 028164916

Call Sign: KA1ZIM
Gene J Soler
26 Williams Crossing Rd

Coventry RI 02816

Call Sign: KB1AFE
Jeremy E Fontes
211 Williams Crossing Rd
Coventry RI 02827

Call Sign: N1VJI
Garry M Noel
123 Windsor Park Dr
Coventry RI 02816

Call Sign: N1IGV
Leonard E Watson
20 Woodland Dr Apt 207
Coventry RI 02816

Call Sign: KB1KOI
Joseph D Matthews
49 Wright Way
Coventry RI 02816

Call Sign: N1WCA
Charles W Tanner Jr
55 Wright Way
Coventry RI 02816

Call Sign: W1QZ
John B Mann
13 York Dr
Coventry RI 02816

Call Sign: KB1QCV
Peter V Corio
46 York Dr
Coventry RI 02816

Call Sign: KB1QCW
Shirley L Corio
46 York Drive
Coventry RI 02816

Call Sign: KD1EJ
David R Perry
Coventry RI 02816

Call Sign: N1PII
Frank V Meglio
Coventry RI 02816

Call Sign: WA1GVM
Stephen T Jurczyk
Coventry RI 02816

Call Sign: KB1MPE
Coventry Mobileers Arc
Coventry RI 02816

Call Sign: K1CCN
Coventry Mobileers Arc
Coventry RI 02816

FCC Amateur Radio Licenses in Cranston

Call Sign: W1PJS
Joseph Pezza
64 A St
Cranston RI 02920

Call Sign: WX1USA
Edward H Cayer Jr
60 Allen Ave
Cranston RI 02910

Call Sign: W1SVE
Edward S Feldman
50 Applegate Rd
Cranston RI 02920

Call Sign: WA1LQA
Edward E Hanson
116 Auburn St
Cranston RI 02910

Call Sign: WA2GFP
Geoffrey H Krauss
71 Bakewell Ct
Cranston RI 02921

Call Sign: WA1WOL
Kenneth J Pickering
39 Balsam Ct.
Cranston RI 02920

Call Sign: N1XAA
Michael P King
330 Bayview Ave
Cranston RI 02905

Call Sign: N1MRH
Thomas P Wallace
226 Beckwith St
Cranston RI 02910

Call Sign: KE2GN
James N Saflund
102 Betsey Williams D
Cranston RI 02905

Call Sign: KA1RFS
Rocco J Grasso
63 Birchwood Dr
Cranston RI 02920

Call Sign: KA1RFT
John R Grasso
63 Birchwood Dr
Cranston RI 02920

Call Sign: N1ZHN
Geraldeen Fay
60 Bluff Ave
Cranston RI 029055106

Call Sign: N1ZZJ
Robert G Felici
85 Briggs Street Apt 706
Cranston RI 02920

Call Sign: KA1QIK
Timothy M Chmura
60 Brookwood Rd
Cranston RI 02910

Call Sign: KB1INT
Amable Gonzalez
80 Burnside St
Cranston RI 02910

Call Sign: K1KDI
Anthony L George Ii
167 Calaman Rd
Cranston RI 02910

Call Sign: KA1WJO
Robert R Barber
34 Celestia Ave
Cranston RI 02920

Call Sign: KB1WUP
Allan R Hilton
35 Cherry Rd
Cranston RI 02905

Call Sign: N1XCY
Scott S Danzer
72 Clark Ave
Cranston RI 02920

Call Sign: KA1KML
James E Yakey
26 Commercial St
Cranston RI 029053634

Call Sign: KB1PVL
Thomas Yakey Sr
26 Commercial St
Cranston RI 029053634

Call Sign: KA1KML
Thomas Yakey Sr
26 Commercial St
Cranston RI 029053634

Call Sign: N1HDB
Marilyn J Suggs
62 Cornell St
Cranston RI 02920

Call Sign: KB1WRK
Christopher J Dillon Sr
184 Cornell St
Cranston RI 02920

Call Sign: N1VZM
Paul M Morena
37 Coulters Rd
Cranston RI 029206003

Call Sign: KB1OQU
Devon R Dubuque
2343 Cranston St
Cranston RI 02920

Call Sign: KZ1K
John R Winman
2453 Cranston St
Cranston RI 02920

Call Sign: N1WVR
Richard M Tovar
2140 Cranston Street
Cranston RI 029203900

Call Sign: AA1JT
Donald L Nichols
222 Crescent Ave Apt 2
Cranston RI 02910

Call Sign: KB1WBC
William F Loux Jr
100 Curtis St
Cranston RI 02920

Call Sign: K1WFL
William F Loux Jr
100 Curtis St
Cranston RI 02920

Call Sign: KE2JY
Donald Andrew Messina
18 Doylston Dr
Cranston RI 02905

Call Sign: KA1FJZ
Joseph F Connetta
443 Dyer Ave
Cranston RI 02920

Call Sign: KA1FKA
Viola I Connetta
443 Dyer Ave
Cranston RI 02920

Call Sign: KB1OIX
Frank A Gardiner
945 Dyer Ave -29
Cranston RI 02920

Call Sign: KB1OHI
David F Gardiner
945 Dyer Ave Apt 29
Cranston RI 02920

Call Sign: N1QL
David F Gardiner
945 Dyer Ave Apt 29
Cranston RI 02920

Call Sign: KB1ADM
John P Isabella Jr
578 Dyer Ave Apt E115
Cranston RI 02920

Call Sign: N1LXN
Gino A Paolucci
16 Edgewood Ave
Cranston RI 029051342

Call Sign: KB1SDL
Carrie A Cullen
100 Elena St Apt 707
Cranston RI 02920

Call Sign: WA1ITU
John K Lesuer
75 Elmhurst Ave
Cranston RI 02920

Call Sign: KB1SAH
Mathew J Ferreira
1310 Elmwood Ave
Cranston RI 02910

Call Sign: KB1SVF
Christina M Motta
1310 Elmwood Ave
Cranston RI 02910

Call Sign: KA1YEX
Zaven R Norigian Jr
20 Everett Rd
Cranston RI 02920

Call Sign: K1JFI
Roger Williams Vhf Society
53 Fairfield Rd
Cranston RI 029105304

Call Sign: N1FKI
Michael G Cardarelli Jr
53 Fairfield Road
Cranston RI 029105304

Call Sign: K1MGC
Michael G Cardarelli Jr
53 Fairfield Road
Cranston RI 029105304

Call Sign: WA1GNW
Robinson O Bellin
26 Fairview Ave
Cranston RI 02905

Call Sign: N1RPZ
Eugene Hassell
26 Fairwood Dr
Cranston RI 02920

Call Sign: KB1ANU
Brenda J Lonquist
32 Fairwood Dr
Cranston RI 02920

Call Sign: KB1ANV
Ronald T Raposa
32 Fairwood Dr
Cranston RI 02920

Call Sign: KA1BBR
William V Polleys
55 Ferncrest Ave
Cranston RI 02905

Call Sign: N3VOY
Peter B Ingles
160 Greenwood St
Cranston RI 02910

Call Sign: N1EJG
Roger A Prata
32 Fairwood Drive
Cranston RI 02920

Call Sign: N1NAB
Thomas M Campbell
120 Forest Ave
Cranston RI 02910

Call Sign: N1HEG
Thomas W Bonnick
156 Hilltop Dr
Cranston RI 02920

Call Sign: KA1YEW
Joshua A Terry
30 Falmouth Rd
Cranston RI 02920

Call Sign: K1MHK
Arthur E Whitcomb
391 Garden City Dr
Cranston RI 029208223

Call Sign: N1MND
Raymond R Antonelli
91 Hollyhock Dr
Cranston RI 029205802

Call Sign: N1UKH
Robert M Di Martino
260 Farmington Ave
Cranston RI 02909

Call Sign: KA1CSU
Paul E Sturtevant
174 Glen Hills Dr
Cranston RI 029203515

Call Sign: K1JHH
Raymond R Antonelli
91 Hollyhock Dr
Cranston RI 029205802

Call Sign: KB1AUA
Christopher Leonard
355 Farmington Ave
Cranston RI 02920

Call Sign: KB1HCO
Kevin P Sturtevant
174 Glen Hills Dr
Cranston RI 02920

Call Sign: N1ATF
Paul M Piekarski
29 Hope Rd
Cranston RI 02920

Call Sign: KB1FTV
Daniel P King
127 Farmington Ave Apt 9
Cranston RI 02920

Call Sign: KB1MJW
James J Sturtevant
174 Glen Hills Dr
Cranston RI 02920

Call Sign: K1TUY
Alfred A Izzo Sr
18 Humbert Ave
Cranston RI 02910

Call Sign: K1VUW
Domenic Loffredo
8 Fernbrook Ct
Cranston RI 02920

Call Sign: K1BCT
George P Carnegis
214 Glen Hills Dr
Cranston RI 02920

Call Sign: K1SGX
Stephen R Fish
59 Imperial Ave
Cranston RI 02920

Call Sign: W1HFC
Charles A Link
8 Fernbrook Ct
Cranston RI 02920

Call Sign: KB1JDD
Jubal O De La Cruz
184 Grand Ave
Cranston RI 02905

Call Sign: W1BG
Stephen R Fish
59 Imperial Ave
Cranston RI 02920

Call Sign: KA1FIG
Herman J Potter
30 Fernbrook Ct Apt 1
Cranston RI 02920

Call Sign: KA1YEV
Michael W Libby
6 Greenview Rd
Cranston RI 02920

Call Sign: KB1ERO
David A Dicenzo
37 Invernia Rd
Cranston RI 029201946

Call Sign: KA1CPX
Joseph N Spagnoli Jr
33 Iroquois Tr
Cranston RI 02920

Call Sign: KB1BCC
Claire Mac Innes
288 Lawnacre Dr
Cranston RI 02920

Call Sign: N1QGN
Paolo L De Petrillo
35 Longview Dr
Cranston RI 02920

Call Sign: W1EOF
John Titterington
20 Irving St
Cranston RI 029101425

Call Sign: N1TDS
James A Mac Innes
288 Lawnacre Dr
Cranston RI 02920

Call Sign: N1QGO
Lawrence R De Petrillo
35 Longview Dr
Cranston RI 02920

Call Sign: KA1ULD
Marc G Le Vasseur
16 Keith Ave
Cranston RI 02910

Call Sign: N1FHZ
Gabriel B San Antonio
205 Legion Way
Cranston RI 02910

Call Sign: KB1SLO
Harry Finkelstein
49 Longview Dr
Cranston RI 02920

Call Sign: W1FPD
Richard E Waugh Sr
79 Keith Ave
Cranston RI 029105742

Call Sign: W1KEM
Harold S Hayward
99 Lincoln Park Ave
Cranston RI 02920

Call Sign: KB1BBZ
Lewis B Lovejoy
55 Longview Dr
Cranston RI 029203317

Call Sign: KD1MR
Kenneth P Potvin
22 Kiki Cir
Cranston RI 02921

Call Sign: KB1MMQ
Richard A Gallo
97 Locust Glen Dr
Cranston RI 02921

Call Sign: K1EGD
Frederick C Dawson
79 Longview Dr
Cranston RI 02920

Call Sign: W1NMH
Marcel J Marchesseault
235 Knollwood Ave
Cranston RI 02910

Call Sign: W1DAG
Richard A Gallo
97 Locust Glen Dr
Cranston RI 02921

Call Sign: N1ZZI
John G Mangasarian
60 Lowell St
Cranston RI 02910

Call Sign: KA1RDL
John W Maki Jr
25 Laconia Rd
Cranston RI 02920

Call Sign: KB1NUK
Marlene D Gallo
97 Locust Glen Dr
Cranston RI 02921

Call Sign: N1ZRD
Dawn Burdick
119 Magnolia St. - Apt #2
Cranston RI 02910

Call Sign: K1SMI
Aram A Plante
15 Lakeside Ave
Cranston RI 02910

Call Sign: N1OPK
Laura A Miniscalco
12 Longhill Dr
Cranston RI 02920

Call Sign: KA1OOL
Robert F Evans
19 Malcolm St
Cranston RI 02910

Call Sign: AA1IF
Craig S Mac Innes
288 Lawnacre Dr
Cranston RI 02920

Call Sign: N1SGG
Christopher Miniscalco
12 Longhill Dr
Cranston RI 02920

Call Sign: KA1DYC
Robert S Casey Ii
210 Mapleton St
Cranston RI 02910

Call Sign: W1WJY
Frank Heiss
117 Maplewood Ave
Cranston RI 02920

Call Sign: K1BDJ
Warren A Chamandy
10 Margaret St
Cranston RI 02907

Call Sign: W1AFO
Stanley W Atkinson
59 Mason Ave
Cranston RI 02910

Call Sign: K1GYW
David H Sholes
32 Mauran St
Cranston RI 02910

Call Sign: KC1GD
Arthur E Anderson
87 Mayfield Ave
Cranston RI 02920

Call Sign: W1BBJ
William A Stempel
425 Meshanticut Vly Pky
Apt 109
Cranston RI 02920

Call Sign: WA1PQX
Arthur O Pelchat
19 Metropolitan Ave
Cranston RI 02920

Call Sign: KA1ORO
Kim A Miller
111 Metropolitan Ave
Cranston RI 02920

Call Sign: N1BDS
Winifred E Miller
111 Metropolitan Ave
Cranston RI 02920

Call Sign: W1IGP
William Miller
111 Metropolitan Ave
Cranston RI 02920

Call Sign: KB1PCD
Richard Forcino
101 Moccasin Trail
Cranston RI 02921

Call Sign: N1ZVW
David W Costantino
58 Mohawk Trl
Cranston RI 029212543

Call Sign: N1HDL
Joseph T Matarese
90 Mollie Drive
Cranston RI 02921

Call Sign: KB1BRF
David A Michel
1406 Narragansett Blvd
Cranston RI 02905

Call Sign: KA1ZQJ
Reuven S Soultanoglou
205 Narragansett St
Cranston RI 02905

Call Sign: W1GPE
George T Underwood
53 Normandy Dr
Cranston RI 02920

Call Sign: KA1YDT
Brian P Flanagan
15 Norton Ave
Cranston RI 02920

Call Sign: KA1YDU
William D Flanagan
15 Norton Ave
Cranston RI 02920

Call Sign: N3UBU
Christopher C Alekna
52 Oakland Avenue
Cranston RI 02910

Call Sign: KB1MYZ
Wayne E Pelletier
111 Oaklawn Ave Apt - 83
Cranston RI 02920

Call Sign: KB1MYS
Wayne E Pelletier Jr
111 Oaklawn Ave - 83
Cransten RI 02920

Call Sign: KB1FML
Joyce S Fleischer
One Selkirk Road
Cranston RI 02905

Call Sign: K1WIR
Francis J Caniglia
40 Packard St
Cranston RI 02910

Call Sign: WA1PSG
Elizabeth P Caniglia
40 Packard St
Cranston RI 02910

Call Sign: KB1AIE
Robert J Peterson
315 Park Ave Apt 220
Cranston RI 02905

Call Sign: KA1MLA
Mark E Wilson
1232 Park Avenue. 2nd
Floor / Rear
Cranston RI 02910

Call Sign: W1NBH
Edmund Orange
19 Pearce Ave

Cranston RI 029105019

Call Sign: W1KNH
Clarence Coppolelli
44 Pengrove
Cranston RI 02920

Call Sign: WA1MQX
Casimiro J Notarianni
53 Pershing St
Cranston RI 02910

Call Sign: N1WQF
Frederick Mancini Jr
250 Phenix Ave
Cranston RI 02920

Call Sign: KB1AKB
Fred L Nelson
801 Pontiac Ave
Cranston RI 02910

Call Sign: KB1IWV
Ari T Foster
825 Pontiac Ave #8101
Cranston RI 02910

Call Sign: K1ZVR
Eugene A Franzen
825 Pontiac Ave Apt 16201
Cranston RI 02910

Call Sign: KA1SUG
Hazel F Krieg
935 Pontiac Ave Apt 77
Cranston RI 02920

Call Sign: W1GTS
Austin Chadwick Jr
132 Poplar Dr
Cranston RI 02920

Call Sign: W1JER
Frank Savicki
284 Poplar Dr

Cranston RI 02920

Call Sign: KB1SJM
Christopher R Lo
98 Potter St
Cranston RI 02910

Call Sign: KA1YFR
Stephen S Barone
39 Preston Dr
Cranston RI 02910

Call Sign: WA1AGV
Angelo Martino
83 Princess Ave
Cranston RI 02920

Call Sign: KA1ZFD
Ronald D Garafano
1 Regina Dr
Cranston RI 02921

Call Sign: N1IIK
David P Williams
55 Regina Dr
Cranston RI 02921

Call Sign: N1KKT
Daniel J Mc Donald Sr
58 Richard St
Cranston RI 02910

Call Sign: KB1OQS
Pasquale S Genco
17 Robinlyn Dr
Cranston RI 02921

Call Sign: KB1OQV
Anthony P Genco
17 Robinlyn Dr
Cranston RI 02921

Call Sign: KB1OQX
Daniel P Genco
17 Robinlyn Dr

Cranston RI 02921

Call Sign: N1EMD
Michael C Iannucelli Jr
100 Royal Ave
Cranston RI 02920

Call Sign: W1SKC
Michael C Iannucelli
100 Royal Ave
Cranston RI 02920

Call Sign: KB1EVH
Michael D Vincent
22 Ruskin Street
Cranston RI 02920

Call Sign: KB1KQG
Shawn D De Cesari
14 Sabra St
Cranston RI 02910

Call Sign: N1YFZ
Thomas M Capirchio
51 Salem Ave
Cranston RI 02920

Call Sign: W1LZY
John F O Rourke
1584 Scituate Ave
Cranston RI 02920

Call Sign: N1RQC
Lewis J Spencer
6403 Scituate Vista Dr
Cranston RI 02921

Call Sign: W1YNE
Gordon F Fox
7219 Scituate Vista Dr
Cranston RI 029211763

Call Sign: KA1QIJ
Jerry L Collette
164 Second Ave

Cranston RI 02910

Call Sign: KB1ADP
Norma C Collette
164 Second Ave
Cranston RI 02910

Call Sign: KB1ADQ
Daniel P Collette
164 Second Ave
Cranston RI 02910

Call Sign: WA1SKQ
Richard G Fleischer
1 Selkirk Rd
Cranston RI 02905

Call Sign: KB1UNJ
John P Fritz
16 Selkirk Rd
Cranston RI 02905

Call Sign: KA1YET
Owen C Mc Dermott
33 Selma St
Cranston RI 02920

Call Sign: KA1YEU
Kevin M Mc Dermott
33 Selma St
Cranston RI 02920

Call Sign: W2IGY
Emmett A Childress
23 Sherwood St
Cranston RI 02920

Call Sign: AB1DJ
Emmett A Childress
23 Sherwood St
Cranston RI 02920

Call Sign: WA1SUB
George F Mc Donald
15 Spenstone Rd

Cranston RI 02920

Call Sign: KA1VXV
Edna B Savage
253 Stony Acre Dr
Cranston RI 02920

Call Sign: KA1BAR
Anthony J Connetta
12 Sunset Ridge Dr
Cranston RI 02920

Call Sign: N1LJP
Roger La Grange
77 Sunset Ter
Cranston RI 029051044

Call Sign: KB1ULY
Christine C Allard
58 Tacoma St
Cranston RI 02920

Call Sign: K1CCA
Christine C Allard
58 Tacoma St
Cranston RI 02920

Call Sign: N1DKF
Sylvester J Gookin
128 Tallman Ave
Cranston RI 029105444

Call Sign: NZ1K
Jane Hathaway Gookin
128 Tallman Ave
Cranston RI 029105444

Call Sign: KA1WPI
Alicia H Hartman
128 Tallman Avenue
Cranston RI 029105444

Call Sign: KA1BRJ
Michael T Maiorano
106 Vallette St

Cranston RI 02920

Call Sign: KB1TIA
Rhode Island Emergency
Team
106 Vallette Street
Cranston RI 02920

Call Sign: KA3RGY
Lauren B Jeweler
14 Valley View Circle
Cranston RI 029211032

Call Sign: KB1AWZ
Frank J Branca
33 Vera St
Cranston RI 02920

Call Sign: KA1NOW
Steven S Ruskin
49 Vigilant
Cranston RI 02920

Call Sign: W1RDM
Raymond D Martin
67 Waldron Ave
Cranston RI 02910

Call Sign: KA1OSP
Everett F Smith
123 Waterman Ave
Cranston RI 02910

Call Sign: KA1YEA
Edna R Farrell
138 Wentworth Ave
Cranston RI 02905

Call Sign: AB2MV
Shadow P Farrell
138 Wentworth Avenue
Cranston RI 02905

Call Sign: KB1GCA
Alfred Der Toumaian

9 Western Hills Lane 4302
Cranston RI 02921

Call Sign: KA1SAF
Charles R Conte
6 Western Hills Ln
Cranston RI 02921

Call Sign: N1OWM
Abby B Cormier
6 Western Hills Ln Apt
3204
Cranston RI 02921

Call Sign: W1IUX
Zaven V Tenkarian
89 Westwood Ave
Cranston RI 02905

Call Sign: KB1HFV
Leonard R Shappy
45 Wheeler Ave
Cranston RI 029052707

Call Sign: KB1EGE
Nicholas A Depetrillo
73 Wheeler Ave
Cranston RI 029052707

Call Sign: W1PRA
Paul R De Petrillo
73 Wheeler Avenue
Cranston RI 029052707

Call Sign: N1CKD
Nicholas A Depetrillo
73 Wheeler Avenue
Cranston RI 029052707

Call Sign: W1BQH
Ernest Moss Jr
280 Woodbine St
Cranston RI 02910

Call Sign: N1FAR

Kenneth A Gaspar
79 Woodland Ave
Cranston RI 02920

Call Sign: N1FKJ
Jamey R Zito
79 Woodland Ave
Cranston RI 02920

Call Sign: KB1KVE
Richard A Degrandpre
20 Zinnia Dr
Cranston RI 02920

Call Sign: K1CR
Joseph F Del Giudice
Cranston RI 02920

Call Sign: K1OS
Ocean State Amateur Radio
Group
Cranston RI 02920

Call Sign: KA1JZS
Michael J Martino
Cranston RI 02920

Call Sign: N1GEB
Adele T Koluch
Cranston RI 029100092

Call Sign: N1GEC
Charles Koluch
Cranston RI 029100092

Call Sign: KB1JQG
Geoffrey L Milner
Cranston RI 029100060

Call Sign: W1ZAP
Geoffrey L Milner
Cranston RI 029100060

Call Sign: KB1KPF
Andrew G Milner

Cranston RI 02910

Call Sign: KB1KQS
Garrett D Milner
Cranston RI 02910

Call Sign: KB1PJO
Richard A Myrick
Cranston RI 02910

Call Sign: KB1TSH
Michael J Flynn
Cranston RI 02920

Call Sign: KA1TBK
Michael Mc Knight
285 Mayfield Ave
Cranstron RI 02920

FCC Amateur Radio Licenses in Cumberland

Call Sign: W1AQA
Harry F Brockington
320 Abbott Run Valley Rd
Cumberland RI 02864

Call Sign: N1VSX
Brian D Boragine
7 Academy Dr
Cumberland RI 02864

Call Sign: WA1PJC
Anthony Muto
17 Arnold Dr
Cumberland RI 02864

Call Sign: WA1TWF
Antonio N Muto
17 Arnold Dr
Cumberland RI 02864

Call Sign: N1HCO
Kathleen M Earley
4 Avon Ave

Cumberland RI 02864   Cumberland RI 02864   Cumberland RI 02864

Call Sign: WA1JEP   Call Sign: KB1MWK   Call Sign: K1LRS
Mark W Earley   John R Brown   Lee R Smith
4 Avon Ave   165 Bryant St   88 Colonial Ave
Cumberland RI 02864   Cumberland RI 02864   Cumberland RI 02864

Call Sign: KB1FZI   Call Sign: KB1CNS   Call Sign: KB1DDV
Brian W Earley   Thomas M Cragin Iii   William R Campbell
4 Avon Ave   12 Buckboard Dr   93 Colonial Ave
Cumberland RI 02864   Cumberland RI 028646152   Cumberland RI 02864

Call Sign: KB1HCN   Call Sign: N1TLH   Call Sign: WA1NVO
David A Pacheco   Thomas M Cragin   Charles Horstman
15 Barn Dr   12 Buckboard Dr   16 Countryside Dr
Cumberland RI 02864   Cumberland RI 02864   Cumberland RI 028642602

Call Sign: KA1WHF   Call Sign: N1DO   Call Sign: AA4PQ
Roger P Scoffone   Richard H Olney   Steven B Arnold
5 Blacksmith Rd   27 Cadoret   150 Crossing Drive Apt 102
Cumberland RI 02864   Cumberland RI 02864   Cumberland RI 02864

Call Sign: KA1WHK   Call Sign: KA1RKU   Call Sign: AF1F
Diane M Scoffone   James M Mc Gilligan   Francis J Souza
5 Blacksmith Rd   15 Cargill Rd   1775 Diamond Hill Rd
Cumberland RI 02864   Cumberland RI 02864   Cumberland RI 02864

Call Sign: K1MKP   Call Sign: KC1BJ   Call Sign: K1JZN
Leo R Varieur   Edward N Sirois   Victor St Laurent
26 Blanche Ave   16 Carlson Dr   465 England St
Cumberland RI 02864   Cumberland RI 02864   Cumberland RI 02864

Call Sign: K1AMG   Call Sign: KB1CHD   Call Sign: K1QIY
Anthony J Sidla   Edward F Glod   Normand P Thibeault
14 Brayton Ct   13 Christine Dr   20 Fairhaven Rd
Cumberland RI 02864   Cumberland RI 028641714   Cumberland RI 028644709

Call Sign: KA1FSU   Call Sign: KB1LHH   Call Sign: K1VXZ
Rudolph S Nawracaj   Ronald J Treanor   Theresa M Thibeault
20 Briarwood Dr   57 Club Dr   20 Fairhaven Rd
Cumberland RI 02864   Cumberland RI 02864   Cumberland RI 028644709

Call Sign: W1NDU   Call Sign: KB1OVM   Call Sign: N1WWG
Garabed G Onoyan   Lee R Smith   Virginia M Jones
25 Britts Ridge   88 Colonial Ave   49 Farm View Dr

Cumberland RI 02864

Cumberland RI 02864

Cumberland RI 02864

Call Sign: WB1P
Robert E Jones
49 Farmview Dr
Cumberland RI 02864

Call Sign: W1MWE
Mark W Earley
51 Hazebrouck St.
Cumberland RI 02864

Call Sign: N1DTG
Theresa M Bouvier
29 Jencks Rd
Cumberland RI 02864

Call Sign: W8PS
Peter A Sichel
13 Fieldside Drive
Cumberland RI 02864

Call Sign: K1KME
Kathleen M Earley
51 Hazebrouck St.
Cumberland RI 02864

Call Sign: KA1UQU
Reggie J Corey
Jencks Rd
Cumberland RI 02864

Call Sign: KB1KWN
Joseph D Guillemette
44 Fisher Rd
Cumberland RI 02864

Call Sign: W1BWE
Brian W Earley
51 Hazebrouck St.
Cumberland RI 02864

Call Sign: N1KNP
Michael J Salinger
45 Knollcrest Dr
Cumberland RI 02864

Call Sign: KB1GJN
Robert E Marois
63 Grandview Dr
Cumberland RI 02864

Call Sign: KA1BVL
Ronald P Chouinard
266 High St
Cumberland RI 02864

Call Sign: K1CBF
James J Dandeneau
59 Laurel Ln
Cumberland RI 02864

Call Sign: KA1QNC
Robert P Cavallaro
20 Green St
Cumberland RI 02864

Call Sign: KA1VXB
Robert R Maurice
370 High St
Cumberland RI 02864

Call Sign: N1EOI
David A Burbine Sr
10 Leach Street Unit B4
Cumberland RI 02864

Call Sign: KB1JNT
Benjamin J Snyder
47 Greenfield Rd
Cumberland RI 02864

Call Sign: KB1DRN
Paul A Young
151 Hilltop Rd
Cumberland RI 02864

Call Sign: AG1O
Eldon E Crawford
96 Leigh Rd
Cumberland RI 02864

Call Sign: KV1O
Roland R St Laurent
48 Greenfield Rd
Cumberland RI 02864

Call Sign: KA1P
Frank J Kelley Jr
145 Hope St
Cumberland RI 028647225

Call Sign: K1VSR
Shawn D De Cesari
185 Leigh Road
Cumberland RI 02864

Call Sign: KB1TNE
Marc P Maria
90 Hadde Ave
Cumberland RI 02864

Call Sign: KB1RYV
Mary A Fontaine
210 Iroquois Ave
Cumberland RI 02864

Call Sign: KB1AUQ
John Pereira
291 Lippitt Ave
Cumberland RI 02864

Call Sign: W1MPM
Marc P Maria
90 Hadde Ave

Call Sign: K1AM
Gerard F Bouvier
29 Jencks Rd

Call Sign: N1HKU
Robert P Kelly Sr
343 Lippitt Ave

Cumberland RI 028644043

Call Sign: KA1UNA
Philip S Mc Grath Jr
Little Pond County Rd
Cumberland RI 02864

Call Sign: KC2CUC
Pablo M Urena
5 Maple St Apt 2f
Cumberland RI 02864

Call Sign: KB1PXI
Matthew J Wollen
10 Matthew Rd
Cumberland RI 02864

Call Sign: KA1JXH
William M Foss
70 Mayfair Rd
Cumberland RI 02864

Call Sign: W1REK
William H Foss
70 Mayfair Rd
Cumberland RI 02864

Call Sign: N1MST
Eugene R Conway
3220 Mendon Rd
Cumberland RI 02864

Call Sign: WB1CPZ
Joseph W Simanski
Mendon Rd
Cumberland RI 02864

Call Sign: KB1KQI
James W Littlefield
2970 Mendon Rd Apt 83
Cumberland RI 02864

Call Sign: WN1X
James W Littlefield
2970 Mendon Rd Apt 83

Cumberland RI 02864

Call Sign: KB1WLB
David W Zagroski
30 Minerva Ave
Cumberland RI 02864

Call Sign: KB1URA
Jonathon T Heaney
306 Minerva Ave
Cumberland RI 02864

Call Sign: KB1LHJ
Stephen Carr
15 N Attleboro Rd
Cumberland RI 02864

Call Sign: W1LQA
G Holmes Wilson
42 Nancy Dr
Cumberland RI 02864

Call Sign: N1JYZ
Arthur J Couture Jr
11 Narragansett Rd
Cumberland RI 02864

Call Sign: KD1RM
Gerard F Foisy
21 Narragansett Rd
Cumberland RI 028645915

Call Sign: KB1LHI
John R Melkonian
6 Nate Whipple Hwy Unit
106
Cumberland RI 028641417

Call Sign: WB1CON
Robert C Norton
67 Newell Dr
Cumberland RI 02864

Call Sign: K1VM
George W Doyle

4 Nixon St
Cumberland RI 02864

Call Sign: KB1NUJ
Jennifer A Galipeau
110 Notre Dame Ave
Cumberland RI 02864

Call Sign: W2DG
Lloyd F Cook
10 Old Diamond Hill Rd
Apt 259
Cumberland RI 02864

Call Sign: K1JYM
Richard H Berthiaume
15 Orchard Dr
Cumberland RI 028645116

Call Sign: WD4AON
Terrence Martin
30 Paine Rd
Cumberland RI 02864

Call Sign: N1WHG
Johnathan D Berard
15 Pine Swamp Rd
Cumberland RI 02864

Call Sign: KC2GAO
Joao D Rodrigues
30 Pleasant St
Cumberland RI 02864

Call Sign: KB1DOY
Zdenko Juskuv
42 Poisson St
Cumberland RI 02864

Call Sign: KB1DRM
Maria Juskuv
42 Poisson St
Cumberland RI 02864

Call Sign: KB1EAQ

Catherine S Juskuv
42 Poisson St
Cumberland RI 02864

Call Sign: KE1LJ
Marian Juskuv
42 Poisson St
Cumberland RI 02864

Call Sign: AA1VU
Marian Juskuv
42 Poisson St
Cumberland RI 02864

Call Sign: KB1WOM
Red Cross Providence
42 Poisson St
Cumberland RI 02864

Call Sign: K1KIK
Arthur E Seidel Jr
124 Pollett St
Cumberland RI 02864

Call Sign: NT1Z
Frank L Di Lorenzo
11 Rebecca Lane
Cumberland RI 02864

Call Sign: KB1KPZ
Lynda F Laplante
21 Roberts St
Cumberland RI 02864

Call Sign: KB1NNG
Southern New England Dx
Association
30 Rocky Crest Dr
Cumberland RI 02864

Call Sign: W1FH
Southern New England Dx
Association
30 Rocky Crest Dr
Cumberland RI 02864

Call Sign: W1YRC
Robert G Beaudet
30 Rocky Crest Rd
Cumberland RI 02864

Call Sign: K1MO
David C Mania
281 Scott Rd
Cumberland RI 02864

Call Sign: WA1ZDY
James F O Leary
148 Shirley Dr
Cumberland RI 028645225

Call Sign: KA1NWY
Harry J Mac Donald
28 Stagecoach Rd
Cumberland RI 028646156

Call Sign: W1HJM
Harry J Mac Donald
28 Stagecoach Rd
Cumberland RI 028646156

Call Sign: KB1QMF
Billy J Charette
16 Sun Valley Drive
Cumberland RI 02864

Call Sign: KA1CYQ
Byron M Kinniburgh
22 Tally Ho Rd
Cumberland RI 02864

Call Sign: KB1RHE
Byron M Kinniburgh
22 Tallyho Rd
Cumberland RI 02864

Call Sign: K1CYQ
Byron M Kinniburgh
22 Tallyho Rd
Cumberland RI 02864

Call Sign: N1FQZ
Joseph F Pugliesi
2 Tanglewood Dr
Cumberland RI 028644128

Call Sign: KA1ZUQ
Louis K Russo
40 Tanglewood Dr
Cumberland RI 02864

Call Sign: N1OMG
Kevin L Morrissey
19 Teakwood Dr
Cumberland RI 02864

Call Sign: KA1WKF
David B Smith
36 Thomas Leighton Blvd N
Cumberland RI 02864

Call Sign: K1SUX
Norman R Sylvester
1 Tiffany Dr
Cumberland RI 02864

Call Sign: KB1TQA
Steven C Lacey
25 Tingley Dr
Cumberland RI 02864

Call Sign: KB1BSA
Narragansett Council Bsa
43 Toboggan Rd
Cumberland RI 02864

Call Sign: N1IHE
Gerard J Lamarsh
43 Toboggan Road
Cumberland RI 028646720

Call Sign: WB1FEX
Carol A Mayer
Tower Hill Rd
Cumberland RI 02864

Call Sign: KA1ZIP
George A Kulz
2 Tower Hill Road
Cumberland RI 02864

Call Sign: KD1XC
Kevin J Kurczy
74 Valley View Drive
Cumberland RI 02864

Call Sign: KB1IQZ
Ralph J Hurst Jr
Victory St
Cumberland RI 02864

Call Sign: KB1MNG
Crissy L Hurst
Victory St
Cumberland RI 02864

Call Sign: N1DJF
Ralph J Hurst Jr
Victory St
Cumberland RI 02864

Call Sign: W1DJF
Crissy L Hurst
Victory St
Cumberland RI 02864

Call Sign: NA1J
Fred A Jeffrey
33 W Barrows St
Cumberland RI 02864

Call Sign: N1UBL
Taras Danyluk
77 Waumsett Ave
Cumberland RI 02864

Call Sign: KB1OCT
David A Queenan
66 West Earle St
Cumberland RI 02864

Call Sign: W1DAQ
David A Queenan
66 West Earle St
Cumberland RI 02864

Call Sign: N1YWY
Paul G Pelletier
111 West Rd
Cumberland RI 02864

Call Sign: WB1FBB
Norma W Aldrich
5 White Pine Dr
Cumberland RI 028643319

Call Sign: WB1FBC
Henry W Aldrich
5 White Pine Dr
Cumberland RI 028643319

Call Sign: WA1UZT
Roland H Sasseville
56 Windsong Road
Cumberland RI 028642727

Call Sign: KA1JXJ
Stephen G Dumont
94 Woodside Ave
Cumberland RI 028646119

Call Sign: KA1OXN
Antonio B Moisao
21 Wysteria Ln
Cumberland RI 02864

FCC Amateur Radio Licenses in Darlington

Call Sign: KB2VZO
Timothy M Cahill
35 Peckham Street
Darlington RI 02861

FCC Amateur Radio Licenses in East Greenwich

Call Sign: N1VTF
Derek H Carlino
140 Adirondack Dr
East Greenwich RI 02818

Call Sign: KC4WUI
Richard A Perry
65 Adirondack Drive
East Greenwich RI 02818

Call Sign: N1IHI
Charles K Shallcross
118 Blueberry Dr
East Greenwich RI 02818

Call Sign: KA1PBK
Kenneth G Tefft
27 Brookside Dr
East Greenwich RI 02818

Call Sign: WB1BZK
Robert E Taylor
363 Cedar Ave
East Greenwich RI 02818

Call Sign: KA1FJI
Ruth Y Chamberland
57 Clemente Dr
East Greenwich RI 02818

Call Sign: WA1RDL
A David Chamberland
57 Clemente Dr
East Greenwich RI 02818

Call Sign: WA2HJJ
Joyce E Hughes
5 Coddington Ct
East Greenwich RI 02818

Call Sign: N1WDK

Thomas J Carbone
10 Deerfield Dr
East Greenwich RI 02818

Call Sign: KA1GJE
Carmine J D Ellena
1490 Diplomat Dr
East Greenwich RI 02818

Call Sign: W1YYQ
Elmer E Angell Jr
Eagle Run
East Greenwich RI
028185075

Call Sign: N1ANQ
Lewis B Jackson Jr
85 Ebony Dr
East Greenwich RI 02818

Call Sign: KA1KWE
Andrew J Stenberg
1149 Frenchtown Rd
East Greenwich RI
028181517

Call Sign: W1LX
Everett S Sunderland
1846 Frenchtown Rd
East Greenwich RI
028181017

Call Sign: W1CJP
Fred S Tanner
1337 Frenchtown Road
East Greenwich RI 02818

Call Sign: N1JVW
Patrick A Luvara
70 Glen Drive
East Greenwich RI 02818

Call Sign: K1CUY
M Estelle O Connell
295 Grand View Rd

East Greenwich RI 02818

Call Sign: K1YGY
Thomas A O Connell
295 Grand View Rd
East Greenwich RI 02818

Call Sign: WB1CRM
Vincent A Green
45 Hamilton Dr
East Greenwich RI 02818

Call Sign: KB1ABW
William L Kimbell Jr
1000 High Hawk Rd
East Greenwich RI
028181360

Call Sign: KA1CND
Larry T Guillemette
9 Howland Farm Road
East Greenwich RI 02818

Call Sign: NU1C
Scott Tagen
30 Huguenot Dr
East Greenwich RI 02818

Call Sign: WA1DOK
Richard J Collins
39 Hunts River Ct
East Greenwich RI 02818

Call Sign: N1WBX
John P Hawley
270 Ives Rd
East Greenwich RI 02818

Call Sign: KA1VZT
John L Newton
25 John Alden Rd
East Greenwich RI 02818

Call Sign: N6SZX
Richard H Friend

70 Kenyon Ave
East Greenwich RI 02818

Call Sign: AA1YT
John C Ufford
216 Kenyon Ave
East Greenwich RI 02818

Call Sign: WE3V
John C Ufford
216 Kenyon Ave
East Greenwich RI 02818

Call Sign: W1LKX
Edward J Staba
69 Lawndale Dr
East Greenwich RI 02818

Call Sign: AA3GA
Matthew D Rokita
37 London Street
East Greenwich RI 02818

Call Sign: K1ZMD
Walter V Jette
33 Long St Apt 110
East Greenwich RI 02818

Call Sign: N1MAA
James A Russo
77 Mawney St. #3
East Greenwich RI 02818

Call Sign: WA1EUM
Kirby A Fritz
157 Middle Rd
East Greenwich RI 02818

Call Sign: N1NMW
Michael J Rossi
400 Middle Rd
East Greenwich RI 02818

Call Sign: W1MJR
Michael J Rossi

400 Middle Rd
East Greenwich RI 02818

Call Sign: KB1RYW
Normand R Langlais
2077 Middle Rd
East Greenwich RI 02818

Call Sign: KB1LLQ
Mark W Gee
99 Middle Road
East Greenwich RI
028182801

Call Sign: KA1RPD
Jonathan Finkle
76 Misty Oak Dr.
East Greenwich RI 02818

Call Sign: W1MKS
Jonathan Finkle
76 Misty Oak Dr.
East Greenwich RI 02818

Call Sign: K8ZFJ
Randall T Jones
33 Nichols Ln
East Greenwich RI 02818

Call Sign: AA1RI
David N Moore
108 Oakwood Dr
East Greenwich RI 02818

Call Sign: W1JPM
James P Mc Guire
21 Overbrook Lane
East Greenwich RI 02818

Call Sign: WA4HIG
Robert N Dochterman
205 Pequot Trail
East Greenwich RI 02818

Call Sign: KB1OYJ

Raymond J Lafrance
5300 Post Rd Apt 263
East Greenwich RI
028183071

Call Sign: KB1PDX
Raymond J Lafrance
5300 Post Rd Apt 263
East Greenwich RI
028183071

Call Sign: K1HGB
Charles W Bare Ii
4430 Post Rd Ste A2
East Greenwich RI
028184136

Call Sign: KA1TJA
Annette M Hinkley
84 Potawomut Rd
East Greenwich RI 02818

Call Sign: WD1N
Michael J Lill Ii
84 Potowomut Rd
East Greenwich RI 02818

Call Sign: N1DWV
Renee L Lebeau
756 Quake Lane Apt 208a
East Greenwich RI
028181666

Call Sign: KC1CY
Robert K Lebeau
756 Quaker Lane Apt 208a
East Greenwich RI
028181666

Call Sign: N1PWU
Robert K Berlyn
43 Rector St
East Greenwich RI 02818

Call Sign: KB1PLM

John O Mcdonald
60 Reynolds St
East Greenwich RI 02818

Call Sign: N1JOM
John O Mcdonald
60 Reynolds St
East Greenwich RI 02818

Call Sign: K2BUI
Eric J Nihill
85 Ridgefield Drive
East Greenwich RI
028183034

Call Sign: K1JD
John G De Primo
7 Rosewood Court
East Greenwich RI 02818

Call Sign: KA1WWY
James P Blanding
199 S Pierce Rd
East Greenwich RI 02818

Call Sign: KB1VRX
Joshua E Fazio
130 Shippeetown
East Greenwich RI 02818

Call Sign: KB1LKX
James N Cummings
150 South Pierce Rd
East Greenwich RI
028183431

Call Sign: N1QDI
William H Hodges Ii
920 South Rd
East Greenwich RI 02818

Call Sign: WA1RXT
Rosalind W Green
156 Spencer Ave

East Greenwich RI
028184016

Call Sign: WA1RXU
Albert E Green
156 Spencer Ave
East Greenwich RI
028184016

Call Sign: WO1W
Eugene M Chicoine
157 Spencer Woods Drive
East Greenwich RI 02818

Call Sign: KB1UNL
John P Pierson
70 Sylvan Dr
East Greenwich RI 02818

Call Sign: K1SD
James M Setzler Jr
131 Sylvan Drive
East Greenwich RI 02818

Call Sign: W1NTE
Robert W Merriam
697 Tillinghast Rd
East Greenwich RI 02818

Call Sign: K1ERG
Clayton W Brooks
81 Valley Rd
East Greenwich RI
028181722

Call Sign: KB1CFO
Henricus J Westland
88 Varnum Dr
East Greenwich RI 02818

Call Sign: N1YHI
Tom Van Oudgaarden
88 Varnum Dr
East Greenwich RI 02818

Call Sign: N1YHJ
Geerdina M Nillesen
88 Varnum Dr
East Greenwich RI 02818

Call Sign: N1ZVU
Arjen J Westland
88 Varnum Dr
East Greenwich RI 02818

Call Sign: AA1SE
John C Smith
East Greenwich RI 02818

FCC Amateur Radio Licenses in East Providence

Call Sign: W1AVO
Harry V Rockwell
61 Aberdeen Rd
East Providence RI 02915

Call Sign: KB1BCJ
Ronald W Suggs
28 Apollo Rd 1p
East Providence RI 02914

Call Sign: KB1EJD
Scott D Aguiar
25 Arlington St
East Providence RI 02914

Call Sign: KA1UVM
Henry V Lacerda
184 B Warren Ave Apt 2
East Providence RI 02914

Call Sign: KA1ZPN
Brian A Perry
70 Bayview Ave
East Providence RI 02915

Call Sign: KA1AIR
John J Almeida

11 Bentley St
East Providence RI 02914

Call Sign: N1SZJ
Anthony M Isidoro
21 Berkeley St
East Providence RI 02914

Call Sign: N1QOY
Jerome R Spinola
154 Bradford Ave
East Providence RI 02914

Call Sign: N1EHX
Gary C Perry
74 Brightridge Ave
East Providence RI 02914

Call Sign: N1XMG
Eduardo Gouveia
205 Brightridge Ave
East Providence RI 02914

Call Sign: K1CWL
John R Sweeney
81 Burgess Ave
East Providence RI 02914

Call Sign: KB1PFD
Orlando M Andrade
24 Church St
East Providence RI 02914

Call Sign: KB1VZY
Kyle E Andrade
24 Church St
East Providence RI 02914

Call Sign: AA1CT
Robert A Guay
16 City View Ave
East Providence RI 02914

Call Sign: KB1AJW
Maria Brito

79 Cotter St
East Providence RI 02914

Call Sign: KB1QVG
Michael A Vanner
18 Cushman Ave
East Providence RI 02914

Call Sign: KB1QVC
Bryan P Galligan
9 Dartmouth Ave
East Providence RI 02915

Call Sign: N1WVM
William J Ciavatta
33 Dover Ave
East Providence RI 02914

Call Sign: N1RWX
Christopher F Cunha
99 Estrell Dr
East Providence RI 02915

Call Sign: N1UWP
Stephen R Cunha
99 Estrell Dr
East Providence RI 02915

Call Sign: K1PGC
Richard H Lopez
107 Estrell Dr
East Providence RI 02915

Call Sign: KA1ERX
Manuel J Ventura Jr
40 Frederick St
East Providence RI 02916

Call Sign: KA1OZF
Henry Perry
82 Garden Dr
East Providence RI 02915

Call Sign: N1SEA
John O Carvalho

99 Goldsmith Ave Apt 305
East Providence RI 02914

Call Sign: KA1UQW
Paul E Duclos
99 Halleck Ave
East Providence RI 02915

Call Sign: KA1ZFC
Paul J Vieira
90 Irving Ave
East Providence RI 02914

Call Sign: K1SJA
Abel Francisco
95 Ivan Ave
East Providence RI
029153743

Call Sign: KB1AIO
Wayne A Manning
146 James Street
East Providence RI
029144310

Call Sign: N1DPY
Wilson L Rollinson
11 Le Roy Dr
East Providence RI 02915

Call Sign: WA1QIO
Donald Meskill
33 Main St
East Providence RI 02915

Call Sign: N1WVO
Frank J Dias
94 Mowry Ave
East Providence RI 02914

Call Sign: KA1AU
Raymond P Jackman
184 Norton Street
East Providence RI 02915

Call Sign: N1NRG
Russell F Pescatore
10 Office Parkway Apt 902
East Providence RI 02914

Call Sign: N1PMV
Bruce C Wilson
12 Oriole St
East Providence RI 02916

Call Sign: KA1KYM
Manuel A Camara
62 Park Dr
East Providence RI 02915

Call Sign: KB1TKF
James V Florio
2 Parker Avenue
East Providence RI 02914

Call Sign: KA1JIM
James V Florio
2 Parker Avenue
East Providence RI 02914

Call Sign: N1WKN
Fred D Britland
90 Pawtucket Ave
East Providence RI 02916

Call Sign: N1JPP
Ronald A Hopkins
Po Box 14378
East Providence RI 02914

Call Sign: KB1KSV
Howard S Long
17 Rachella Ct
East Providence RI 02914

Call Sign: AB1EZ
Howard S Long
17 Rachella Ct
East Providence RI 02914

Call Sign: KB1DGV
Jose R Cabral
19 Roslyn Ave
East Providence RI 02914

Call Sign: KA1ZPM
Scott A Lewis
45 Russell Ave
East Providence RI 02914

Call Sign: W1LU
Scott F Oakland
1317 S Broadway
East Providence RI
029144987

Call Sign: W1AL
Scott F Oakland
1317 S Broadway
East Providence RI
029144987

Call Sign: KB1AHZ
John M Newsham
58 Silver Spring Ave
East Providence RI 02915

Call Sign: N1FHK
Gerald G Greaves
1287 South Broadway
East Providence RI 02914

Call Sign: KB1FLM
Island Hunters Amateur
Radio Club
1317 South Broadway
East Providence RI 02914

Call Sign: KC4AAG
Island Hunters Amateur
Radio Club
1317 South Broadway
East Providence RI 02914

Call Sign: K1MQ

Island Hunters Amateur
Radio Club
1317 South Broadway
East Providence RI 02914

Call Sign: N1SO
Island Hunters Amateur
Radio Club
1317 South Broadway
East Providence RI 02914

Call Sign: AA1J
Island Hunters Amateur
Radio Club
1317 South Broadway
East Providence RI 02914

Call Sign: K1AN
Island Hunters Amateur
Radio Club
1317 South Broadway
East Providence RI 02914

Call Sign: AJ1Q
Island Hunters Amateur
Radio Club
1317 South Broadway
East Providence RI 02914

Call Sign: N1SMI
Robert R Maher Jr
13 Spicer St
East Providence RI 02904

Call Sign: KA1MBX
Henry F Walther
38 Stephen St
East Providence RI 02915

Call Sign: WA1TXY
James S Mendes
63 Sterling St
East Providence RI
029143857

Call Sign: KA1YYP
Alexander Avila
131 Sutton Ave
East Providence RI 02914

Call Sign: N1FGI
Edward W Collins
73 Terrace Ave
East Providence RI 02915

Call Sign: KA1OBO
Joseph L Ploettner
138 Terrace Ave
East Providence RI 02915

Call Sign: N1RMI
Greg M Amaral
62 Town House Rd
East Providence RI 02914

Call Sign: K7RSH
Stephen R Rush
69 Vine Street
East Providence RI 02914

Call Sign: N1KDD
William H Minardi
34 Viola Avenue
East Providence RI 02915

Call Sign: N1HWJ
John R Mc Murry
47 Walnut St
East Providence RI 02914

Call Sign: WA1RYK
Raymond V Quirk Jr
156 Walnut St
East Providence RI 02914

Call Sign: W1PCQ
Harrie L Davenport Jr
15 Wampanoag Trl
East Providence RI 02915

Call Sign: K1EPS
Joseph S Duarte
34 West St
East Providence RI 02914

Call Sign: N1QQY
Alfonso T Moniz
9 Williams Ave
East Providence RI 02914

Call Sign: KA1OBS
Barry A Ramer
44 Woodland Ave
East Providence RI 02914

Call Sign: KA1FDA
Raymond Jordan
14 Woodward Ave
East Providence RI
029143429

Call Sign: WA1IIM
Anthony V Sousa
15 Woodward Ave
East Providence RI 02914

FCC Amateur Radio Licenses in Edgewood

Call Sign: N1COR
Charles O Read
131 Shaw Ave
Edgewood RI 02905

FCC Amateur Radio Licenses in Esmond

Call Sign: N1KHD
Gerald E Smith
29 Esmond St
Esmond RI 029173005

Call Sign: N1ADM
Robert A Huntley
35 Fenwood Ave

Esmond RI 029173907

Call Sign: KA1TZS
Ernest J Aldrich
12 Mountaindale Rd
Esmond RI 02917

Call Sign: W1EI
Russell F Smith
96 Stillwater Rd
Esmond RI 029173339

Call Sign: N1SAF
William A Small Sr
9 Warren St
Esmond RI 02917

Call Sign: W1FTO
Elmer V Swift
Esmond RI 02917

FCC Amateur Radio Licenses in Exeter

Call Sign: KA1RVJ
Dorothy C Brunelli
Austin Farm Rd
Exeter RI 02822

Call Sign: KB1GCT
Raymond J Tarbox
Bates School House Rd
Exeter RI 02822

Call Sign: KB1KQT
Frank S Klus Jr
131 Beechwood Hill Trail
Exeter RI 02822

Call Sign: K1LUS
Frank S Klus Jr
131 Beechwood Hill Trail
Exeter RI 02822

Call Sign: KD1WD

Normand M Hamel
103 Black Plain Rd
Exeter RI 028222137

Call Sign: KB1KVC
Brian J Shippee
Black Plain Rd
Exeter RI 02822

Call Sign: KB1GBS
Samuel D Simpkins
175 Black Plain Road
Exeter RI 02822

Call Sign: WA1QCE
Ronald P Di Salvo
54 Briarwood Hill Road
Exeter RI 02822

Call Sign: N1JSF
Richard E Booth Jr
77 East Shore Drive
Exeter RI 028221929

Call Sign: KA1RDJ
George H Lafond Jr
559 Escoheag Hill Rd
Exeter RI 02821

Call Sign: N1AGG
Michael P De Francesco
87 Hallville Rd
Exeter RI 02822

Call Sign: K1PN
Michael P De Francesco
87 Hallville Rd
Exeter RI 02822

Call Sign: W1BA
Michael P De Francesco
87 Hallville Rd
Exeter RI 02822

Call Sign: KB1EXU

Carl W Reiner
266 Hallville Rd
Exeter RI 02822

Call Sign: KB1JPM
Ernest Jeffrey Hutchinson
5 Locust Valley
Exeter RI 02822

Call Sign: K1EJH
Ernest Jeffrey Hutchinson
5 Locust Valley
Exeter RI 02822

Call Sign: WA1BSB
Bradley S Brown
465 Mail Road
Exeter RI 02822

Call Sign: KB1GGE
Bradley S Brown
469 Mail Road
Exeter RI 02822

Call Sign: K9BSB
Bradley S Brown
469 Mail Road
Exeter RI 02822

Call Sign: KB1VBK
Jarrett W Devine
6 Maryann Dr
Exeter RI 02822

Call Sign: AA1AZ
Thomas N Dobbing
21 Queens Fort Ln
Exeter RI 02822

Call Sign: N1QIE
Nathaniel S Blanchard
166 Sheffield Hill Rd
Exeter RI 02822

Call Sign: KB1BXZ

Washington County
Amateur Radio Assn
6 Short Rd
Exeter RI 02822

Call Sign: WA1HAH
John A Palmborg
6 Short Rd
Exeter RI 02822

Call Sign: NM1G
Charles S Secrest
433 Ten Rod Rd
Exeter RI 02822

Call Sign: K1RWK
Robert W Knott
480 Ten Rod Rd
Exeter RI 02822

Call Sign: KA1MTI
Bryan B Hawkins
Ten Rod Road
Exeter RI 02822

Call Sign: KE2US
Ann L Olszewski
188 Tripes Corner Rd
Exeter RI 02822

Call Sign: KB1VYG
John F Brady
17 Tripps Corner Rd
Exeter RI 02822

Call Sign: WA1ZAT
Glenn R Gardner
288 Widow Sweets Rd
Exeter RI 02822

Call Sign: AA1LW
Ben R Smith
449 Widow Sweets Rd
Exeter RI 028223100

Call Sign: KA1NXF
James S Glawson
892 Widow Sweets Rd
Exeter RI 02822

Call Sign: N1DXB
Charles Rogers
357 William Reynolds Rd.
Exeter RI 02822

Call Sign: KB1HLP
Matthew G Newcomb
73 Wolf Rock Rd
Exeter RI 02822

Call Sign: N1RQD
Joyce E Bastien
320 Yawgoo Valley Road
Exeter RI 02822

Call Sign: WB1FVU
Ronald A De Francesco
Exeter RI 02822

Call Sign: KB1LLB
Karen A Comeroski Rn
46 Beechwood Hill Tr
Exter RI 028225232

Call Sign: KB1LLC
John P Comeroski
46 Beechwood Hill Tr
Exter RI 028225232

Call Sign: KB1LKZ
Kimberly J Langello
647 Gardner Rd
Exter RI 02822

Call Sign: KB1LLD
James R Hallene
1 James Pl
Exter RI 028223750

Call Sign: KB1LKY

John M Lotocki
28 Reuben Brown Ln
Exter RI 02822

Call Sign: KB1FFO
Edward M Austin
1775 Ten Rod Rd
Exter RI 02822

FCC Amateur Radio Licenses in Fiskeville

Call Sign: N1PDU
Donat J Labrie
Hall Ave 6
Fiskeville RI 02823

Call Sign: NE1E
Robert L Ritoli
8 Locust Ct
Fiskeville RI 02823

Call Sign: KB1KFW
Classic Wireless Amateur
Radio Club
8 Locust Ct
Fiskeville RI 02823

Call Sign: KB1HBU
Eric I Hanson
Fiskeville RI 028230195

Call Sign: KB1RXP
Brandon P Landry
Fiskeville RI 028230188

Call Sign: N1QMI
Brandon P Landry
Fiskeville RI 028230188

FCC Amateur Radio Licenses in Forestdale

Call Sign: KB1ACW
James J O Brien Jr

Forestdale RI 02824

FCC Amateur Radio Licenses in Foster

Call Sign: N1REZ
Michaela Ferreira
193a Hartford Pike
Foster RI 02825

Call Sign: KB1QIM
Wilfred T Demoranville
155 B South Killingly Road
Foster RI 02825

Call Sign: KB1EBI
William A Esser
15 Balcom Rd.
Foster RI 028251405

Call Sign: N1AGU
Terrence M O Shea
21 Burgess Rd
Foster RI 02825

Call Sign: KB1HFW
William F Rose
13 Central Pike
Foster RI 02825

Call Sign: W1HPH
William F Rose
13 Central Pike
Foster RI 028251407

Call Sign: KA1YTN
Richard B Tassone
61 Central Pike
Foster RI 02825

Call Sign: K1EWP
Marion D Lowden
Cucumber Hill Rd
Foster RI 02825

Call Sign: WB1GPZ
Howard O Wood
63 Cucumber Hl Rd
Foster RI 028251211

Call Sign: KA1VDC
Larry S Olivo
Danielson Pike
Foster RI 02825

Call Sign: NU1Z
Walter M Jehu
41 E Killingly Rd
Foster RI 02825

Call Sign: K1MFZ
Raymond A Allard
32 Foster Center Rd
Foster RI 02825

Call Sign: K1TXP
Robert J Peterson
114 Foster Center Rd
Foster RI 02825

Call Sign: N1XTR
Chris T King
115 Foster Center Rd
Foster RI 02825

Call Sign: N1XTS
Richard T King Jr
115 Foster Center Rd
Foster RI 02825

Call Sign: K1QZW
Frederick A Huse
Foster Center Rd
Foster RI 02825

Call Sign: W1CA
Peter C Johnson
17 Howard Hill Rd
Foster RI 02825

Call Sign: N1SGI
William B Chatterly
13 Kennedy Rd
Foster RI 02825

Call Sign: WA1V
Edward M Ciaramello Jr
33 Kennedy Rd
Foster RI 028251615

Call Sign: N2LMO
Kathleen M Fagas
57 Kennedy Road
Foster RI 02825

Call Sign: WB2VVV
John C Fagas
57 Kennedy Road
Foster RI 02825

Call Sign: KA1WDP
Brendan S Mara
11 Mill Road
Foster RI 02825

Call Sign: K1MDH
John H Gould
19 Mill Road
Foster RI 02825

Call Sign: W1KJN
Kevin J Weeks
40 Mount Hygeia Road
Foster RI 02825

Call Sign: W1KJW
Kevin J Weeks
40 Mount Hygeia Road
Foster RI 02825

Call Sign: N1FOT
Phillip S Stern
23 Mt Hygeia Rd
Foster RI 02825

Call Sign: N1JFH
Clifford C Cost
North Rd
Foster RI 02825

Call Sign: K1FIG
Robert G Salsberry
177 Old Plainfield Pike
Foster RI 02825

Call Sign: K1YVN
Warren A Crookes
44 Plainfield Pike
Foster RI 02825

Call Sign: W1HI
Edmond S Zuromski
54 Plainfield Pike
Foster RI 02825

Call Sign: AA1KH
Thomas A Durvin Jr
49 Stanley Mowry Rd
Foster RI 02825

Call Sign: ND1O
Thomas A Durvin Jr
49 Stanley Mowry Rd
Foster RI 02825

Call Sign: KC0AYO
Gary L Pickard
1 T. Parker Road
Foster RI 02825

Call Sign: KA1YXN
Edward J Smith
7 Walker Rd
Foster RI 02825

Call Sign: KD4SFY
Lynda Daley
66 Winsor Rd
Foster RI 02825

Call Sign: WA1ABC
Community College Of Ri
Radio Club
Foster RI 028250007

FCC Amateur Radio Licenses in Glendale

Call Sign: K1TOP
Alice M Lavigne
Box 158
Glendale RI 02826

Call Sign: KA1QXH
Norman J Bennett
Glendale RI 02826

Call Sign: W1CJF
Chris J Foti
Glendale RI 02826

FCC Amateur Radio Licenses in Glocester

Call Sign: WA1UNQ
Richard A Calkins
76 Cherry Valley Rd
Glocester RI 02814

FCC Amateur Radio Licenses in Greene

Call Sign: N1VQA
Stephen W Hawley
486 Lewis Farm Rd
Greene RI 02827

Call Sign: KB1TND
Neal E Liddle
1119 Maple Valley Rd
Greene RI 02827

Call Sign: KA1ABI
Duane C Burnham
235 Pig Hill Rd

Greene RI 028271634

Call Sign: KB1USI
Jessica S Burnham
235 Pig Hill Rd
Greene RI 02827

Call Sign: N1VEY
Barry J Robinson
998 Plainfield Pike
Greene RI 02827

Call Sign: KA1RVB
Scott J Murray
210 Sisson Rd
Greene RI 02827

Call Sign: K8BGZ
David U Maier
580 Sisson Rd
Greene RI 02827

Call Sign: WD8NOX
Joyce J Sodman
580 Sisson Rd
Greene RI 02827

Call Sign: W1BAT
David U Maier
580 Sisson Rd
Greene RI 02827

Call Sign: N1MAD
Peter L Beauchaine
126 Waterman Hill Rd
Greene RI 02827

Call Sign: W1SVQ
David H Underwood
Greene RI 02827

**FCC Amateur Radio
Licenses in Greenville**

Call Sign: KA1VFC

Scott D Caron
21 Austin Ave
Greenville RI 02828

Call Sign: N1MAB
Leo F Kennedy
43 Beverly Cir
Greenville RI 02828

Call Sign: W1NEH
John J Kaminski Sr
17 Cider Ln
Greenville RI 02828

Call Sign: K1PZY
John F Murphy
16 Cortland Ln
Greenville RI 02828

Call Sign: N1KET
Christopher M Trainor
8 Crestview Dr
Greenville RI 02828

Call Sign: KB1PUG
David C Johnson
4 David St
Greenville RI 02828

Call Sign: KB1OJN
Paul C Barbato
2 Fair Oaks Court North
Greenville RI 02828

Call Sign: KA1YZP
Paul E Mendence Sr
4 Maplecrest Dr
Greenville RI 02828

Call Sign: KA1DKI
Kathleen E Pora
3 Pamela Dr
Greenville RI 02828

Call Sign: KA1DKJ

Stanley F Pora
3 Pamela Dr
Greenville RI 02828

Call Sign: KA1ZAM
Patricia A Pora
3 Pamela Dr
Greenville RI 02828

Call Sign: KB1RTA
James E Beanland
29 Peach Blossom Lane
Greenville RI 02828

Call Sign: W1JEB
James E Beanland
29 Peach Blossom Lane
Greenville RI 02828

Call Sign: KB1RWM
Glenn R Brown
46 Pleasant View Ave
Greenville RI 02828

Call Sign: KB1NJE
George P Tessier
21 Pleasant View Circle
Greenville RI 02828

Call Sign: KB1WAI
Brian A Mailloux
515 Putnam Pike
Greenville RI 02828

Call Sign: KB1PZD
Oriance R Godfroy
662 Putnam Pike
Greenville RI 02828

Call Sign: KB1LPQ
Stephen D Godfroy
662 Putnam Pk
Greenville RI 02828

Call Sign: KD1UA

John A Hawkins Jr
26 Sprague Street
Greenville RI 02828

Call Sign: N1EYE
Ernest H Piette Jr
27 Steere Rd
Greenville RI 02828

Call Sign: N1ERG
Charles V Mc Mahon Jr
6 Tippling Rock Rd
Greenville RI 02828

Call Sign: KB1GYR
Paul F Durocher
23 Tucker Rd
Greenville RI 028282217

Call Sign: KB1CJS
Glenn P Caron
17 Valley View Dr
Greenville RI 02828

Call Sign: N1PYH
John L Nimmo
19 West Prospect St.
Greenville RI 02828

Call Sign: KB1RCK
Julie A Lepore
5 Willow Rd
Greenville RI 02828

Call Sign: KB1VKH
Smithfield Emergency
Management Agency
5 Willow Rd
Greenville RI 02828

Call Sign: WS1EMA
Smithfield Emergency
Management Agency
5 Willow Rd
Greenville RI 02828

Call Sign: WA1GGD
Timothy S Chilinski
30 Willow Rd
Greenville RI 02828

Call Sign: N1MIX
Michael J Lepore
5 Willow Road
Greenville RI 02828

Call Sign: KA1QXQ
William P Tocco Jr
Greenville RI 02828

Call Sign: WA1PYX
John L Currier
Greenville RI 02828

Call Sign: WI1I
Bernard G Quartaroli
Greenville RI 02828

FCC Amateur Radio Licenses in Harmony

Call Sign: KB1SC
Steven A Hokeness
94 Phillips Ln
Harmony RI 028290081

Call Sign: K1DOC
Steven A Hokeness
94 Phillips Ln
Harmony RI 028290081

Call Sign: K1SKC
Irmgard L O Connors
62 Tucker St
Harmony RI 02829

Call Sign: K1QVF
Patrick F O Connors
Harmony RI 02829

Call Sign: KB1DRK
Keith R Barrette
Harmony RI 02829

FCC Amateur Radio Licenses in Harragansett

Call Sign: WB1FDL
Edward L Calamar Sr
93 Cedar Island Rd
Harragansett RI 02882

FCC Amateur Radio Licenses in Harrisville

Call Sign: KA1QYP
William A Rossi
250 Brook Rd
Harrisville RI 02830

Call Sign: KB1LPU
Joseph W Quiray Jr
405 Brook Rd
Harrisville RI 02830

Call Sign: KB1GUT
Walter J Mycroft
12 Carol Dr
Harrisville RI 02830

Call Sign: WA1PJD
Lucien R La Montagne
264 Central St
Harrisville RI 02830

Call Sign: KA1YPW
Marc P Dupre
525 Cherry Farm Road
Harrisville RI 02830

Call Sign: N1VHN
Edith M Plante
104 Colonial Rd
Harrisville RI 02830

Call Sign: N1VHO
Roland G Plante
104 Colonial Rd
Harrisville RI 02830

Call Sign: KA1ZUO
David G Leduc
1355 Douglas Pike
Harrisville RI 02830

Call Sign: KB1PVB
Richard H Langlois Phd
864 Douglas Pk
Harrisville RI 02830

Call Sign: W1TBR
Richard H Langlois Phd
864 Douglas Pk
Harrisville RI 02830

Call Sign: KA1YVE
David P Aubin
275 East Ave
Harrisville RI 02830

Call Sign: KC0EES
Christopher R Trudel
9 Franconia Drive
Harrisville RI 02830

Call Sign: N1RGK
Kenneth D Trudel
9 Franconia Drive
Harrisville RI 02830

Call Sign: KB1SQD
Burrillville Emergency
Management Agency
105 Harrisville Main St
Harrisville RI 02830

Call Sign: WB2EMA
Burrillville Emergency
Management Agency
105 Harrisville Main St

Harrisville RI 02830

Call Sign: N1YWZ
Wilfred P Pimental Jr
554 Ironmine Rd
Harrisville RI 02830

Call Sign: KB1WV
Don C Wolfe
75 North Hill Rd
Harrisville RI 02830

Call Sign: KD1HA
Denis J Couture
4 Paula Dr
Harrisville RI 02830

Call Sign: KB1SXR
Jason M Rhodes
64 Round Top Rd
Harrisville RI 02830

Call Sign: KB1RHC
James H Alix
1160 Round Top Rd
Harrisville RI 02830

Call Sign: NK1S
James H Alix
1160 Round Top Rd
Harrisville RI 02830

Call Sign: KA1ODI
Marie E Federici
1624 Round Top Rd
Harrisville RI 02830

Call Sign: WA1Y
John N Federici
1624 Round Top Rd
Harrisville RI 02830

Call Sign: N1BJF
Brian J Falvey
8 Sandy Lane

Harrisville RI 028301341

Call Sign: WA1UKR
Harry Thanos
720 Sherman Farm Rd
Harrisville RI 02830

Call Sign: N1KOJ
Gerard R Cournoyer
100 Whipple Ave
Harrisville RI 02830

Call Sign: AA1PV
Albert F Dorval Jr
Harrisville RI 02830

FCC Amateur Radio Licenses in Hope

Call Sign: N2RTK
Benjamin L Steinberg
23 Audubon Lane
Hope RI 02831

Call Sign: N1KKU
Ronald G Carter
214 Burnt Hill Rd
Hope RI 02831

Call Sign: N1WDL
David C Leo
425 Carpenter Rd
Hope RI 02831

Call Sign: KA1EZE
Richard E La Banca
86 Eagle Dr
Hope RI 02831

Call Sign: KI1G
Malcolm E Davenport Jr
477 Hope Furnace Rd
Hope RI 02831

Call Sign: NB1V

Henry Tomaszewski
88 Jackson Flat Rd
Hope RI 02831

Call Sign: KA1EMH
Robert S Janus
68 Nottingham Drive
Hope RI 02831

Call Sign: K1VFD
Agnes M Nelson
43 Orchard Dr
Hope RI 028311224

Call Sign: W1LWB
Arthur W Nelson
43 Orchard Dr
Hope RI 028311224

Call Sign: K1LA
Leonard A Audet
9 Pineknoll Dr
Hope RI 028310102

Call Sign: N1GKE
Myrton T Smith Ii
37 Ryefield Rd
Hope RI 028310256

Call Sign: WA1USN
Uss Saratoga Arc
37 Ryefield Rd
Hope RI 02831

Call Sign: KB1KVB
Debra L Smith
37 Ryefield Rd
Hope RI 02831

Call Sign: W1GKE
Debra L Smith
37 Ryefield Rd
Hope RI 02831

Call Sign: KB1LEF

Alexander A Ruggieri
37 Ryefield Rd
Hope RI 02831

Call Sign: K1GKE
Alexander A Ruggieri
37 Ryefield Rd
Hope RI 02831

Call Sign: N1VOC
Jose A Severino
22 Set-N-Sun Drive
Hore RI 02831

Call Sign: KB1GCB
John J Munko
45 Trout Brook Lane
Hope RI 02831

Call Sign: KA1WIP
David R Howes
114 Trout Brook Ln
Hope RI 02831

Call Sign: N1JAU
Theresa A Howes
114 Trout Brook Ln
Hope RI 02831

Call Sign: KB1KCX
Marc D Abeshaus
203 Trout Brook Ln
Hope RI 028311416

Call Sign: KA1QLL
Barbara R Miller
385 Tunk Hill Rd
Hope RI 02831

Call Sign: KA1ZJA
Matthew M Miller
385 Tunk Hill Rd
Hope RI 02831

Call Sign: NG1H

Mark H Miller
385 Tunk Hill Rd
Hope RI 02831

Call Sign: KA1RCY
Roland A Barratt Sr
Hope RI 02831

Call Sign: KA1ZRJ
Leona Barratt
Hope RI 028310357

Call Sign: N1UTB
John T Babiec
Hope RI 02831

Call Sign: KB1JFD
Michele L Podvin
Hope RI 02831

Call Sign: KB1TXY
Larwence S Lemanquais Iii
Hope RI 02831

FCC Amateur Radio Licenses in Hope Valley

Call Sign: KA1ZZS
Preston Lawhorne
126 Arcadia Rd
Hope Valley RI 02832

Call Sign: KA1ZZT
Lori A Lawhorne
126 Arcadia Rd
Hope Valley RI 02832

Call Sign: AA1EM
Kazimierz E Bogusz
5 Bank Street - Apt 5
Hope Valley RI 02832

Call Sign: KA1LMX
William J Mc Allister Iii
30 Cherry Lane

Hope Valley RI 02832

Call Sign: N1ZJF
Vincent J Alianiello Jr
202 Fenner Hill Rd
Hope Valley RI 02832

Call Sign: AA1PL
Peter J Harrison
24 Forest Glen Dr
Hope Valley RI 02832

Call Sign: KB1AWV
Kenneth J Carr
26 Karen Drive
Hope Valley RI 02832

Call Sign: N1WRZ
Camille K Carr
26 Karen Drive
Hope Valley RI 02832

Call Sign: N1TMT
Douglas P Marcil
10 Kenney Hill Rd
Hope Valley RI 02832

Call Sign: N1LLY
Ralph C Caddick
15 Ridley Lane
Hope Valley RI 02832

Call Sign: WA1ZPK
Norman A Phillips
346 Smith Ln
Hope Valley RI 02832

Call Sign: WB1CEU
Marjorie F Olsen
320 Switch Rd
Hope Valley RI 02832

Call Sign: WA1SVG
Roy O Dubs
10 Wicasta Farm Rd

Hope Valley RI 02832

Call Sign: KB1BDD
Kathryn A Koziol
199 Woodville Alton Rd
Hope Valley RI 02832

Call Sign: KD1NW
Kevin J Koziol
199 Woodville Alton Rd
Hope Valley RI 028322421

Call Sign: KB1ARC
Brian J Turner
118 Woodville Alton Rd.
Hope Valley RI 02832

Call Sign: KN1GBN
William C Watson
122 Woodville Rd
Hope Valley RI 02832

Call Sign: WA1PWA
Mark E Titterington
Hope Valley RI 02832

Call Sign: WB2VEV
Robert W Minchin
Hope Valley RI 02832

FCC Amateur Radio Licenses in Hopkinton

Call Sign: K1ZXR
Paul M Depetrillo
150 Fenner Hill Rd
Hopkinton RI 02832

Call Sign: KB1HNN
John E Heinold
36 Lawton Foster Rd
Hopkinton RI 02833

Call Sign: KB1DMF
Carolyn A Thompson

33 Lawton Foster Rd S
Hopkinton RI 02833

Call Sign: N1WVJ
Sylvia K Thompson
33 Lawton Foster Rd S
Hopkinton RI 02833

Call Sign: KB1EJF
Meridith J Thompson
33 Lawton Foster Rd S
Hopkinton RI 02833

Call Sign: N1VJ
Sylvia K Thompson
33 Lawton Foster Rd S
Hopkinton RI 02833

Call Sign: N1SMW
Gabriel Lengyel
548 Main St
Hopkinton RI 028330162

Call Sign: KA1AJF
George M Abbott
169 North Rd
Hopkinton RI 02833

Call Sign: W1GMA
George M Abbott
169 North Rd
Hopkinton RI 02833

FCC Amateur Radio Licenses in Jamestown

Call Sign: WA1VAJ
Benedetto A Cerilli Jr
6 America Way
Jamestown RI 02835

Call Sign: N4FXS
David J Dunwoodie
20 Bayview Dr
Jamestown RI 02835

Call Sign: WB2REY
Nancy W Bennett
434 Beavertail Rd
Jamestown RI 02835

Call Sign: N2ULF
Mike D Smith
16 Courageous Ct
Jamestown RI 02835

Call Sign: KB1PJQ
Samra Pease
29 Maple Ave
Jamestown RI 02835

Call Sign: AB1KC
Bruce R Beard Jr
1 Blueberry Lane
Jamestown RI 02835

Call Sign: W1DEC
David E Cain Mr
11 Court Street
Jamestown RI 02835

Call Sign: KA1LA
Richard A Ventrone
12 Nautilus Street
Jamestown RI 02835

Call Sign: N1QCB
Audra J Piotti
24 Bryer Ave
Jamestown RI 02835

Call Sign: W1JYF
William E Caldarone
473 E Shore Rd
Jamestown RI 02835

Call Sign: W1XY
Gerald B Bay
27 Newport St
Jamestown RI 02835

Call Sign: N1UCH
Joseph A Piotti Jr
24 Bryer Ave
Jamestown RI 02835

Call Sign: N1PRJ
George W Waterman
5 Fox Run
Jamestown RI 02835

Call Sign: K1DA
Charles H Di Luglio
34 Nun Ave
Jamestown RI 02835

Call Sign: KA1GHC
V Rose Karentz
2 Clarke Village Ln
Jamestown RI 02835

Call Sign: W1TEM
Ronald E Drake
60 Garboard St
Jamestown RI 02835

Call Sign: WA1UHO
Keller P Di Luglio
34 Nun Ave
Jamestown RI 02835

Call Sign: W1YLB
Varoujan Karentz
2 Clarke Village Ln
Jamestown RI 02835

Call Sign: W1YMH
Victor C Richardson
165 Hamilton Avenue
Jamestown RI 02835

Call Sign: KB1LJR
Adam C Diluglio
34 Nun Ave
Jamestown RI 02835

Call Sign: KB1PJT
Joan P Mccauley
148 Columbia Lane
Jamestown RI 02835

Call Sign: AA1XQ
Michael K Seil
25 Howland Avenue
Jamestown RI 028351219

Call Sign: K2QXX
Howard T Krainin
78 Pemberton Ave
Jamestown RI 02835

Call Sign: KB1PJU
John J Mccauley
148 Columbia Lane
Jamestown RI 02835

Call Sign: KB1OYK
Carol A Peltier
44 Hull St
Jamestown RI 02835

Call Sign: N1VXO
Raleigh E Utterback
194 Seaside Dr
Jamestown RI 02835

Call Sign: W1UFC
Margaret R Soukup
6 Coronado St
Jamestown RI 02835

Call Sign: KB1PJR
Fred F Pease
29 Maple Av
Jamestown RI 02835

Call Sign: KB1RWQ
William C Pierce
58 Seaside Drive
Jamestown RI 02835

Call Sign: KC9HUT
Alexander B Knowles
108 Southwest Avenue
Jamestown RI 02835

Call Sign: N1NJK
Ruth E Burns
20 Spanker St
Jamestown RI 02835

Call Sign: K1BER
Ruth E Burns
20 Spanker Street
Jamestown RI 02835

Call Sign: W1LY
William H Maclean Jr
74 Stern St
Jamestown RI 028350547

Call Sign: N3JWY
John W Yarger
7 Valley Street
Jamestown RI 02835

Call Sign: W2ILA
Thomas J Mackie
14 Washington St
Jamestown RI 02835

Call Sign: KB1SDV
Thomas M Brendlinger
178 West Reach Dr
Jamestown RI 02835

Call Sign: KB1SLQ
Richard W Brendlinger
178 West Reach Dr
Jamestown RI 02835

Call Sign: N3RWB
Richard W Brendlinger
178 West Reach Dr
Jamestown RI 02835

Call Sign: N3TMB
Thomas M Brendlinger
178 West Reach Dr
Jamestown RI 02835

Call Sign: KB1SPO
Michael E Brendlinger
178 West Reach Dr
Jamestown RI 02835

Call Sign: KB1SRH
Lisa D Brendlinger
178 West Reach Dr
Jamestown RI 02835

Call Sign: W1MEB
Michael E Brendlinger
178 West Reach Dr
Jamestown RI 02835

Call Sign: N3LDB
Lisa D Brendlinger
178 West Reach Dr
Jamestown RI 02835

Call Sign: KB1PJS
Thomas P Tighe
4 West St
Jamestown RI 02835

Call Sign: W1NZR
Mark W Beezer
Jamestown RI 02835

Call Sign: KB1EUK
Joyce E Miller
Jamestown RI 02835

Call Sign: W1JPK
Ara Uss Joseph P Kennedy
Jr Dd 850
Jamestown RI 02835

Call Sign: KB1TYA

Heather E Smith
Jamestown RI 02835

Call Sign: KB1TYB
Rachel K Ohara
Jamestown RI 02835

FCC Amateur Radio
Licenses in Johnston

Call Sign: AI1L
Anthony L Ionata
5 Alcazar Ave.
Johnston RI 029194038

Call Sign: KA3WLV
Robert J Simoneau
21 Alden St
Johnston RI 02919

Call Sign: N3LCF
Teresita J Simoneau
21 Alden St
Johnston RI 02919

Call Sign: KA1TOA
Fernando C Correia
20 Angelico St
Johnston RI 02919

Call Sign: KA1PVB
Dennis R Rotondo
28 Audubon St
Johnston RI 02919

Call Sign: N1XVL
Sonja Rotondo
28 Audubon St
Johnston RI 02919

Call Sign: WB1DEX
Neil S Golditch
15 Barbato Dr
Johnston RI 02919

Call Sign: N1KOA
Jose A Rodriguez Jr
3 Becker Ave
Johnston RI 02919

Call Sign: KE1JA
Frederick J Pocai Jr
41 Bishop Rd
Johnston RI 02919

Call Sign: KB1FWP
Ronald L Shappy
728 Central Ave
Johnston RI 02919

Call Sign: N1GOP
Robert S Barcellos
68 Belfield Dr
Johnston RI 029191802

Call Sign: N1KRU
Linda Pocai
41 Bishop Rd
Johnston RI 02919

Call Sign: K1XGT
Ronald L Shappy
728 Central Ave
Johnston RI 02919

Call Sign: WA1AHK
Frank E Barcellos
68 Belfield Dr
Johnston RI 02919

Call Sign: K1IXU
Colin W Leath
14 Blueberry Ln
Johnston RI 029191902

Call Sign: W1NAB
Robert H Richard
24 Cherry Hill Rd
Johnston RI 02919

Call Sign: KB1JEF
Marvin C Hanson
15 Bigelow Rd
Johnston RI 02919

Call Sign: K1UTK
Mary K Leath
14 Blueberry Ln
Johnston RI 02919

Call Sign: W1FJG
Frank J Grzych
31 Chestnut St
Johnston RI 02919

Call Sign: KB1JGC
Donna L Allcock
15 Bigelow Rd
Johnston RI 02919

Call Sign: KB1HJV
Kenneth A Botelho
27 Buchanan
Johnston RI 02919

Call Sign: WF1U
Frank J Grzych
31 Chestnut St
Johnston RI 02919

Call Sign: N1YDR
William P Derita
32 Birchtree Dr
Johnston RI 02919

Call Sign: N1TWA
Michael G Pescatore
7 Buratti Rd
Johnston RI 02919

Call Sign: KB1BHR
Danielle E Ruest
10 Christopher Dr
Johnston RI 02919

Call Sign: W1POP
Robert C Sprague
121 Bishop Hill Rd
Johnston RI 029192822

Call Sign: N1CYX
Raymond M Stanford Jr
7 Carlisle Ave
Johnston RI 02919

Call Sign: N1YDT
Christopher R Lisi
10 City View Pkwy
Johnston RI 02919

Call Sign: W1NJ
Marc A Spardello Jr
39 Bishop Rd
Johnston RI 02919

Call Sign: W1IJ
August R Gulli
1 Celona Drive
Johnston RI 02919

Call Sign: W1YRY
Robert N Johnson
4 Dexter St
Johnston RI 02919

Call Sign: AA1II
Frederick J Pocai
41 Bishop Rd
Johnston RI 02919

Call Sign: KA1SRV
James D Hinkley
166 Central Ave
Johnston RI 02919

Call Sign: N1IUC
Ralph R A Russo
12 Edna St
Johnston RI 02919

Call Sign: N1HCZ
David M A Russo Sr
33 Edna St
Johnston RI 02919

Call Sign: KA1SGV
Carl M Brunt
2776 Hartford Ave
Johnston RI 02919

Call Sign: KB1FSD
Joseph Femminella
4 Jaime Drive
Johnston RI 02919

Call Sign: KB1BTQ
Brendin J Gould
5 Elwin Ave
Johnston RI 02919

Call Sign: WB1ANJ
Paul J Kelly
1010 Hartford Ave Apt F
Johnston RI 02919

Call Sign: N1KOQ
James I Greenhalgh
40 John St
Johnston RI 02919

Call Sign: KA1JRJ
Joseph E Provencal
41 Fairmont Ave
Johnston RI 02919

Call Sign: WA1MHI
Paul J Kelly
1010 Hartford Ave Apt F
Johnston RI 029195074

Call Sign: K5RJI
Edward S Haskell
7 Juniper Ln
Johnston RI 02919

Call Sign: KG4MWY
Kevin M Carson
184 Federal Way Apt 201
Johnston RI 02919

Call Sign: KB1MRC
Cynthia A Silverman
2484 Hartford Avenue
Johnston RI 029191705

Call Sign: W1PN
Edward S Haskell
7 Juniper Ln
Johnston RI 02919

Call Sign: KB1IRA
Susan A Femminella
16 Flanders St
Johnston RI 02919

Call Sign: KB1MCM
David A Farrar
103 Hedley Ave
Johnston RI 02919

Call Sign: KC1C
George W Bowder
645 Killingly St
Johnston RI 02919

Call Sign: K1IAL
Thomas E Cummings
6 Freedom Ct
Johnston RI 02919

Call Sign: KA1OSQ
William E Connolly
31 Highland Ave
Johnston RI 02919

Call Sign: K1GIL
Gilbert E Bishop
7 Lakeview Ave
Johnston RI 029192901

Call Sign: KB1HSJ
Michael S Owens
454 George Waterman Ave
Johnston RI 02919

Call Sign: KD1QA
Cosimo S Galasso Sr
20 Hill St
Johnston RI 02919

Call Sign: NN1G
Gilbert E Bishop
7 Lakeview Ave
Johnston RI 029192901

Call Sign: AI1K
John A Szelka Jr
3 Granite St
Johnston RI 02919

Call Sign: KA1APG
Frank A Gracie Jr
370 Hilltop Dr
Johnston RI 02919

Call Sign: AB1JV
Gilbert E Bishop
7 Lakeview Ave
Johnston RI 029192901

Call Sign: KA1FKG
Kelly A Szelka
3 Granite St
Johnston RI 02919

Call Sign: KB1IAS
Kenneth Turner
33 Jackson Ave
Johnston RI 02919

Call Sign: W1OP
Providence Radio
Association Inc
1 Ludlow St
Johnston RI 02919

Johnston RI 02919

Johnston RI 02919

Call Sign: N1VRN
Stephen J Riccitelli
1 Lusi Dr
Johnston RI 02919

Call Sign: AA1PQ
Steven B Arnold
3 Meriline St
Johnston RI 02920

Call Sign: W1ICE
Gary G Peterson Mr
P.O. Box 19161
Johnston RI 02919

Call Sign: N1XVK
Maureen H Riccitelli
1 Lusi Dr
Johnston RI 02919

Call Sign: KC1FL
William E Guilmette
310 Morgan Ave
Johnston RI 02919

Call Sign: AA1JK
John H Chester
36 Peck Hill Rd
Johnston RI 02919

Call Sign: KA1PVC
Joyce A Draine
4 Luther Ct
Johnston RI 02919

Call Sign: W1JFT
Gerald F Morin
19 Morton Ave
Johnston RI 02919

Call Sign: N1XVI
Cecile A Chester
36 Peck Hill Rd
Johnston RI 02919

Call Sign: W1PHR
Pine Hill Amateur Radio
Repeater Group Inc
4 Luther Ct
Johnston RI 02919

Call Sign: KB1AIN
John R Sarro
21 Mulberry Cir
Johnston RI 02919

Call Sign: KA1NVO
Anthony C Palumbo
29 Pine Hill Road
Johnston RI 02919

Call Sign: WA1QHL
John A Draine
4 Luther Ct
Johnston RI 02919

Call Sign: N1NJM
Melissa J Pallotta
42 N Fairview
Johnston RI 02919

Call Sign: KA1OQQ
Marie R Palumbo
29 Pine Hill Road
Johnston RI 02919

Call Sign: N1HHV
Leo E O Donnell
21 Lynnwood Dr
Johnston RI 02919

Call Sign: N1NJH
Bruce A Pallotta
42 N Fairview Ave
Johnston RI 02919

Call Sign: KD1UH
Gaetano Forte
1609 Plainfield Pike Apt
215
Johnston RI 02919

Call Sign: N1XLV
Richard R Ruggiero
78 Manuel Ave
Johnston RI 02919

Call Sign: N1LZW
Corey M Franco
4 Nicole Ln
Johnston RI 02919

Call Sign: N1RQB
Todd C Ryone
214 Putnam Pike
Johnston RI 02919

Call Sign: K1AOS
John Mc Allister
1 Mathewson St
Johnston RI 029192023

Call Sign: N1OPI
James M Ruscito
229 Normandy St
Johnston RI 02919

Call Sign: KC1RI
Judith A Nelson
12 Roosevelt Ave
Johnston RI 02919

Call Sign: KB1FFQ
Elaine M Lamontagne
17 Mathewson St

Call Sign: KA1PBM
Lindsay T Chandler
46 Orchard Ave

Call Sign: N1GOR
John F Nelson Jr

12 Roosevelt Ave
Johnston RI 02919

Call Sign: W1USM
John F Nelson Jr
12 Roosevelt Ave
Johnston RI 02919

Call Sign: WA4GND
James D Johnson Jr
28 Shore Drive
Johnston RI 02919

Call Sign: K1GND
James D Johnson Jr
28 Shore Drive
Johnston RI 02919

Call Sign: N1ALH
Stephen J Harrison
20 Steere Dr
Johnston RI 02919

Call Sign: KB1GSF
Anthony George
7 Steere St
Johnston RI 02919

Call Sign: KA1RYU
Kenneth T Testa
12 Stevenson Ave
Johnston RI 02919

Call Sign: N1YHD
Christopher Paolella
6 Stromberg Ct
Johnston RI 02919

Call Sign: KB1SUG
Gary G Peterson
61 Union Ave
Johnston RI 02919

Call Sign: WB1FLX
Albino F Conte

55 Walnut St
Johnston RI 02919

Call Sign: KA1ZQH
Robert N Simmons Sr
41 Waveland St
Johnston RI 02919

Call Sign: KA1ZQI
Robert N Simmons Jr
41 Waveland St
Johnston RI 02919

Call Sign: K1QZV
James L Harrington
17 Winsor Ave
Johnston RI 02919

Call Sign: K1YQY
Joseph S Browning Sr
39 Winsor Ave
Johnston RI 02919

Call Sign: N1JER
Kelli M Fisher
52 Winsor Ave
Johnston RI 02919

Call Sign: KA1POB
Carlo J Jacavone
16 Wood Haven Dr
Johnston RI 02919

Call Sign: N1VJJ
Joseph L Giudici
24 Woodlake Dr
Johnston RI 02919

Call Sign: KB1EJG
Roger A Prata
Johnston RI 029199653

**FCC Amateur Radio
Licenses in Kingston**

Call Sign: N8LI
Salim S Hameed
131 Biscuit City Road
Kingston RI 02881

Call Sign: KB1BQG
Bethany G Vaccaro
24 Campus Ave
Kingston RI 02881

Call Sign: N1VBA
Richard J Vaccaro
24 Campus Ave
Kingston RI 02881

Call Sign: KB1JZO
Adam B Juda
71 Conant Ln
Kingston RI 02881

Call Sign: N1CFY
J M Nuzum
46 Crestwood Rd
Kingston RI 028811508

Call Sign: N1QNR
Keith A Mac Innes
70 Diane Dr
Kingston RI 02881

Call Sign: KB1LLH
Lucian Dobrot
2900 Kingstown Road Apt
533
Kingston RI 02881

Call Sign: WA1YDR
Ralph W England Jr
144 Linden Dr
Kingston RI 02881

Call Sign: KB1ULT
Harry W Bock Iii
30 Rolens Dr Apt A1
Kingston RI 02881

Call Sign: W1MKF
Daniel Martin Jr
53 Rolens Dr Apt B1
Kingston RI 02881

Call Sign: KB1IBE
David S Lesh
30 Rolens Drive Apt C1
Kingston RI 028811738

Call Sign: N1SMV
Gustavo O Ruiz Riquer
Kingston RI 02881

Call Sign: NS1Y
David L Cherlin
Kingston RI 02881

Call Sign: W1KMV
Memorial Union Univ
Rhode Island University Of
Rhode Island Amateur
Radio Club
Kingston RI 028810804

Call Sign: W1LUJ
Thomas J Keefe Jr
Kingston RI 02881

Call Sign: KB1IMB
Niels Rorhelm
Kingston RI 02881

**FCC Amateur Radio
Licenses in Lincoln**

Call Sign: KD1YE
Francis P Mc Donald
69 Arnold St
Lincoln RI 028651903

Call Sign: KB1NET
Scott M Butler
8 Beverly Dr

Lincoln RI 02865

Call Sign: WA1SCH
Robert Gorman
10 Franklin St Apt 349
Lincoln RI 02865

Call Sign: W1PEV
Paul E Vanasse
628 George Washington
Highway
Lincoln RI 02865

Call Sign: KB1TOT
Wa1qca Repeater Club
628 George Washington
Hwy
Lincoln RI 02865

Call Sign: KB1JAQ
Jonathan E Davis
1 Glendale Way
Lincoln RI 02865

Call Sign: N1WSK
Thomas J Griffin
135 Grandview Ave
Lincoln RI 02865

Call Sign: KB1EQT
Bruce R Mccabe
474 Great Rd
Lincoln RI 02865

Call Sign: KB1EWJ
Colin J Mccabe
474 Great Rd
Lincoln RI 02865

Call Sign: W1CJM
Colin J Mccabe
474 Great Rd
Lincoln RI 02865

Call Sign: W1BRM

Bruce R Mccabe
474 Great Rd
Lincoln RI 02865

Call Sign: W1FIG
Maarten Broess
17 Greenwood Ln
Lincoln RI 02865

Call Sign: N1DZ
Maarten Broess
17 Greenwood Ln
Lincoln RI 02865

Call Sign: N1WBZ
Diane M Nelson
67 Jenckes Hill Rd
Lincoln RI 02865

Call Sign: WV1H
David H Nelson
67 Jenckes Hill Rd
Lincoln RI 02865

Call Sign: KA1SJW
Kenneth J Robbio
98 Jones St
Lincoln RI 02865

Call Sign: KB1PUI
Timothy R Cabbabe
31 Kilburn Ave
Lincoln RI 02865

Call Sign: WA1NWV
Theron A Bone
23 Kirkbrae Dr
Lincoln RI 02865

Call Sign: KB1UNM
Melissa Gamage
17 Knowles St
Lincoln RI 02865

Call Sign: N1ZO

John C Mc Manus
5 Laurel Lane
Lincoln RI 028651211

Call Sign: KA1TXY
John C Mc Manus
5 Laurel Ln
Lincoln RI 02865

Call Sign: KA1MYV
Michael P Cervone
13 Lladnar Dr
Lincoln RI 02865

Call Sign: W1MPC
Michael P Cervone
13 Lladnar Dr
Lincoln RI 02865

Call Sign: W1RFQ
Lewis A Prescott Jr
15 Loring Dr
Lincoln RI 028651623

Call Sign: N1FAB
Gary D Costello
2 Mitris Blvd
Lincoln RI 028653611

Call Sign: WB1FCG
Mark D Lucia
10 Nottingham Drive
Lincoln RI 02865

Call Sign: KB1LHL
Francesco D Scaramuzzi
7 Oakwood Ave
Lincoln RI 02865

Call Sign: W1KWY
Frank M Sikocinski
16 Oakwood Ave
Lincoln RI 02865

Call Sign: KJ1S

Robert M Mooney
1731 Old Louisquisset Pike
Lincoln RI 028654507

Call Sign: K1DWY
Normand J Boutin
80 Old River Rd
Lincoln RI 02865

Call Sign: N1KOC
David A Paolantonio
200 Old River Rd.
Lincoln RI 028651141

Call Sign: KA1ZAH
Carlos J Ramos
6 Rollingwood Dr
Lincoln RI 02865

Call Sign: W1CJR
Carlos J Ramos
6 Rollingwood Dr
Lincoln RI 02865

Call Sign: KA1KJ
James W Duffell
12 Sherman Ave
Lincoln RI 02865

Call Sign: N1SUN
Frederic C Allen
22 Sherman Ave
Lincoln RI 02865

Call Sign: KB1RWO
Gerald Gormley
12 Steeple Lane
Lincoln RI 02865

Call Sign: K1RPC
Robert H Grundner
17 Sunview St
Lincoln RI 02865

Call Sign: K1UJX

Samuel F Ward
9 Sutcliffe Ave
Lincoln RI 02865

Call Sign: WA2RHR
Wayne E Coats
3 Sylvaia Ln
Lincoln RI 02865

Call Sign: KA1RCI
Steven M Hodell
98 Wilbur Rd
Lincoln RI 02865

Call Sign: KA1RXB
Sandra A Hodell
98 Wilbur Rd
Lincoln RI 02865

Call Sign: KA1VKD
William R Hodell
98 Wilbur Rd
Lincoln RI 02865

Call Sign: K1RSR
Rhode Island State React
98 Wilbur Rd
Lincoln RI 02865

Call Sign: KB1OMO
Narragansett Bay Amateur
Radio Club
98 Wilbur Rd
Lincoln RI 02865

Call Sign: NB1RI
Narragansett Bay Amateur
Radio Club
98 Wilbur Rd
Lincoln RI 02865

Call Sign: W1NRI
Northern Rhode Island
Radio Club
27 Woodward Rd 56

Lincoln RI 02865

Call Sign: K1PYJ
Laurence J Godek
Lincoln RI 02865

Call Sign: KB1VHW
Anthony Marchetti Ii
Lincoln RI 02865

FCC Amateur Radio Licenses in Little Compton

Call Sign: WA1VHW
David R Hammer
22 Bramblewood Cross
Little Compton RI 02837

Call Sign: WA1LTL
Roger P Lord
29 Bramblewood Cross
Little Compton RI
028372004

Call Sign: WA1BYL
Carlton Wilkie
93 E Main Rd
Little Compton RI 02837

Call Sign: KB1OHC
Amanda M Carr
296 Long Highway
Little Compton RI 02837

Call Sign: WA1QKB
John M O Neil
Long Hwy
Little Compton RI
028371825

Call Sign: KA1VFY
Franklin H Pond
45 Maple Ave
Little Compton RI 02837

Call Sign: K1CVH
Charles R Ogren Jr
51 Oak Forest Dr
Little Compton RI 02837

Call Sign: N1BO
Charles R Ogren Jr
51 Oak Forest Dr
Little Compton RI 02837

Call Sign: W1CRO
Charles R Ogren Jr
51 Oak Forest Dr
Little Compton RI 02837

Call Sign: K1CVH
Charles R Ogren Jr
51 Oak Forest Dr
Little Compton RI 02837

Call Sign: KA1VSE
John J Arruda
Old Main Rd
Little Compton RI 02837

Call Sign: WA6BMO
Richard P Bowen
3 Old Stone Church Rd
Little Compton RI 02837

Call Sign: KD1MW
Bruce N Gavin
220 Peckham Rd
Little Compton RI 02837

Call Sign: KB1FZF
Stephen G Johnson
32 Sakonnet Trail
Little Compton RI 02837

Call Sign: K1CCK
Kenneth T Powers
1 Simmons Rd

Little Compton RI
028371521

Call Sign: WA1QXL
Marion F Powers
1 Simmons Rd
Little Compton RI
028371521

Call Sign: KB1NRA
Thomas J Carson Jr
6 South Shore Rd
Little Compton RI
028370323

Call Sign: K1XGM
Thomas J Carson Jr
6 South Shore Rd
Little Compton RI
028370323

Call Sign: WA1BXY
Donald A Rosinha Ii
50 Tompkins Lane
Little Compton RI 02837

Call Sign: KB1LJI
Andrew P Marks
450 W Main Rd
Little Compton RI 02837

Call Sign: N1OHS
Jack B Crook
461 W Main Rd
Little Compton RI 02837

Call Sign: W1UCU
Manuel Renasco
666 W Main Rd
Little Compton RI
028371124

FCC Amateur Radio Licenses in Manville

Call Sign: KB1EUT
Rene J Fortier
20 Central St
Manville RI 028381025

Call Sign: KB1RJF
Rene J Fortier
20 Central St
Manville RI 028381025

Call Sign: KA1SRO
Roger E Menard
37 Central St
Manville RI 02838

Call Sign: N2RDF
Douglas Troughton
17 Joyce Ann Dr
Manville RI 02838

Call Sign: KB1APC
James L Akers
25 Main St
Manville RI 02838

Call Sign: KB1IAR
James M Surprenant
28 Portland Street
Manville RI 02838

Call Sign: AB1DQ
James M Surprenant
28 Portland Street
Manville RI 02838

Call Sign: KA1TYO
Frank A Rule
Manville RI 02838

FCC Amateur Radio Licenses in Mapleville

Call Sign: N1AXB
Lawrence G Pignolet
362 Cooper Hill Rd

Mapleville RI 02839

Call Sign: N1WVL
John M Capparrille
766 Lapham Farm Rd
Mapleville RI 02839

Call Sign: N1NGW
Robert J Archambault
28 Rexmere Rd
Mapleville RI 02839

FCC Amateur Radio Licenses in Middletown

Call Sign: AA1LG
Robert G Day
6 Acacia Dr
Middletown RI 02842

Call Sign: KC2IQV
Charles C Blocher
1 Admirality Dr - Apt 1
Middletown RI 02842

Call Sign: AB1IY
Christopher D
Korzeniowski
2 Admiralty Dr. Apt 5
Middletown RI 02842

Call Sign: KA6ALH
Raoul H Payette Sr
85 Briarwood Ave Apt 2
Middletown RI 02840

Call Sign: KD4RXR
Angela P Rudisill
17 Brookdale Rd
Middletown RI 02842

Call Sign: KB1IVH
Angela P Rudisill
17 Brookdale Rd
Middletown RI 02842

Call Sign: K1IMJ
James G Edward Jr
15 Circle Dr
Middletown RI 02840

Call Sign: KB1WJP
Samuel B Schwemin
3 Circle Dr.
Middletown RI 02842

Call Sign: KA1MAT
Robert A Dixon
7 Collins Ter
Middletown RI 02842

Call Sign: KG6TDO
Robbie H Scott Jr.
1 Columbia Ct
Middletown RI 02842

Call Sign: KB1KLZ
Basile Panoutsopoulos
12 Connecticut Ave
Middletown RI 02842

Call Sign: N1DCU
Stephen C Damas
103 Corey Lane
Middletown RI 02842

Call Sign: KA1DVJ
Robert A Cilette
223 Corey Ln
Middletown RI 02840

Call Sign: WA1DET
Robert A Miller
1302 Fairway Drive
Middletown RI 02842

Call Sign: N1XVV
Jonathan C Zerbus
245 Forest Ave
Middletown RI 02842

Middletown RI 028424670

Call Sign: KA7QJU
Gene V Bodenberger
22 Gravely Dr
Middletown RI 02842

Call Sign: N1TBU
Phillip B Thow
1425 Green End Ave
Middletown RI 02842

Call Sign: KA1FYA
Richard E Ross
7 Halsey Ave
Middletown RI 02842

Call Sign: KC0NSV
Daniel P Halsig Jr
29 Harbor Village Dr - Apt
4
Middletown RI 02842

Call Sign: N1XZH
George A Wardwell
1 Hickory Ave
Middletown RI 028425309

Call Sign: KC1SD
James W Kyle
2 Howland Ave
Middletown RI 02840

Call Sign: N1CCP
Avery Seaman
357 Indian Ave
Middletown RI 028425765

Call Sign: KA1VHP
Robert C Thompson
5 James St
Middletown RI 02840

Call Sign: KB1DMN
Paul L Bongiovanni
774 Jepson Lane

Call Sign: N1IAB
Alexander Lirakis
62 Kane Ave
Middletown RI 02840

Call Sign: W1PDL
James F Bartram
94 Kane Ave
Middletown RI 02842

Call Sign: WA1WKK
Edna D Bartram
94 Kane Ave
Middletown RI 02842

Call Sign: WB1FMB
Earl H Jameson
32 King Rd
Middletown RI 02842

Call Sign: WB1GVH
Mary S Jameson
32 King Rd
Middletown RI 02840

Call Sign: KA1YFK
David J Walker
212 Maffit St
Middletown RI 02840

Call Sign: W1WDD
Peter C Card
29 Maple Ave
Middletown RI 028424898

Call Sign: KA1FXZ
Robert T Smith
113 Maple Ave
Middletown RI 02840

Call Sign: KA1ZHZ
Rita F Stearns
10 Maple Ter

Middletown RI 02842

Call Sign: N1DHH
Richard M Dunlap
452 Mitchell Ln
Middletown RI 028425349

Call Sign: K1CFQ
Thomas L Murphy
16 Namquid Dr
Middletown RI 02840

Call Sign: KB1PPN
Walter M Wasowski
8 Osage Dr
Middleton RI 02842

Call Sign: K7VOU
Conrad E Overy
11 Philips Ave
Middletown RI 02840

Call Sign: N1FKK
William A Buell
468 Purgatory Rd
Middletown RI 028425974

Call Sign: N1DQD
Michael J Pelczarski
8 Samson Ln
Middletown RI 02842

Call Sign: KA1QYK
Barbara Miller
3 Squantum Ct
Middletown RI 02842

Call Sign: WA1CSO
Joseph A Silveira
3 Squantum Ct
Middletown RI 02842

Call Sign: KA2CDK
Thomas A Frank
40 Swan Dr

Middletown RI 02842

Call Sign: KB1GTU
Anne M Frank
40 Swan Dr
Middletown RI 02842

Call Sign: N1DDB
Edward E Hogan
Ui Mardford River Rd
Middletown RI 02840

Call Sign: W1LNC
Malcolm E Berrett
Valley Rd Apt 230
Middletown RI 02842

Call Sign: AA1GP
Pierre R Demange
35 View Avenue
Middletown RI 02842

Call Sign: KB1LQK
Peter J Sterczela
13 Vigilant St
Middletown RI 02842

Call Sign: WA1NBG
Thomas F Rosa
25 Ward Ave
Middletown RI 028425512

Call Sign: KB1UZB
Alys Dufrey
325 West Main Rd
Middletown RI 02842

Call Sign: KB1UZI
James L Siedman
325 West Main Rd
Middletown RI 02842

Call Sign: WA1VTZ
Gary D Paquette
37 White Ter

Middletown RI 028425952

Call Sign: KB1PP
Donald C Hood
24 William Dr
Middletown RI 02842

Call Sign: W1JCF
Leonard J Vandermyde
24 Willow Ave
Middletown RI 02842

Call Sign: KF1D
Michael A Bunker
11 Winthrop Dr
Middletown RI 02840

Call Sign: KA1PQA
Vince Cermak
24 Wood Rd
Middletown RI 02840

Call Sign: KA1ZJT
Corey Gene Vittucci
Middletown RI 02840

Call Sign: KD6KWK
Jamin L Taibo
Middletown RI 02842

FCC Amateur Radio Licenses in Misquamicut

Call Sign: N1WQE
Richard F Fontana Sr
2 Third St
Misquamicut RI 02891

FCC Amateur Radio Licenses in Naragansett

Call Sign: AB1MT
George J Szarka Jr
17 Spicebush Trail
Naragansett RI 02882

Call Sign: N1HAS
Leonard A Cuoco
29 Azalea Rd
Narragansett RI 02882

Call Sign: KA1YNF
Laurence K Walsh
17 Bonnet View Dr
Narragansett RI 02882

Call Sign: K1VOB
Robert J Kerr
31 Bonnet View Dr
Narragansett RI 02882

Call Sign: KB1JCT
James E Minnich Ii
45 Burnside Ave
Narragansett RI 02882

Call Sign: KB1KQL
Southern R. I. Dx Club
45 Burnside Ave
Narragansett RI 02882

Call Sign: WB1EEW
Richard P Flynn
69 Carver Ln
Narragansett RI 02882

Call Sign: KB1JDC
Leopold J Demarco
35 Caswell St
Narragansett RI 02882

Call Sign: KA1NJI
David W Pierce
164 Caswell St
Narragansett RI 02882

Call Sign: W1NZH
John H Cook
45 Central St
Narragansett RI 02882

Call Sign: K4IJK
Janice E Lentz
200 Clarke Rd - A108
Narragansett RI 028824544

Call Sign: N1FUZ
Raymond H Bliss
235 Col John Gardner Rd
Narragansett RI 02882

Call Sign: KZ1B
Robert W Beatrice
235 Foddering Farm Road
Narragansett RI 028824105

Call Sign: KB1LLG
Gerald Reynolds
36 Fox Drive
Narragansett RI 02882

Call Sign: N1VFG
Priscilla T Chappell
12 Highland Ave
Narragansett RI 02882

Call Sign: N1HVW
Andrew T Mignanelli
2 Hillview Dr
Narragansett RI 02882

Call Sign: KB1OYM
Jeffrey M Simshauser
115 Iroquois Rd
Narragansett RI 02882

Call Sign: W1OGY
Gerard Moor
39 Major Arnold Rd
Narragansett RI 02882

Call Sign: KA1QLH
Edna L O Rourke
59 Oak Ave
Narragansett RI 02882

Call Sign: K1CRN
Walter G Fontaine Jr
101 Ocean Rd U205
Narragansett RI 02882

Call Sign: K1TAV
Richard Broomfield
32 Overlook Rd
Narragansett RI 02882

Call Sign: K1OUN
John D Evans
46 Pontiac Rd
Narragansett RI 02882

Call Sign: KB1UZC
Donna L Andrews
91 Pt Judith Rd Suite 104
Narragansett RI 02882

Call Sign: N1ECL
William L Johnson Sr
44 Shag Bark Rd
Narragansett RI 02882

Call Sign: N1HJM
Brian J Falvey
34 Shagbark Rd
Narragansett RI 02882

Call Sign: K1JIV
William J Thomas
1 Stevenson Way
Narragansett RI 02882

Call Sign: N1XLD
Jill Hynes
5 Treasure Rd
Narragansett RI 02882

Call Sign: N1WGH
Walter R Langlois
67 Treasure Rd
Narragansett RI 02882

Call Sign: W1FOV
Edgar F Robinson
26 Walnut St
Narragansett RI 02882

Call Sign: N1WVX
Michael W Carty
67 What Cheer Rd
Narragansett RI 02882

Call Sign: N1GOQ
Kurt Tedeschi
27 Wheatfield Cove Rd
Narragansett RI 02882

Call Sign: KB1IMA
Shangri-La At Seaweed
Beach Radio Club
49 Willow Ave
Narragansett RI 02882

Call Sign: N1AAH
Paul A Peterson
Narragansett RI 02882

FCC Amateur Radio Licenses in Newport

Call Sign: KB1VEL
Kendall A Crutcher
5 Albro St
Newport RI 02840

Call Sign: N1VAZ
Joseph S Robinson
20 Ayrault St
Newport RI 02840

Call Sign: N1TWQ
Jonathan L Cohen
6 B Braman St
Newport RI 028402502

Call Sign: WE1H

John H Siegrist
15 Bay View Ave
Newport RI 02840

Call Sign: WB6LQQ
Michael J Cullen
19 Bayside Ave
Newport RI 028401552

Call Sign: K1NPT
Michael J Cullen
19 Bayside Ave
Newport RI 028401552

Call Sign: KB1BUL
Terry R Lane
64 Bedlou Ave
Newport RI 028401444

Call Sign: KC6LSN
David W Houghton
270 Bellevue Ave - #337
Newport RI 02840

Call Sign: WA1RJE
James C Poppenhouse
553 Bellevue Ave Apt 15
Newport RI 02840

Call Sign: KC2FMI
Joseph M Miklovic Jr
270 Bellevue Ave Apt 361
Newport RI 02840

Call Sign: N1BQB
Joseph D Haddad
5 Blackwell
Newport RI 02840

Call Sign: KB1SZX
Elizabeth A Silvia
6 Boughton Road 2
Newport RI 02840

Call Sign: KB1DUZ

Jeffrey J Gomes
30 Brewer St. Apt 2
Newport RI 02840

Call Sign: W2MRH
John H Cabot
282 Broadway
Newport RI 02840

Call Sign: KA1ERW
Larry J Bettencourt
315 Broadway Apt 2
Newport RI 02840

Call Sign: N1JCP
Michael B Rabinowitz
26 Brown & Howard Wharf
#205
Newport RI 02840

Call Sign: W1UQN
Bruce F Braga
17 Byrnes St
Newport RI 02840

Call Sign: KB1PPJ
Stephen Kane
19 Carroll Ave
Newport RI 02840

Call Sign: WW4OK
Victor J Farmer
19 Catherine St.
Newport RI 02840

Call Sign: KB1MOH
Candy A Dumond
19 Chapel St Apt 523
Newport RI 02840

Call Sign: W1JFF
Fred E Evans
14 Clarke St
Newport RI 028403024

Call Sign: KB1UZH
Timothy M Mcmahon
Coddington Cove
Newport RI 02840

Call Sign: N1UHP
Julian P Plowright
11 Coddington Street
Newport RI 028402507

Call Sign: K2LDS
Matthew S Gull
1 Commercial Wharf
Newport RI 02840

Call Sign: N1WLZ
Jose M Torres
29 Cowie St
Newport RI 02840

Call Sign: KB1IF
Richard A Mauceri
11 Defenders Row
Newport RI 02840

Call Sign: KA1WGB
Herman L Dawson
11 Division St
Newport RI 02840

Call Sign: KB1OJO
John J Pudloski
49 Division St
Newport RI 02840

Call Sign: N1QAA
Charles Y Duncan
65 Dr Marcus Wheatland
Blvd
Newport RI 02840

Call Sign: KB1PPI
Wayne Robinson
25 Dudley Ave
Newport RI 028401207

Call Sign: KA1IPR
Robert E Emerson
41 E Bowery St
Newport RI 02840

Call Sign: KA1YHM
Sean P Powers
Eastcourt Bellevue Ct
Newport RI 02840

Call Sign: N1USR
Walter A Merchant Jr
211 Eustis Ave
Newport RI 02840

Call Sign: KB1FSQ
Gregory P Lavoy
51 Everett St Apt 1
Newport RI 02840

Call Sign: WA1JHV
Phillip A Ellis
4 Farewell St Box 164
Newport RI 02840

Call Sign: KA1NTJ
Mark A Chramiec
45 Friendship St
Newport RI 02840

Call Sign: AA1TN
Leo Radchenko
218 Goddard Row
Newport RI 02840

Call Sign: KB7YHV
Andrew N Chesnokov
218 Goddard Row
Newport RI 02840

Call Sign: N1RTW
Igor B Booklan
218 Goddard Row
Newport RI 02840

Call Sign: N1UO
Leo Radchenko
218 Goddard Row
Newport RI 02840

Call Sign: KA2EDZ
Charles S Adams
15 Greenough Place
Newport RI 02840

Call Sign: KB1FDC
Janet M Turner
62 Halsey St Unit A
Newport RI 02840

Call Sign: KA1RF
Anthony P Caputi
15 Hammersmith Rd Unit
31
Newport RI 028404215

Call Sign: KB1SDN
Albert W Cory
59 John H Chafee Blvd Ste
309
Newport RI 02840

Call Sign: KC1VH
Charles E Evans
91 Kay St
Newport RI 02840

Call Sign: W1ABE
Lester E Kendall
8 Lakeview Ave
Newport RI 02840

Call Sign: KA8ETY
Ernest C Ware Jr
11 Leonard Ter
Newport RI 02840

Call Sign: N1PGM
Laszlo Kiss

4 Longwood Pl
Newport RI 02840

Call Sign: KC8QQT
Nicholas S Logothets
27 Middleton Avenue
Newport RI 02840

Call Sign: AA1AC
Mark L Stenning
97 Narragansett Ave - M5
Newport RI 02840

Call Sign: KB4DUC
Gary Dobis
Naval Justice School Netc
Newport RI 02841

Call Sign: KA4TDG
Michael J Tracy
Netc
Newport RI 02841

Call Sign: WA1AUL
Robert F Barlow
2 Nicol Ter
Newport RI 02840

Call Sign: WA1OSL
Norman R Anderson
14 Norman St
Newport RI 028403830

Call Sign: KB1AGJ
Toshio Ogami
34 Norman St
Newport RI 02840

Call Sign: KA1YVH
Jay C Grutman
83 Ocean Dr
Newport RI 02840

Call Sign: KA1IYQ
Paul A Lindh

9 Pell St
Newport RI 02840

Call Sign: AC6TE
Jon M Anderson
26 Polk Ct
Newport RI 028403716

Call Sign: KB1NHK
Christopher J Hubbard
85 Pope St
Newport RI 02840

Call Sign: N1QMH
Patrick A Padillia
20 Poplor St
Newport RI 02840

Call Sign: KA1UQL
Joseph F Mc Enness
68 Prairie Ave
Newport RI 02840

Call Sign: KB1JDE
Tim L Ferguson
20 Rhode Island Ave
Newport RI 02840

Call Sign: WA1KUU
Daniel W Marvelle
Roseneath Ave
Newport RI 02840

Call Sign: KE6STQ
Nigel G Philips
30 Second St
Newport RI 02840

Call Sign: KE6STR
Dale E Philips
30 Second St
Newport RI 02840

Call Sign: AA1CH
Elmer E Zborofsky

23 Spouting Rock Dr
Newport RI 02840

Call Sign: WA4COA
Grace L Zborofsky
23 Spouting Rock Dr
Newport RI 02840

Call Sign: WB4TBK
Kim E Zborofsky
23 Spouting Rock Dr
Newport RI 02840

Call Sign: KB1KFH
Mary E Wood
580 Thames St 249
Newport RI 02840

Call Sign: WC1R
Robert C Vlasaty
29 Thurston Ave
Newport RI 02840

Call Sign: KB1KTI
Lance C Shavers
Van Zandt
Newport RI 02840

Call Sign: KA1MTS
Richard Konkolski
23 Warner St
Newport RI 02840

Call Sign: WA1YDT
Alan A Schwartze
60 Warner St Apt 5
Newport RI 028402082

Call Sign: KF4KHC
Andrew J Cogswell
Weaver Ave
Newport RI 02840

Call Sign: KB1WQP
David Eikeland

35 Wellington Ave
Newport RI 02840

Call Sign: KB1PPK
Henry T Wrobel
45 William St
Newport RI 02840

Call Sign: W1GRI
Henry T Wrobel
45 William St
Newport RI 02840

Call Sign: WA6VCT
Claude A Lavarre
15 Willow St
Newport RI 02840

Call Sign: N1IBK
Maurice J Spillane
25 Young St
Newport RI 02840

Call Sign: AI1F
Paul M Baggenstoss
Newport RI 02840

Call Sign: KA1RKO
Diane J Rabinowitz Ms
Newport RI 02840

Call Sign: KA5FTH
Albert Felton
Newport RI 02840

Call Sign: KB1EEG
Doris M Oliveira
Newport RI 02840

Call Sign: KC1EE
Dean B Bullard
Newport RI 02840

Call Sign: N1DKL
Peter A Johnson

Newport RI 02840

Call Sign: W1SYE
Newport County Radio
Club
Newport RI 02840

Call Sign: W6JZZ
Millard A Harris
Newport RI 02840

Call Sign: KB1KQF
Douglas B Bernon
Newport RI 02840

Call Sign: KB1PPP
Richard W Gallipeau
Newport RI 02840

Call Sign: KB1RYG
Newport County Radio
Club
Newport RI 02840

Call Sign: W1AAD
Newport County Radio
Club
Newport RI 02840

FCC Amateur Radio Licenses in North Kingston

Call Sign: KB1HEI
Christopher E Emerson
412 Butternut Dr
North Kingston RI 02852

Call Sign: W1JTO
Christopher E Emerson
412 Butternut Dr
North Kingston RI 02852

Call Sign: WB1FKY
Norman E Sweeney

112 Lake Dr
North Kingston RI
028522030

Call Sign: KB1IMC
George W Gillott
North Kingston RI 02852

Call Sign: N2KV
Kosaku Sugiura
Abeywardane 75dawn
Marie Court
North Kingstown RI 02852

Call Sign: KA1WPR
Mark S Knapp
98 Allen Ave
North Kingstown RI 02852

Call Sign: KA1EVB
Thomas V Morrissey
646 Annaquatucket Road
North Kingstown RI
028525604

Call Sign: N1YKG
Albert A Denis
36 Arcadia Dr
North Kingstown RI 02852

Call Sign: WA1BVB
Peder A Johnsen
20 Arrow Ln
North Kingstown RI 02852

Call Sign: N1HRK
Gordon P Daglieri
104 Audubon Rd
North Kingstown RI 02852

Call Sign: KB1HXV
Neil R Whitehouse
46 Audubon Road
North Kingstown RI 02852

Call Sign: N1ZDB
Maurice O Quinlan
179 Beach St
North Kingstown RI 02852

Call Sign: WA1DPF
Richard G Albright
25 Beachwood Dr
North Kingstown RI 02852

Call Sign: N1WGD
Gregory B Blasbalg
53 Belle Air Dr
North Kingstown RI 02852

Call Sign: KB1SXS
Donald S Atkin
530 Boston Neck Rd
North Kingstown RI 02852

Call Sign: K6JRY
Gerald T Plemmons
46 Breakwater Lane
North Kingstown RI 02852

Call Sign: WA1BO
Robert W Obenauf
8 Bromley Court
North Kingstown RI
028523509

Call Sign: W1QLO
Roger B Chapman
49 Buena Vista Dr
North Kingstown RI 02852

Call Sign: KB1HQY
William K Wray Sr
93 Cara Ct
North Kingstown RI 02852

Call Sign: KB1HQZ
Nancy H Wray
93 Cara Ct
North Kingstown RI 02852

Call Sign: KB1HRA
William K Wray Jr
93 Cara Ct
North Kingstown RI 02852

Call Sign: WA1MQO
Robert W Obenauf
98 Cardinal Dr
North Kingstown RI 02852

Call Sign: WB4SON
Robert M Beatty
32 Carrie Ln
North Kingstown RI 02852

Call Sign: KB1AAW
Robert W Chille
29 Cole Dr
North Kingstown RI 02886

Call Sign: N1VAX
Zachariah D Gleason
56 Concord Ave
North Kingstown RI 02852

Call Sign: W1OFO
William D Acton
126 Cynthia Dr
North Kingstown RI 02852

Call Sign: W1AXU
Roger W Klages
24 Dahlia Dr
North Kingstown RI 02852

Call Sign: WJ1H
L Kevin O Connor
231 Daniel Dr
North Kingstown RI 02852

Call Sign: WX1X
Scott A Tillotson
150 Eastwick Rd
North Kingstown RI 02852

Call Sign: WA1ZGO
Norman J Wrigley
56 Ellis Rd
North Kingstown RI 02852

Call Sign: K2ET
James J Kassal
70 Esker Lane
North Kingstown RI 02852

Call Sign: N1TAF
Sandra B Lepore
105 Ewing Rd
North Kingstown RI 02852

Call Sign: KA1TNY
Robert E Hazard
511 Fletcher Rd
North Kingstown RI 02852

Call Sign: N1EKA
George A Bates
85 Gateway Rd
North Kingstown RI 02852

Call Sign: N1IDT
Noah J Mendelson
20 Georgia Av
North Kingstown RI 02852

Call Sign: N1ICU
Adam J Mendelson
20 Georgia Ave
North Kingstown RI 02852

Call Sign: N1JMA
Martin Mendelson
20 Georgia Ave
North Kingstown RI
028526022

Call Sign: WB1FDG
Warren J Lema
22 Grant Dr

North Kingstown RI 02852

Call Sign: WA1MNO
Charles Caroselli
75 Grant Dr
North Kingstown RI 02852

Call Sign: N1ECT
Albert J Dimascolo Jr
19 Grove Ave
North Kingstown RI 02852

Call Sign: N1TDT
Donald G Pick
33 Grove Ave
North Kingstown RI 02852

Call Sign: KA1ZOU
James I Sammons Iii
271 Hamilton Allenton Rd
North Kingstown RI 02852

Call Sign: W1LLS
G Richard Wills
51 Harrison St
North Kingstown RI 02852

Call Sign: KB1TSI
Jeffrey A Potter
215 Harrison St
North Kingstown RI 02852

Call Sign: N1SMZ
Eric W Bryson
56 Hickory Dr
North Kingstown RI 02852

Call Sign: KB1NVW
David T Glinka
130 Hickory Dr
North Kingstown RI 02852

Call Sign: KA2QYW
Fyzodeen Khan
127 Hideaway Ln

North Kingstown RI 02852

Call Sign: W1EOF
Mark E Titterington
74 Hornet Rd
North Kingstown RI 02852

Call Sign: N1SMX
John R Jackman
113 Huckleberry Road
North Kingstown RI 02852

Call Sign: KB1BJA
Carl S King Jr
52 Intrepid Rd
North Kingstown RI
028524911

Call Sign: KB1OAM
David O Card
48 King Phillip Dr
North Kingstown RI 02852

Call Sign: KA1GYC
Samuel O Baldwin
77 Lawton Ave
North Kingstown RI 02852

Call Sign: KE4NZD
Gregory A Blasdell Sr
63 Lindsay Lane
North Kingstown RI 02852

Call Sign: KB1ULR
Tyler M Whittaker
41 Linwood Dr
North Kingstown RI 02852

Call Sign: KB1APE
David S Wrenn
21 Loop Drive
North Kingstown RI 02852

Call Sign: KD1IZ
James D Lent

13 Martha Drive
North Kingstown RI 02852

Call Sign: N1SNG
Glenn C Miller
107 Meadowland Dr
North Kingstown RI 02852

Call Sign: KB1FWO
Paul M Depetrillo
71 Mt Laurel Way
North Kingstown RI 02854

Call Sign: W1TMZ
Robert Wild
600 Oak Hill Rd
North Kingstown RI 02852

Call Sign: WA1YZD
Joan A Wild
600 Oak Hill Rd
North Kingstown RI 02852

Call Sign: N1RPT
Patrick H Barrows
740 Oak Hill Rd
North Kingstown RI 02852

Call Sign: AC0CQ
David M Sagamang
41 Oakdale Rd
North Kingstown RI 02852

Call Sign: KB1OYL
Geoffrey B Sagamang
41 Oakdale Rd
North Kingstown RI 02852

Call Sign: WA1ZGT
Jean W Abar
59 Pojac Point Rd
North Kingstown RI 02852

Call Sign: KB1HTX
Ralph Lawson Iii

45 Pojac Pt
North Kingstown RI 02852

Call Sign: W1LAB
Ralph Lawson Iii
45 Pojac Pt
North Kingstown RI 02852

Call Sign: KB1SUE
Daniel C Miller
8225 Post Rd
North Kingstown RI 02852

Call Sign: N1WVN
Esther M Clark
6705 Post Rd D12
North Kingstown RI 02852

Call Sign: KA1PPX
Paul A Raiche
381 Potter Rd
North Kingstown RI 02852

Call Sign: WA1ZAR
Leon B Salisbury
40 Queen
North Kingstown RI 02852

Call Sign: N1QON
Craig J Thalhauser
235 Rollingwood Dr
North Kingstown RI 02852

Call Sign: KB1LLE
Jose A Flores
94 Sachem Rd
North Kingstown RI 02852

Call Sign: N1OHR
Patrick S Roach
105 Sachem Rd
North Kingstown RI 02852

Call Sign: KB1LLA
Ronald H Depietro

134 Sachem Rd
North Kingstown RI 02852

Call Sign: WB1CRQ
Peter L Cavanaugh
77 Sea Grass Way
North Kingstown RI
028524041

Call Sign: WA1PNM
Peter M Mc Donough
1320 Stony Ln
North Kingstown RI 02852

Call Sign: KB1JIK
Ralph M Henry Jr
217 Ten Rod Rd
North Kingstown RI 02852

Call Sign: W1KFD
Ralph M Henry Jr
217 Ten Rod Rd
North Kingstown RI 02852

Call Sign: K1QFD
Phyllis S Hoffman
274 Ten Rod Rd
North Kingstown RI 02852

Call Sign: KE1JP
Steven S Corbett
382 Ten Rod Rd
North Kingstown RI 02852

Call Sign: K1GZM
William B Mc Kay
61 Virginia Ave
North Kingstown RI 02852

Call Sign: K4EIS
Mark H Eisenbies
119 Waldron Ave
North Kingstown RI 02852

Call Sign: N1MDW

Lila H Carney
19 Waterwheel Ln
North Kingstown RI 02852

Call Sign: N1XQ
Gregory B Blasbalg
70 Whitman Drive
North Kingstown RI 02852

Call Sign: N1LEA
Kirk T Dyer
60 Woodland Dr
North Kingstown RI 02852

Call Sign: WB1ADG
James J Grueb Sr
68 Woodmont Dr
North Kingstown RI 02852

Call Sign: WE1W
Walter W Campbell
26 Worsley Ave
North Kingstown RI 02852

Call Sign: K1QL
John C Flynn
North Kingstown RI 02852

Call Sign: KB1SNJ
Christopher C Prata
North Kingstown RI 02852

Call Sign: KB1FFR
Charles E Pick
33 Grove Ave
North Kinstown RI 02852

**FCC Amateur Radio
Licenses in North
Providence**

Call Sign: KC1XF
Frederick E Bassett Jr
33 Alexander Street
North Providence RI 02911

Call Sign: KA1QLR
Edward F Laurendeau
11 Allendale Ave
North Providence RI 02911

Call Sign: K1CBO
Frank J Kelley Sr
5 Atlantic Ave
North Providence RI 02904

Call Sign: W1YXL
Charles E Smith Jr
26 Beach St
North Providence RI 02904

Call Sign: W1OOG
Luigi Zannini
28 Bellevue Ave
North Providence RI 02911

Call Sign: KA1VOJ
Leo E Charette Sr
31 Bellevue Ave
North Providence RI 02911

Call Sign: KD1GM
David G Gauthier
20 Bennett St
North Providence RI 02904

Call Sign: W1CFE
David A Paolantonio
1765 Bicentennial Way #N
North Providence RI 02911

Call Sign: N1WNU
Robert W Savitsky
1 Bourne Ave
North Providence RI 02911

Call Sign: KA1QYE
William A Vota
41 Brookside Ave
North Providence RI 02911

Call Sign: W1GVQ
Marco M Marchetti
26 Centredale Ave
North Providence RI
029111636

Call Sign: N1WKB
John D Mc Neill Ii
996 Charles St
North Providence RI 02904

Call Sign: KA1WJM
David P Andreozzi
14 Coes St
North Providence RI 02904

Call Sign: N1HPS
Michael Carruolo
23 Coes St
North Providence RI 02904

Call Sign: KB1PEZ
Narcisco Almeida
206 Dorman Ave
North Providence RI 02904

Call Sign: KB1IAQ
Dante R Calise
1117 Douglas Ave Unit 113
North Providence RI 02904

Call Sign: KA1DKR
Bruce L Berkholtz
15 Douglas Ter Apt 602
North Providence RI 02904

Call Sign: KB1AKD
Robert A Calise
22 Fera St
North Providence RI 02904

Call Sign: K1RAC
Robert A Calise
22 Fera St

North Providence RI 02904

Call Sign: W1RAC
Robert A Calise
22 Fera St
North Providence RI 02904

Call Sign: N1JAT
John A Fascitelli
17 Franklin St
North Providence RI 02904

Call Sign: N1NRJ
Jacyee A Fascitelli
17 Franklin St
North Providence RI 02904

Call Sign: KA1VPN
Jose P Tavares
31 Highlande Ave
North Providence RI 02911

Call Sign: WA1KET
Joseph Torrusio
57 Jacksonia Dr
North Providence RI 02911

Call Sign: W1EIG
Joseph J Aquilante
52 John St
North Providence RI 02904

Call Sign: KC1CF
Timothy J Mc Laughlin
18 Leah St
North Providence RI 02911

Call Sign: KB1EXT
Dawn T Mclaughlin
18 Leah St
North Providence RI 02911

Call Sign: KC1C
Timothy J Mc Laughlin
18 Leah St

North Providence RI 02911

Call Sign: KT1M
Timothy J Mc Laughlin
18 Leah St
North Providence RI 02911

Call Sign: N1GXJ
John R Primeau
47 Meadow View Blvd
North Providence RI 02904

Call Sign: N1GFF
Joseph Fontana
57 Metcalf Ave
North Providence RI 02911

Call Sign: N1XAD
Dorothy L Savitsky
1042 Mineral Spring Ave
North Providence RI 02904

Call Sign: N1VRH
John W O Brien
1081 Mineral Spring Ave
North Providence RI 02904

Call Sign: KC1HI
John D Masso Jr
34 Monticello St
North Providence RI 02904

Call Sign: N1BAQ
Robert J Egan Jr
Nipmuc Trail
North Providence RI 02904

Call Sign: N1XZY
Christopher Rao
132 Palm St
North Providence RI 02904

Call Sign: KB1EKB
Fernando J Chaves
66 Pearl Ave

North Providence RI 02904

Call Sign: KA1AVQ
Sheila M Giardino
17 Rena St
North Providence RI 02911

Call Sign: KC1G
Anthony F Giardino
17 Rena St
North Providence RI 02911

Call Sign: K1AEE
Frederick E Bassett Jr
19 Rose St Apt 1
North Providence RI 02904

Call Sign: KB1KOE
Matthew J Puglia
44 Rosner Ave
North Providence RI
029044446

Call Sign: N1ZTG
Christina L Donovan
1909 Smith St
North Providence RI 02911

Call Sign: KA1YYA
Mirna Nieves
2 Smithfield Rd Apt B1
North Providence RI 02904

Call Sign: N1YKV
Kevin J Nobles
300 Smithfield Road
North Providence RI 02904

Call Sign: N1ELX
Gail M Tretton
17 Spicer Street
North Providence RI 02904

Call Sign: K1WJO
Paul H Roy

70 Superior View Blvd
North Providence RI 02911

Call Sign: KB1EKC
Ludgerio A Fernandes
28 Terry St
North Providence RI 02904

Call Sign: K1LAF
Ludgerio A Fernandes
28 Terry St
North Providence RI 02904

Call Sign: NI1S
Ralph J Sullivan Sr
13 Twins Ln
North Providence RI 02904

Call Sign: KB1IGG
Paul A Silvestri
7 Wenscott Ln
North Providence RI 02904

Call Sign: WA1QNO
Harry Ajemian
68 Westriver Pky
North Providence RI 02904

Call Sign: KA1OIG
Anthony Tudino
17 Woodcliffe Ave
North Providence RI 02911

Call Sign: KB1HUJ
Frank C Velleco Jr
306 Woonasquatucket Ave
North Providence RI 02911

Call Sign: KB1IYE
Gary D Fagnant
405 Woonasquatucket Ave
North Providence RI 02911

**FCC Amateur Radio
Licenses in North Scituate**

Call Sign: N1NKR
Jeffrey A Darche
27 Apple Hill Dr
North Scituate RI 02857

Call Sign: W1QL
Jeffrey A Darche
27 Apple Hill Dr
North Scituate RI 02857

Call Sign: KA1EDP
David G Crowell
40 Briarwood Rd
North Scituate RI 02857

Call Sign: KA1TKF
Shelley R Austin
97 Central Pike
North Scituate RI 02857

Call Sign: KB1PFA
Skye A Pechie
479 Central Pike
North Scituate RI 02857

Call Sign: KB1PFB
Steven J Pechie
479 Central Pike
North Scituate RI 02857

Call Sign: K1RI
Robert A Elliot
11 Cooke Dr
North Scituate RI
028571609

Call Sign: KA1OAC
Linda F Elliot
11 Cooke Dr
North Scituate RI
028571609

Call Sign: KB1CRR
Mason D Briggs

167 Danielson Pike
North Scituate RI 02857

Call Sign: N1XVJ
Angelo A Riccitelli
175 Danielson Pike
North Scituate RI 02919

Call Sign: KB1EJE
George Kuzmowycz
37 Esek Hopkins Rd
North Scituate RI 02857

Call Sign: K1GPD
Stephen W Goulet
Gleaner Chapel Rd
North Scituate RI 02857

Call Sign: WA1PUP
Robert E Sweet
35 Hartford Pike
North Scituate RI 02857

Call Sign: KB1LYT
Alvaro J Torres
1189 Hartford Pike
North Scituate RI 02857

Call Sign: KA1QVS
Thomas F Devine
1225 Hartford Pike
North Scituate RI 02857

Call Sign: N1TYQ
George E Edwards
15 Hesse Ln
North Scituate RI 02857

Call Sign: N1JFM
Brian P Cost
179 Ide Rd
North Scituate RI 02857

Call Sign: KD1A
David P Laferriere

Old Hartford Pike
North Scituate RI
028571068

Call Sign: N1VHM
David E Manni
43 Old Hartford Pk
North Scituate RI 02857

Call Sign: WB1FWJ
Frank Dolyak
134 Peeptoad Rd
North Scituate RI 02857

Call Sign: W1WIU
James P Greenwood
30 Pinecrest Rd
North Scituate RI 02857

Call Sign: KB1OVO
Howard S Feingold
800 Plainfield Pike
North Scituate RI 02857

Call Sign: KA1BGG
David H Clark
135 Quaker Ln
North Scituate RI 02857

Call Sign: K1VEX
Preston C Spicer
76 Rockland Rd
North Scituate RI
028571927

Call Sign: K1HWS
Donald A Mc Call
247 Rockland Rd
North Scituate RI
028571926

Call Sign: KD1TS
Robert H Netzer
476 Rocky Hill Rd
North Scituate RI 02857

Call Sign: N1RPY
Carol J Collins
476 Rocky Hill Rd.
North Scituate RI 02857

Call Sign: KB1RPX
Sarah J Brown
406 Snake Hill Rd
North Scituate RI 02857

Call Sign: KB1CUI
Paul A Charron
250 Snake Hill Road
North Scituate RI 02857

Call Sign: N1NRK
Keith R Brown
406 Snake Hill Road
North Scituate RI 02857

Call Sign: KB1LYZ
Alex J Schenck
36 St James Ln
North Scituate RI
028672982

Call Sign: KB1SJP
Cheryl A Mowry
19 Trimtown Rd
North Scituate RI 02857

Call Sign: W1EYH
Frank S Depetrillo Mr.
548 Trimtown Rd
North Scituate RI 02857

Call Sign: KB1RRB
William F Brown
210 Westcott Rd
North Scituate RI 02857

Call Sign: KB1CMC
Thomas Winnard Jr
350 Westcott Rd

North Scituate RI 02857

Call Sign: N1AVZ
Kenneth P Borden Sr
7 Wilkinson Rd
North Scituate RI 02857

Call Sign: KB1DFC
Gary Ives Tapner
57 William Henry Rd
North Scituate RI
028572040

Call Sign: K1UKQ
Harris J Kenner
222 William Henry Rd
North Scituate RI 02857

Call Sign: KA1KUU
Armand L Masse
299 William Henry Rd
North Scituate RI 02857

Call Sign: KA1AWW
Ellen L Kenner
222 Wm Henry Rd
North Scituate RI 02857

Call Sign: KB1OQW
Barbara W Los
North Scituate RI 02857

Call Sign: AA1HZ
Thomas C Williams
North Scituate RI 02857

Call Sign: KB1BPV
Nn1u Radio Club
North Scituate RI 02857

Call Sign: N1TAG
James Brown
North Scituate RI 02857

Call Sign: KB1UXG

Uss John F Kennedy Arc
North Scituate RI 02857

Call Sign: WA2USN
Uss John F Kennedy Arc
North Scituate RI 02857

Call Sign: NN1U
Alfonso M Paolantonio
North Situate RI 02857

**FCC Amateur Radio
Licenses in North
Smithfield**

Call Sign: KB1QFH
Judson J Mitsock
232 Black Plain Rd
North Smithfield RI 02896

Call Sign: W1JMZ
Judson J Mitsock
232 Black Plain Rd
North Smithfield RI 02896

Call Sign: KB1LUH
Robert B Cesario
669 Black Plain Rd
North Smithfield RI 02896

Call Sign: K1NED
Harold H Morris
850 Black Plain Rd
North Smithfield RI 02896

Call Sign: W1PH
P Joseph Barrett
902 Black Plain Rd
North Smithfield RI 02896

Call Sign: KB1NSG
Walter J Trombly
898 Black Plain Road
North Smithfield RI 02896

Call Sign: KB1RYS
Carmine Iacuone
15 Bourget Ct
North Smithfield RI 02896

Call Sign: WA1PHB
Lionel H Poissant
19 Cynthia Dr
North Smithfield RI 02895

Call Sign: N1FJB
Daniel C Halloran
62 Douglas Pike
North Smithfield RI 02896

Call Sign: K1KEE
Conrad J Laflamme
199 Eddie Dowling Hwy
North Smithfield RI 02896

Call Sign: K1FKJ
Richard M Perron
1138 Eddie Dowling Hwy
North Smithfield RI 02896

Call Sign: KA1SJE
Robert V Allard
478 Greenville Rd
North Smithfield RI 02895

Call Sign: KB1BDE
Joseph E Perry
850 Iron Mine Hill Rd
North Smithfield RI 02895

Call Sign: KB1GIQ
Barbara E Devivo
1275 Iron Mine Hill Road
North Smithfield RI 02896

Call Sign: KB1GIR
Ralph A De Vivo Sr
1275 Iron Mine Hill Road
North Smithfield RI 02896

Call Sign: N1PCR
Robert L Savard
3 Julie Ave
North Smithfield RI 02895

Call Sign: KA1TPA
Carlton J Cabral
5 Julie Ave
North Smithfield RI 02895

Call Sign: KA1SST
James L Brown
28 Lamoureux Blvd
North Smithfield RI 02895

Call Sign: W1EIZ
Charles R Boudreau
62 Mechanic St
North Smithfield RI
028967724

Call Sign: W1DSG
Robert F Taylor
25 Mowry Ave
North Smithfield RI
028967109

Call Sign: W1VH
William G Ewan
175 Old Great Rd
North Smithfield RI
028967743

Call Sign: K1VTA
Veeta A Ewan
175 Old Great Road
North Smithfield RI 02896

Call Sign: W1FJC
William M Edwards
675 Old Smithfield Rd
North Smithfield RI 02895

Call Sign: WA1NCS
Peter E Branconnier

805 Pound Hill Rd
North Smithfield RI 02896

Call Sign: WC1ABW
North Smithfield
Emergency Management
Agency
805 Pound Hill Rd
North Smithfield RI 02896

Call Sign: KB1OFF
Northern Rhode Island
React
805 Pound Hill Rd
North Smithfield RI 02896

Call Sign: K1NSR
Northern Rhode Island
React
805 Pound Hill Rd
North Smithfield RI 02896

Call Sign: KA1JJV
Michael R Cote
1313 Pound Hill Rd
North Smithfield RI
028969525

Call Sign: WA1IWJ
George R Archambault
715 Poundhill Rd
North Smithfield RI 02896

Call Sign: K1AVL
Leo R Antaya
197 Providence Pike
North Smithfield RI
028968013

Call Sign: KD5BXH
Derek R Brodeur
10 Railroad St. #207w
North Smithfield RI 02896

Call Sign: W1MB

Merrill P Budlong
10 Rhodes Avenue
North Smithfield RI 02896

Call Sign: KA1KHO
Joan M Hutchins
12 Ridge Rd
North Smithfield RI 02876

Call Sign: K1SKA
Lawrence H Poitras
190 St Paul St Apt 24a
North Smithfield RI 02896

Call Sign: N1ECJ
Ann A Nyhan
41 Summit Ave
North Smithfield RI 02895

Call Sign: N1LRR
Arthur E Burton Sr
355 Victory Hwy
North Smithfield RI 02896

Call Sign: WA1E
Frederick O Klockars
2 Village Way - The
Meadows - Apt 239
North Smithfield RI
028967248

Call Sign: KB1RYT
Ronald R Blais
8 Wedgewood Dr
North Smithfield RI 02896

Call Sign: KB1RYY
Brian G Vanhouwe
135 Woonsocket Hill Rd
North Smithfield RI 02896

Call Sign: WA1WHJ
Normand R Piette
1281 Woonsocket Hill Rd
North Smithfield RI 02895

Call Sign: KB1CME
Richard G Caya
95 Donahue Rd
Pascoag RI 02859

Call Sign: N1WZZ
Lori A Caya
95 Donahue Rd
Pascoag RI 02859

Call Sign: N1ONY
Wendy M Hysko
1085 Hill Rd
Pascoag RI 02859

Call Sign: KB1EKL
James K Wingren
145 Jackson School House
Rd
Pascoag RI 02859

Call Sign: N1YHB
Kristopher A Keeble
1640 Jackson School House
Rd
Pascoag RI 02859

Call Sign: KB1ODX
Timothy D Lynch
394 Knibb Rd
Pascoag RI 02859

Call Sign: KE1KN
Ronald E Harbour
78 Lee Cir
Pascoag RI 028591313

Call Sign: N1SEE
William G Hill
147 Reservoir Ave
Pascoag RI 02859

Call Sign: NE1W
Joseph L Houle Jr
321 Reservoir Rd
Pascoag RI 02859

Call Sign: K1IA
Raymond T Trinque
605 Reservoir Rd
Pascoag RI 02859

Call Sign: WA1LLO
John S Emidy Sr
242 Sayles Ave
Pascoag RI 02859

Call Sign: KB1TNJ
Kenneth G Biron
235 Union Ave
Pascoag RI 028593308

Call Sign: K5KEN
Kenneth G Biron
235 Union Ave
Pascoag RI 028593308

Call Sign: N1EJQ
Emily F King
601 Victory Hwy
Pascoag RI 02859

Call Sign: N1EJR
James L King
601 Victory Hwy
Pascoag RI 02859

Call Sign: WA1KME
Elmer G Jenks
290 Wallum Lake Rd
Pascoag RI 02859

Call Sign: KB1MWM
Eric M Fontenault
515 Wallum Lake Rd
Pascoag RI 02859

Call Sign: WA1TRG
Harold P Shalou
935 Wallum Lake Rd
Pascoag RI 02859

Call Sign: KA1QYF
Robert J Vota
2575 Wallum Lake Rd
Pascoag RI 02859

Call Sign: WA1CGS
John R Cowles
630 Wallum Lake Rd Box
53
Pascoag RI 02859

Call Sign: WA1MGM
Sophia A Cowles
630 Wallum Lake Rd Box
53
Pascoag RI 02859

Call Sign: N1SEG
Gerald S Pomes
254 Warner Ln
Pascoag RI 02859

Call Sign: KB1BFN
Nicole C Dumin
81 Arland Dr
Pawtucket RI 02861

Call Sign: N1ICW
Linda K Dumin
81 Arland Dr
Pawtucket RI 02861

Call Sign: K1RXN
Albert Sharples
685 Armistice Blvd
Pawtucket RI 02861

Call Sign: N1IFD
Eileen M Di Lorenzo
185 Balch St
Pawtucket RI 02861

Call Sign: KA1BJJ
John C Hemminger
24 Balloo St
Pawtucket RI 02860

Call Sign: K1OYK
J Raymond Mc Nerney
15 Bart Dr
Pawtucket RI 028611506

Call Sign: KA1ZHJ
David N Melo
7 Bassett St
Pawtucket RI 02861

Call Sign: KB1CRS
William F Allen
566 Benefit St
Pawtucket RI 02861

Call Sign: W1WAC
Gilbert A Slater Sr
25 Benjamin St
Pawtucket RI 02861

Call Sign: W1NJD
Walter R Zagroski
55 Birchland Ave
Pawtucket RI 02860

Call Sign: WA1SVH
Amateur Radio Club Troop 37
55 Birchland Ave
Pawtucket RI 02860

Call Sign: KB1MOL
Gary J Donovan
42 Blackburn St

Pawtucket RI 02861

Call Sign: AF1O
Takao Sato
22 Blaisdell Ave C/O J Anderson
Pawtucket RI 02860

Call Sign: KB1UYU
Tomas P Elphick
34 Blodgett Ave
Pawtucket RI 02860

Call Sign: W1ABB
Andrew B Butler
104 Blodgett Ave
Pawtucket RI 02860

Call Sign: KX1Y
Stanley Kurzynski Sr
171 Bloodgood St
Pawtucket RI 028611416

Call Sign: W1YUT
Albert H Robitaille Jr
12 Bloomfield St
Pawtucket RI 028612928

Call Sign: W1ISR
Matthew J Sokolowski
207 Bloomfield St
Pawtucket RI 02861

Call Sign: WA1JLA
John P Palagi
230 Bloomfield St
Pawtucket RI 02861

Call Sign: KC1EV
Francisco Oliveira Jr
53 Brookdale Blvd
Pawtucket RI 02861

Call Sign: KA1YM
Fred T Willett

180 Burgess Ave
Pawtucket RI 02861

Call Sign: KB1BKF
Richard A Suls
57 Capwell Ave
Pawtucket RI 02860

Call Sign: N1UPN
Brian B Provost
793 Central
Pawtucket RI 02861

Call Sign: K1KYI
Richard B Fairweather
106 Chaplin St
Pawtucket RI 02861

Call Sign: K1AGA
Rene E Rancourt
32 Clark Ave
Pawtucket RI 02860

Call Sign: KB1BKG
Jeremy B Stein
220 Cleveland St
Pawtucket RI 02860

Call Sign: KB1BKJ
Jeremy B Stein
220 Cleveland St
Pawtucket RI 02860

Call Sign: W1SMU
Francis P Vivier
40 Clinton St
Pawtucket RI 02861

Call Sign: KD5DDV
Shawn C Whitmore
68 Clyde St
Pawtucket RI 02860

Call Sign: KB1ENY
Shawn C Whitmore

68 Clyde St
Pawtucket RI 02860

228 East St
Pawtucket RI 02860

12 Greene St
Pawtucket RI 02860

Call Sign: W1UKI
John T Costa
11 Crane
Pawtucket RI 02860

Call Sign: K1TUZ
Milton Marks
45 Edgemere Rd
Pawtucket RI 02861

Call Sign: KA1WOF
Michael A George
78 Greene St
Pawtucket RI 02860

Call Sign: N1BMP
Francis R Costa
11 Crane St
Pawtucket RI 02860

Call Sign: KB1GOY
Mark L Humphrey
122 Englewood Ave Apt 1
Pawtucket RI 028605438

Call Sign: WA1FOL
Laurent H Coutu
38 Hanover Ave
Pawtucket RI 02861

Call Sign: KB1G
William J Boyes Jr
35 Desmarais Ave
Pawtucket RI 02861

Call Sign: N1TNS
Christopher A Morin
39 Fern St
Pawtucket RI 02860

Call Sign: KD1FI
Harold E Vine Jr
157 Hughes Ave
Pawtucket RI 028612010

Call Sign: KB1KA
Gary F Powers
122 Dewey Ave
Pawtucket RI 02861

Call Sign: KB1KWJ
Joanne F Ramsey
8 Foster St
Pawtucket RI 02861

Call Sign: KB1OHT
Robert A Littlefield
80 Japonica St
Pawtucket RI 02860

Call Sign: W1LFW
Horace W Coe
15 Diana Dr
Pawtucket RI 028611516

Call Sign: WA1QBD
Alpha J Cantara
Goff Ave Apt 601
Pawtucket RI 02860

Call Sign: KB1AAR
Kellie L Fletcher
55 John St 3rd Flr
Pawtucket RI 02861

Call Sign: W1DJO
Aime J C E Brissette Sr
48 Dickens St
Pawtucket RI 02861

Call Sign: K1TPG
Stanley C Ptak
8 Gooding
Pawtucket RI 02860

Call Sign: KB1ERT
Robert D Octeau
47 Kepler St
Pawtucket RI 02860

Call Sign: W1PLL
Aaron M Finkle
10 Dryden Ave
Pawtucket RI 02860

Call Sign: KB1PFC
Andrew B Kinnecom
39 Gould St
Pawtucket RI 02861

Call Sign: N1EOK
David A Robitaille
32 Kirk Drive
Pawtucket RI 02861

Call Sign: N1DMK
Steven E Snow
81 Dryden Ave
Pawtucket RI 02860

Call Sign: K1UUW
Beatrice M Piche
14 Grandview Rd
Pawtucket RI 02860

Call Sign: KA1GNB
Andreas G Mahlecke
209 London Ave
Pawtucket RI 02861

Call Sign: N1QFX
Jay A Taylor

Call Sign: KB1LER
Earlene M Hines

Call Sign: N1UOL
Matthew T Listenfelt

11 Longfellow St
Pawtucket RI 02861

Call Sign: W1SIK
Edwin Z Wattman
182 Magill Street
Pawtucket RI 02860

Call Sign: N1VXN
Donald S Dumond
574 Main St
Pawtucket RI 02860

Call Sign: N1JWI
Charlotte D Drescher
301 Main St Apt 505
Pawtucket RI 02860

Call Sign: AA1JC
John B Drescher Sr
301 Main St Apt617
Pawtucket RI 02860

Call Sign: N1YHC
Jeffrey N Martin
225 Manton St
Pawtucket RI 02861

Call Sign: K1QOV
Robert Harris
245 Manton St 218
Pawtucket RI 02861

Call Sign: WA1HBA
Adrian I Costantino
70 Maplewood Dr
Pawtucket RI 02861

Call Sign: K1OBZ
Arlow D Sampson
95 Mc Aloon St
Pawtucket RI 02861

Call Sign: KB1QCX
Robert M Gagne

38 Mccabe Ave
Pawtucket RI 02861

Call Sign: KB1RMG
Robert M Gagne
38 Mccabe Ave
Pawtucket RI 02861

Call Sign: N1GHU
Augustine P Chin
200 Mineral Spring
Pawtucket RI 02860

Call Sign: KB1BCA
John W Eastwood
154 Newell Ave
Pawtucket RI 02860

Call Sign: KA1SP
Ovid Vezza
236 Newport Ave
Pawtucket RI 02861

Call Sign: KE3PX
Michael J Emerling
426 Newport Avenue
Pawtucket RI 02861

Call Sign: AB1HR
Michael J Emerling
426 Newport Avenue
Pawtucket RI 02861

Call Sign: WE1Q
Michael J Emerling
426 Newport Avenue
Pawtucket RI 02861

Call Sign: KB1ARL
Jessica L L Heureux
218 Norfolk Ave
Pawtucket RI 02861

Call Sign: KB1FKN
David P Sweeney

58 Olympia Ave
Pawtucket RI 02861

Call Sign: K1PPA
Donald B Morris
86 Ordway St
Pawtucket RI 028611636

Call Sign: KB1BBG
Jason D Williams
13 Orth St
Pawtucket RI 02860

Call Sign: KB1ITQ
Robert A Babbitt
320 Owen Ave
Pawtucket RI 02860

Call Sign: KB1QWO
William G Benn
45 Pallen Ave
Pawtucket RI 02861

Call Sign: W1HLU
Joseph R Santos Sr
40 Paris St
Pawtucket RI 02860

Call Sign: KB1KOD
Jeffery A Miller
26 Parkside Ave Apt 2r
Pawtucket RI 02861

Call Sign: N1YZM
Joao A Garcia
301 Pawtucket Ave
Pawtucket RI 02860

Call Sign: K1NQC
Raymond J Ambrose
27 Pembroke Ave
Pawtucket RI 02860

Call Sign: K1ALI
Anthony L Ionata

159 Pidge Ave Apt 5
Pawtucket RI 028606030

Call Sign: KB1LEQ
Arthur Shlevin
106 Pinecrest Dr
Pawtucket RI 028611524

Call Sign: K1YWS
Stanley Stefanik Jr
121 Pinecrest Dr
Pawtucket RI 02861

Call Sign: KB1EKD
Edward Zawacki
6 Pond St
Pawtucket RI 028604402

Call Sign: N1XNL
Robert D Willows
121 Power Rd
Pawtucket RI 02860

Call Sign: N1ZEW
Jo Anne Chuck
121 Power Rd
Pawtucket RI 02860

Call Sign: KA1UYK
Danielle A Paquette
358 Power Rd
Pawtucket RI 02860

Call Sign: WA1VPC
Ronald E Paquette
358 Power Rd
Pawtucket RI 028603922

Call Sign: W1TAQ
James G Nield
15 Pullen Ave
Pawtucket RI 02861

Call Sign: KA3PNX
Prithwish Basu

60 Ridge St
Pawtucket RI 02860

Call Sign: KA1YOP
Roger L Tetreault
81 Rocco Ave
Pawtucket RI 02860

Call Sign: WA1ZZA
Francisco Oliveira Sr
214 Roosevelt Ave.
Pawtucket RI 02860

Call Sign: KA1XA
Adrien A Bourassa
93 Rosemere Rd
Pawtucket RI 02861

Call Sign: W1HY
Paul F Cavanaugh
233 Rowe Ave
Pawtucket RI 02861

Call Sign: KB1ETH
Russell Refino
80 S Union St
Pawtucket RI 02860

Call Sign: KB1QFG
George Green Jr
197 Sabin St
Pawtucket RI 02860

Call Sign: KD8BUZ
Jason Deines
50 Sisson St Apt 103
Pawtucket RI 02860

Call Sign: W1BMG
Romeo A Robitaille
53 Slade St
Pawtucket RI 02861

Call Sign: KA1ERL
Russell J Ferland

126 Slater Park Ave
Pawtucket RI 02861

Call Sign: KB1PPT
David G Najac
185 Slater Park Ave
Pawtucket RI 02861

Call Sign: K1PAM
Robert Foulkes Iii
11 Tashmoo Way
Pawtucket RI 02861

Call Sign: KB1JDF
Yolima Perez
11 Thomas Ave
Pawtucket RI 02860

Call Sign: KA1ZSD
Armando P Santos
37 Tobie Ave
Pawtucket RI 02861

Call Sign: KD1ZX
Harold E Vine Iii
70 Toledo Avenue
Pawtucket RI 028604730

Call Sign: KA1ZBT
Albert S Koenig
41 Utton Ave
Pawtucket RI 02860

Call Sign: KB1LES
Thomas E Tenney
52 Vale St
Pawtucket RI 02860

Call Sign: KB1LET
Heidi M Tenney
52 Vale St
Pawtucket RI 02860

Call Sign: N1FKZ
Susan M Pierini

554 Walcott St
Pawtucket RI 02861

Call Sign: KB1WAD
Robert L Renshaw
378 Weeden St
Pawtucket RI 02860

Call Sign: W1YVW
Lawrence H Young
698 Weeden St
Pawtucket RI 02860

Call Sign: KB1IDD
Scott Duckworth
14 Wendell St
Pawtucket RI 02861

Call Sign: K1LM
Edward J Janowski
110 Windsor Rd
Pawtucket RI 02861

Call Sign: K1TSV
James R Santos
950 York Ave
Pawtucket RI 02861

Call Sign: KB1LEO
Stephanie A Needham
995 York Ave
Pawtucket RI 02861

Call Sign: KB1LEP
Thomas J Needham
995 York Ave
Pawtucket RI 02861

Call Sign: KB1AXG
David R Roberts
1041 York Ave
Pawtucket RI 02861

Call Sign: KB1ARP
Donna F Manfredi

Pawtucket RI 02908

Call Sign: W1YIF
Frank V Costa Sr
Pawtucket RI 02861

Call Sign: KB1MLA
Richard D Diggett Jr
Pawtucket RI 02861

Call Sign: KB1PXG
James J Allard
Pawtucket RI 02862

FCC Amateur Radio Licenses in Peace Dale

Call Sign: WB9ZMA
Paul A Bizer
62 Church St.
Peace Dale RI 02879

Call Sign: N1JOC
Lawrence A Washburn
920 Curtis Corner Rd
Peace Dale RI 02879

Call Sign: N1JAS
Dale J Taylor
1625 Kingston Rd
Peacedale RI 02879

Call Sign: WA1FLM
Carolyn L Tourgee
157 North Rd
Peace Dale RI 02883

Call Sign: WD9AJR
William D Kovacs
25 Oak Hill Rd
Peace Dale RI 02883

Call Sign: N1ODU
Eric J Bushee
121 Rose Hill Rd

Peace Dale RI 02879

Call Sign: N1DAF
Eugene E Addison
1221 Saugatucket Rd 101a
Peacedale RI 02879

Call Sign: WA1YLP
Shaun Curry
53 Spring St
Peace Dale RI 02883

Call Sign: N1AGP
David J Giles Sr
27 Stedman Ct
Peace Dale RI 02883

Call Sign: KD1QV
Swami Kumaresan
150 W Wind Rd
Peace Dale RI 02883

Call Sign: N1COM
Eugene B Warren
Peace Dale RI 02883

FCC Amateur Radio Licenses in Portsmouth

Call Sign: KB1OAT
Patrick H Agin
62 Alan Ave
Portsmouth RI 02871

Call Sign: KB1LRG
Bsa Amateur Radio Club
Narragansett Council
70 Alan Ave
Portsmouth RI 02871

Call Sign: KB1NUX
Robert E Cosgrove
70 Alan Ave
Portsmouth RI 02871

Call Sign: KB1OFX
Christopher A Cosgrove
70 Alan Ave
Portsmouth RI 02871

Call Sign: KB1HKY
Richard G Cunningham
1909 Alden Landing
Portsmouth RI 02871

Call Sign: KB1HKZ
Elke H Cunningham
1909 Alden Landing
Portsmouth RI 02871

Call Sign: N1PYA
Joseph Baccaro
87 Anson Dr
Portsmouth RI 02871

Call Sign: N1MVS
Theodore F Whittier
1045 Anthony Rd
Portsmouth RI 02871

Call Sign: KA1GKS
Kirsten S Parker
28 Aquidneck Ave
Portsmouth RI 02871

Call Sign: W1RDH
Kenneth J Grinnell Sr
2 Atlantic Ave
Portsmouth RI 02871

Call Sign: KA1HDY
Harold P Andrews
3 Bancroft Dr
Portsmouth RI 02871

Call Sign: WX2T
Richard N Wells Jr
168 Bayview Ave.
Portsmouth RI 02871

Call Sign: W1YZU
William H Weed Jr
84 Belmont Dr
Portsmouth RI 02871

Call Sign: KA1JCS
George M Schwartze Sr
97 Belmont Dr
Portsmouth RI 02871

Call Sign: N1APF
Takayuki Hiroshima
5 Benedict Ave
Portsmouth RI 02871

Call Sign: W1HCQ
Harold B Belson
5 Benedict Ave
Portsmouth RI 02871

Call Sign: W1BNW
Takayuki Hiroshima
5 Benedict Ave
Portsmouth RI 02871

Call Sign: KA1HZH
Shirley A Heywood
127 Berkeley Ave
Portsmouth RI 02871

Call Sign: KO1V
Donald T Heywood
127 Berkeley Ave
Portsmouth RI 02871

Call Sign: WB1HIV
Thomas A Brown
634 Black Point Ln
Portsmouth RI 02871

Call Sign: N1NEZ
Charles G Weymouth
78 Bramans Ln
Portsmouth RI 02871

Call Sign: WA1HXK
Gordon J Stenning
36 Brant Rd
Portsmouth RI 028711802

Call Sign: N1QME
William B Bliss
105 Bristol Ferry Rd
Portsmouth RI 02871

Call Sign: W1WBB
William B Bliss
105 Bristol Ferry Rd
Portsmouth RI 02871

Call Sign: WA1YDU
Richard E Hart
228 Bristol Ferry Rd
Portsmouth RI 028711906

Call Sign: KB1QZP
James J Gaston
240 Bristol Ferry Rd
Portsmouth RI 02871

Call Sign: W1NRI
James J Gaston
240 Bristol Ferry Rd
Portsmouth RI 02871

Call Sign: KB1IDE
Donald M Berrett
4 Cliff Ave
Portsmouth RI 02871

Call Sign: W1LNC
Donald M Berrett
4 Cliff Ave
Portsmouth RI 02871

Call Sign: N1PGJ
George B Gomes Jr
27 Corys Ct
Portsmouth RI 02871

Call Sign: N1PGK
Rachel L Gomes
27 Corys Ct
Portsmouth RI 02871

Call Sign: W1DUC
Frank H Morgan
284 Corys Ln
Portsmouth RI 02871

Call Sign: N1SRR
Erik B Muehlenkamp
285 Corys Ln
Portsmouth RI 02871

Call Sign: KB1UJP
Michael Thombs
171 Cottontail Dr
Portsmouth RI 02871

Call Sign: AB1NM
Michael Thombs
171 Cottontail Dr
Portsmouth RI 02871

Call Sign: KB1WMZ
Amy Thombs
171 Cottontail Dr
Portsmouth RI 02871

Call Sign: W9DAD
Michael Thombs
171 Cottontail Dr
Portsmouth RI 02871

Call Sign: KA7LRA
Juliette M Berriault
9 De Bra Dr
Portsmouth RI 02871

Call Sign: WB1ESY
Robert J Berriault
9 De Bra Dr
Portsmouth RI 02871

Call Sign: N1XBC
Jennifer L O Neill
222 Dexter St
Portsmouth RI 02871

Call Sign: KA1YVC
Robert L Voisinet
11 Dubois Street
Portsmouth RI 02871

Call Sign: WA1HXJ
Forster E Chase
285 E Main Rd
Portsmouth RI 02871

Call Sign: K1IG
Jack P Garforth
2126 E Main Rd
Portsmouth RI 02871

Call Sign: NA1B
Jack P Garforth
2126 E Main Rd
Portsmouth RI 028711290

Call Sign: N1JK
Jack P Garforth
2126 E Main Rd
Portsmouth RI 028711290

Call Sign: KB1OVT
Terry L Wanstreet
3311 E Main Rd - Apt C
Portsmouth RI 02871

Call Sign: W1BLS
Frank A Irish Jr
2368 E Main Rd Apt A2
Portsmouth RI 02871

Call Sign: N1CSE
Jeffrey C Allen
168 East Main Rd
Portsmouth RI 02871

Call Sign: K1LSD
Deborah A Ellis
East Main Rd
Portsmouth RI 02871

Call Sign: N5MVU
David R Ferreira
East Main Rd.
Portsmouth RI 028712426

Call Sign: KB1GZV
Deborah A Ellis
E Main Rd
Portmouth RI 02871

Call Sign: KA1TYB
Richard T Skinger
46 Education Ln
Portsmouth RI 02871

Call Sign: N1TBT
Brian D Cottle
5 First St
Portsmouth RI 02871

Call Sign: N1SRV
Lloyd P Sanborn
7 First St
Portsmouth RI 02871

Call Sign: K1TWN
George M Walsh
61 Fischer Circle
Portsmouth RI 02871

Call Sign: N1TSR
Richard A Moranville
93 Foxboro Ave
Portsmouth RI 02871

Call Sign: N1JJG
Robert A Young
92 Greenfield Ave
Portsmouth RI 02871

Call Sign: WB1FNH
Jerry W Kluba
58 Hilltop Dr
Portsmouth RI 02871

Call Sign: N1SFI
Robert J Barden
113 Hilltop Dr
Portsmouth RI 02871

Call Sign: K3IU
Kenneth E Wagner
124 Hilltop Dr
Portsmouth RI 02871

Call Sign: WA1ABI
John A King
23 Hope Ave
Portsmouth RI 02871

Call Sign: K1VBT
Joseph B Thorpe
135 Hummock Ave
Portsmouth RI 02871

Call Sign: KB1BIZ
Matthew R Yriart
75 Independence Ct
Portsmouth RI 02871

Call Sign: KA1TS
Stephen J Koeberle
75 Joanne Ave
Portsmouth RI 02871

Call Sign: K1LIQ
Arthur G Weeks Jr
5 Karen St
Portsmouth RI 02871

Call Sign: W1AGW
Arthur G Weeks Jr
5 Karen St
Portsmouth RI 02871

Call Sign: KB1RFL
Gary R Crosby
51 Kirduglyn Rd
Portsmouth RI 02871

Call Sign: W1ZAR
Forest B Golden
50 Lambie Cir
Portsmouth RI 02871

Call Sign: W1MPB
Michael P Bielecki
52 Lee Ave
Portsmouth RI 02871

Call Sign: KB1FZG
Christopher T Bielecki
52 Lee Ave
Portsmouth RI 02871

Call Sign: W1AXO
George W Wilkinson
66 Linda Ave
Portsmouth RI 02871

Call Sign: W1RHG
Ralph H Gaze
35 Linda Terrace
Portsmouth RI 02871

Call Sign: KB1IVB
Ronald A Franklin
8 Long Meadow Rd
Portsmouth RI 02871

Call Sign: AA9AL
Christopher B Lirakis
38 Malee Ter
Portsmouth RI 02871

Call Sign: KB1LLN
John F Nickerson Jr
195 Mc Corrie Ln
Portsmouth RI 02871

Call Sign: KB1BIY
Christopher J Thompson
15 Michael Dr
Portsmouth RI 02871

Call Sign: N1GHH
Peter J Dunning Sr
51 Middle Rd Anthony
House Apt 318
Portsmouth RI 02871

Call Sign: K1UFR
Edith R Davis
51 Middle Rd Apt 206
Portsmouth RI 02871

Call Sign: KA3CWV
Kevin J High
1 Mount View Rd
Portsmouth RI 02871

Call Sign: K1CWV
Kevin J High
1 Mount View Rd
Portsmouth RI 02871

Call Sign: KB1GPM
Anthony L Weatherford
31 Narragansett Blvd.
Portsmouth RI 02871

Call Sign: KA1TPS
David J Duggan
6 Norseman Dr
Portsmouth RI 02871

Call Sign: KB1SJN
Stephen E Macdonald
124 Old Mill Lane
Portsmouth RI 02871

Call Sign: W1TXH
William A Gillett
548 Park Ave
Portsmouth RI 028710805

Call Sign: W1UVF
Rosario E Cushera
5 Peleg Road
Portsmouth RI 02871

Call Sign: W1HHH
Kevin D O Brien
34 Porters Ln
Portsmouth RI 02871

Call Sign: K1IUM
Geoffrey Chase
Portsmouth Abbey School
Portsmouth RI 028711352

Call Sign: KB1BMK
Allan M Heatherly
67 Power St
Portsmouth RI 02871

Call Sign: KE1AK
Corry M Thibault
77 President Ave
Portsmouth RI 02871

Call Sign: KA1LRS
Richard M Viggiano
297 R I Blvd
Portsmouth RI 02871

Call Sign: W1ZLU
James A Burton
31 Redwood Rd
Portsmouth RI 02871

Call Sign: AF1I
Robert A Poniatowski
70 Richard Dr
Portsmouth RI 02871

Call Sign: K1TZQ
Howard S Naugle
95 Robin Rd
Portsmouth RI 02871

Call Sign: K1MUB
Thomas Stoupis
59 Roger Williams Ct
Portsmouth RI 02871

Call Sign: AA1JS
John D Francis
294 Rolling Hill Rd
Portsmouth RI 02871

Call Sign: W1NQH
Edward P Gosling Iii
484 Sandy Point Ave
Portsmouth RI 028713514

Call Sign: K4YJC
Joseph F Smith
515 Sandy Point Ave
Portsmouth RI 02871

Call Sign: AA1RD
Frank S Santos Iii
533 Sandy Point Ave
Portsmouth RI 02871

Call Sign: W1MFS
Michael F Santos
533 Sandy Point Avenue
Portsmouth RI 028710101

Call Sign: AB1KR
Michael F Santos
533 Sandy Point Avenue
Portsmouth RI 028710101

Call Sign: KM1S
Michael F Santos
533 Sandy Point Avenue
Portsmouth RI 028710101

Call Sign: AA1RC
Sandra A Santos
533 Sandy Pt Ave
Portsmouth RI 02871

Call Sign: WA1GLP
Albert E Neves
181 Seaconnet Blvd
Portsmouth RI 02871

Call Sign: KB1QXS
Jason A Gaston
16 Second St
Portsmouth RI 02871

Call Sign: KB1QXV
Jason A Gaston
16 Second St
Portsmouth RI 02871

Call Sign: WA1OHK
Robert N Bieber Sr
39 Seneca Rd
Portsmouth RI 02871

Call Sign: W1IIC
Robert F Gunning
22 Sherman Ave
Portsmouth RI 02871

Call Sign: WA1FTB
John M Richardson
95 Sherwood Terrace
Portsmouth RI 02871

Call Sign: KB1EAV
Michael E Montecalvo
54 Soares Dr
Portsmouth RI 028712915

Call Sign: KA8EMS
John W Le Favour
135 Spring Hill Road
Portsmouth RI 02871

Call Sign: KC1HM
Lofton E Clark Jr
21 Stagecoach Rd
Portsmouth RI 02871

Call Sign: N6LSZ
Don B Mills
36 Stewart Dr
Portsmouth RI 02871

Call Sign: N1RIY
Abel R Massa
248 Union St
Portsmouth RI 02871

Call Sign: W1NWX
Philip A Recupero
265 Union St
Portsmouth RI 02871

Call Sign: AJ1B
Mark J Munkacsy
379 Vanderbilt Lane
Portsmouth RI 028712322

Call Sign: WA1LQF
William B Robinson Sr
82 Viking Dr
Portsmouth RI 02871

Call Sign: KB1PPL
William J Ramey
340 W Main Rd
Portsmouth RI 02871

Call Sign: KB1DWO
Thomas G Spence
1220 W Main Rd
Portsmouth RI 02871

Call Sign: WY1L
Thomas G Spence
1220 W Main Rd
Portsmouth RI 02871

Call Sign: KA1HGR
Valorie J Hatch
44 Wamsutta Ln
Portsmouth RI 02871

Call Sign: KB2KTO
Kevin P Bongiovanni
39 Warrens Way
Portsmouth RI 02871

Call Sign: KB1FZH
Maurice W Warren
120 Water St
Portsmouth RI 02871

Call Sign: KA1LRL
Marlin E Keefer
172 Water St
Portsmouth RI 02871

Call Sign: KA1LRM
Maria I F Gomes
172 Water St
Portsmouth RI 02871

Call Sign: N1SFZ
John S Mills
297 Water St Unit D1
Portsmouth RI 02871

Call Sign: N1NFA
Stephen J Desnoyers
70 Watson Dr
Portsmouth RI 02871

Call Sign: KD4ONW
James J Lowrimore
58 Weetamoe Lane
Portsmouth RI 02871

Call Sign: KB1SGW
Paula M Aldrich
42 Willow Lane
Portsmouth RI 02871

Call Sign: W1CVU
Rogers High School
Amateur Rad Clb
42 Willow Ln

Portsmouth RI 02871

Call Sign: W1WLG
John D Aldrich
42 Willow Ln
Portsmouth RI 02871

Call Sign: WA1UWU
David W Smith
103 Windward Dr
Portsmouth RI 02871

Call Sign: KA1JLW
Richard L Stafford Ii
Portsmouth RI 02871

FCC Amateur Radio Licenses in Providence

Call Sign: KA1JZD
Robert J Gonicberg
88 11th St
Providence RI 02906

Call Sign: KB1PPM
Jeffrey W Stevens
38 12th St
Providence RI 02906

Call Sign: KB1ATZ
Salvatore R Palumbo
721 Academy Ave
Providence RI 02908

Call Sign: N1XOZ
David J Ranucci
764 Admiral St
Providence RI 02908

Call Sign: W1WVK
Leonard M Perkins Jr
192 Alabama Ave
Providence RI 02905

Call Sign: KB1LQI

Robert F Amato
11 Aldine St
Providence RI 02909

Call Sign: KB1ICY
Derek J Hallam
124 Almy St. Apt C
Providence RI 02909

Call Sign: KB1NRV
Robert H Gillissie
73 Alverson Ave -3
Providence RI 02909

Call Sign: KB1PIV
Petar V Horvatic
12 Andrew St -1
Providence RI 02909

Call Sign: KC9LDC
Justin B Savage
96 Arnold St.
Providence RI 02906

Call Sign: KB1CGG
Robin L Ward
52 Ascham Street 3rd Floor
Front
Providence RI 02904

Call Sign: N1UWO
Herminio Severino
23 Atlantic Ave
Providence RI 02907

Call Sign: KC5NLT
Kevin D Greene
16 Aurelia Dr
Providence RI 02909

Call Sign: KB1LXU
Kevin D Greene
16 Aurelia Dr
Providence RI 02909

Call Sign: KB1WWX
William H Anger Jr
12 Balmoral Ave
Providence RI 02908

Call Sign: W1MU
Alfred M Hughes
46 Barnes St
Providence RI 02906

Call Sign: KB1ANY
Denise J Hahn
160 Benedict St Apt 620
Providence RI 02909

Call Sign: K1FGK
Emma Lawton
30 Bergen St
Providence RI 02908

Call Sign: KA1OCG
John C Gargaro
43 Berlin St
Providence RI 02908

Call Sign: KB1SYA
Russell E Pescatore
20 Bernon St
Providence RI 02908

Call Sign: KB1ARE
Medric H Maynard Jr
Box 40097
Providence RI 02940

Call Sign: N1OHO
Matthew A Coolidge
12 Bradley St
Providence RI 02908

Call Sign: KB1ARB
Michael J Zarlenga
964 Branch Ave
Providence RI 02904

Call Sign: KB1GTZ
Gabriel Read
2 Brighton Street
Providence RI 02909

Call Sign: N1VJK
Richard P Boutin
162 Broad St 416
Providence RI 029034052

Call Sign: N1UID
James A Shahbaz
224 Broadway
Providence RI 02903

Call Sign: N1VBE
Robert S Shahbaz Ii
224 Broadway 2nd Fl
Providence RI 02903

Call Sign: W1SGA
Malcolm C Bromberg
27 Brookway Rd
Providence RI 02906

Call Sign: N1RMN
David E Langworthy
Brown
Providence RI 02912

Call Sign: KV6K
Kevin A Bravo
Brown Medical
Providence RI 02912

Call Sign: N1TEK
Joshua R Rai
Brown Univ Box 3271
Providence RI 02912

Call Sign: KB1DAT
Soren C Spies
Brown University
Providence RI 029122354

Call Sign: N1JGU
LAURA L Cavanaugh
108 Burlington St
Providence RI 02906

Call Sign: N1JGW
Jeffrey P Cavanaugh
108 Burlington St
Providence RI 02906

Call Sign: W1BGM
Ansel Cleinman
1 Butler Ave Unit 315
Providence RI 029065144

Call Sign: K1IJU
C Norman Peacor
1 Butler Ave Unit 328
Providence RI 029065144

Call Sign: N1XCU
Paul A Palrao
240 California Ave
Providence RI 02905

Call Sign: KB1UHC
Jose A Rivera
8 Carver Ct
Providence RI 02906

Call Sign: KA1TNE
James F Grundner
5 Cathedral Sq.
Providence RI 02903

Call Sign: KA1QXR
Ralph C Gemma
39 Celia St
Providence RI 02909

Call Sign: KJ6ARR
Georg O P Eschert
38 Chaffee Street
Providence RI 02909

Call Sign: N1WCX
Robert A Holton
912 Chalkstone Ave
Providence RI 02908

Call Sign: N1WCY
Donna J Holton
912 Chalkstone Ave
Providence RI 02908

Call Sign: N1RAI
Christopher J Harwood
111 Colonial Rd
Providence RI 029062549

Call Sign: W1IUP
Thomas L De Petrillo
7 Constitution Hill
Providence RI 02904

Call Sign: KA1RCZ
Amable A G Gonzalez
485 Cranston St
Providence RI 02907

Call Sign: K1JA
James A Anderson
9 Creighton Street
Providence RI 02906

Call Sign: KB1DJD
Pedro M Arias
120 Cumberland St
Providence RI 02908

Call Sign: N1RWX
Pedro M Arias
120 Cumberland St
Providence RI 02908

Call Sign: N1DYB
Kenneth L Wennberg
23 Cutler St
Providence RI 02909

Call Sign: KB1AUH
Paul F Maurice
18 Daboll St
Providence RI 02907

Call Sign: N1WSI
George W Zabel Iii
79 Dana St
Providence RI 02906

Call Sign: N1PZV
Alfred J Cicillini
175 Devonshire St
Providence RI 02908

Call Sign: W1NCA
Anthony J Klumbis
360 Douglas Ave
Providence RI 02908

Call Sign: KA5ORV
Peter J Lech
96 Dover St
Providence RI 02908

Call Sign: W1OTE
John J Dwyer
11 Eames St
Providence RI 029063303

Call Sign: W1FBV
James W Hackett
70 Elmgrove Ave
Providence RI 02906

Call Sign: W1TQW
Robert H Rothman
710 Elmgrove Ave
Providence RI 029064900

Call Sign: W2IFA
Robert H Groh
41 Elmway St
Providence RI 02906

Call Sign: KB1HXA
Carol Annette Cooke
86 Elton St
Providence RI 02906

Call Sign: KB1NCA
Philip Lieberman
141 Elton St
Providence RI 02906

Call Sign: KB1PPO
Robert M Pesapane
153 Emeline St
Providence RI 02906

Call Sign: WA1DWN
Bruce O Anderson
136 Evergreen St
Providence RI 02906

Call Sign: KB1BKI
Richard A Suls
98 Evergreen St Apt 1
Providence RI 02906

Call Sign: N1RWU
Angel L Diaz
30 Fallon Ave
Providence RI 02908

Call Sign: N1YAA
Angel L Pacheco
102 Florence St.   Apt. 2
Providence RI 02909

Call Sign: N1LWV
Edward T Johnson
58 Forbes Street
Providence RI 02908

Call Sign: KB1BIL
Sophearak Huy
176 Ford St
Providence RI 02909

Call Sign: KA1FDN
Mark S Abrams
72 Fosdyke St
Providence RI 02906

Call Sign: K1MBO
David Potter
84 Fosdyke Street
Providence RI 02906

Call Sign: KA1JKE
Fernando A Silva
47 Furnace St
Providence RI 02903

Call Sign: KB1MTJ
Robert G Felici
40 Glossop St
Providence RI 02920

Call Sign: N1OHF
Louis A Gianfrancesco
33 Gloucester St
Providence RI 02908

Call Sign: KA1ZBN
Pedro J Ayala
200 Gordon Ave
Providence RI 02905

Call Sign: KB1KIQ
Jeffrey V Rose
69 Governor St
Providence RI 02906

Call Sign: KA1OHO
Genevieve E Gabriele
20 Gridley St
Providence RI 02904

Call Sign: N1FFK
Luigi Gabriele
20 Gridley St
Providence RI 02904

Call Sign: KB1UHE
Angel L Cecilia
28 Hamilton St
Providence RI 02907

Call Sign: WA1QMX
Anthony L Ionata
63 Henrietta St
Providence RI 029041011

Call Sign: KA1WIT
Joseph A Rohelia
20 Hereford St
Providence RI 02908

Call Sign: N1UWN
Jeffrey A Walsh
11 Hilarity Street
Providence RI 029095708

Call Sign: KB1JLV
Anthony Fascia
45 Hillview Ave
Providence RI 02908

Call Sign: KB1RGH
East Coast Birds On Patrol
549 Hope St
Providence RI 02906

Call Sign: KB1SRG
Oral O Clarke
428 Hope St Apt 4
Providence RI 02906

Call Sign: WB1DSJ
Robert E Crossette
549 Hope St.
Providence RI 02906

Call Sign: K1NHG
Michael D Troiano
337 Jastram St
Providence RI 02908

Call Sign: KB1QVF
Derek T Mcgarry
69 Job St
Providence RI 02904

Call Sign: KA1SVW
William B Shipp
224 Medway St
Providence RI 02906

Call Sign: KB1UKQ
John Duksta
94 Mount Pleasant Ave
Providence RI 02908

Call Sign: KD1S
Anthony S Pelliccio
197 Knight St
Providence RI 02909

Call Sign: KB1SUF
Matthew M Miller
222 Melrose St Apt 2
Providence RI 02907

Call Sign: W1WKO
Armand De Fusco
393 Mount Pleasant Ave
Providence RI 029083325

Call Sign: N1ZMG
Carlos R Rios
170 Laurel Hill St
Providence RI 02909

Call Sign: N1LLZ
Steven J Richard
38 Mercy St
Providence RI 02909

Call Sign: KB1PGQ
Brian W Morrison
2 Moy St
Providence RI 029042113

Call Sign: WB1DES
Stuart H Altman A
15 Lauriston St
Providence RI 02906

Call Sign: KB8FKF
Katherine M Begin
38 Meridian St
Providence RI 02908

Call Sign: KA1WWU
David R Johnston
35 Moy St
Providence RI 02904

Call Sign: N1DYA
John M Randall Jr
25 Lecia Dr
Providence RI 029096035

Call Sign: KB1WMT
Caeli I Carr-Potter
25 Messer St
Providence RI 02909

Call Sign: K1GOW
Joseph F Dupre
766 Mt Pleasant Ave
Providence RI 02908

Call Sign: N1WGE
Stephen A Metcalf
100 Lloyd Ave
Providence RI 02906

Call Sign: N1WMK
Glen A Waterman
145 Modena Ave
Providence RI 02908

Call Sign: N1LZV
Paul E Stolle
670 N Main St 6e
Providence RI 02904

Call Sign: N1GEE
Wayne D Wilbur
Manchester Pl
Providence RI 02903

Call Sign: N1ZJL
Carolyn L Waterman
145 Modena Ave
Providence RI 02908

Call Sign: KB1AYF
Diane P Deignan
136 Nelson St
Providence RI 02908

Call Sign: KB1WRM
Thomas K Kettenmann
31 Mather Ave
Providence RI 02905

Call Sign: KB1ERU
Sheri A Ward
26 Monticello St
Providence RI 02904

Call Sign: KB1LKA
Gianna M Richer
64 Oak St
Providence RI 02909

Call Sign: N1RUP
Peter A Duhme
197 Medway St
Providence RI 02906

Call Sign: W1SQG
Anthony Sisti
148 Moorefield St
Providence RI 02909

Call Sign: KA1EHZ
Philip A Speare
25 Orchard Pl
Providence RI 02906

Call Sign: KB1DRQ
Pablo R Mendez
262 Orms St
Providence RI 02908

Call Sign: N1VDI
Steven D Foster
5 Rowley St
Providence RI 02909

Call Sign: KA1ZKA
William D Lema
65 Sheldon St
Providence RI 02906

Call Sign: KP4VQ
Yassey Rodriguez
181 Ortoleva Drive
Providence RI 02909

Call Sign: N1VVV
Jeffrey T Foster
5 Rowley St
Providence RI 02909

Call Sign: N1EGU
Richard J Brito
36 Shepard Ave
Providence RI 02904

Call Sign: KB2ABZ
Britt H Tonnessen
11 Pittman St
Providence RI 02906

Call Sign: WA1BCW
Donald J Place
56 Rutherglen Ave
Providence RI 02907

Call Sign: KA1VJZ
Paul E Bevilacqua
77 Sherwood St
Providence RI 02908

Call Sign: N1ZWN
Julian Valdez
143 Prudence Ave
Providence RI 02909

Call Sign: W1ESQ
Neville J Bedford Esq
321 S. Main St. Fl5
Providence RI 029037108

Call Sign: KB1BCK
Mark W Moran
203 Sinclair Ave
Providence RI 02907

Call Sign: KA1OWY
Walter E Little
49 Ravenswood Ave
Providence RI 02908

Call Sign: KB1ARO
Deborah A Alessandro
114 Salina St
Providence RI 02908

Call Sign: KB1WJD
Jack Mendez
11 South Angell St 106
Providence RI 02906

Call Sign: KA1OGO
Laurie A Mc Laughlin
176 Regent Ave
Providence RI 02908

Call Sign: N1MIU
John J Nichols
56 Samoset Ave
Providence RI 029083816

Call Sign: N1HCM
Anthony S Di Folco
46 Stella St
Providence RI 02909

Call Sign: WA1DOH
Paul J Giorgio
285 River Ave
Providence RI 02908

Call Sign: KA1JRL
Eduino N Silva
27 Schofield St
Providence RI 02903

Call Sign: WA1LLP
Edward Handy Jr
10 Stephen Hopkins Ct
Providence RI 02904

Call Sign: W1QCF
Raymond T Warner
129 Roger Williams Ave
Providence RI 029073326

Call Sign: W1LKH
Paul D Carignan
9 School St
Providence RI 02909

Call Sign: N1JXB
Angel G Batista
46 Sumter St
Providence RI 02907

Call Sign: KA1ZQZ
Richard H Yearwood
128 Roosevelt St
Providence RI 02909

Call Sign: KA1QCI
Richard F Santopietro
23 Shafter St
Providence RI 02909

Call Sign: W1JII
Norman La Croix
Sunset Ave
Providence RI 02909

Call Sign: WE1RD
Michael P Deignan
Repeater Association
39 Sutton St Apt 1
Providence RI 02903

Call Sign: K1NJT
Clinton H Lawton
700 Union Ave
Providence RI 02909

Call Sign: N1HDD
Vicke D Bryant
73 Wisdom St 2
Providence RI 02908

Call Sign: N1VOD
Clayton J Keiser
80 Terrace Ave
Providence RI 02909

Call Sign: KB1UZ
James M Arruda
15 Verdic Ave
Providence RI 02909

Call Sign: N1ZTW
Luis A Diaz
33 Wood St
Providence RI 02909

Call Sign: KC9COB
Donald W Kendall
307 Thayer St 1st Floor
Providence RI 02906

Call Sign: N1JYY
Braulio Barinas
297 Vermont Ave
Providence RI 02925

Call Sign: N1HBG
Jose A Perez
118 Wood St
Providence RI 02909

Call Sign: KB1NPD
Konstantin Salikhov
151 Thayer St Box 1917
Providence RI 02912

Call Sign: N1TWB
Larry A Spencer
26 Wallace St
Providence RI 029093055

Call Sign: KB1CVT
Maria E Perez
118 Wood St 2floor
Providence RI 02909

Call Sign: N1KBK
Herman A Ralph Jr
5 Ticknor St
Providence RI 029084008

Call Sign: W1CVE
Bruce H Brundage
28 Wayne Street
Providence RI 02908

Call Sign: WA1SER
James L Tourigny
197 Wyndham Ave
Providence RI 029082831

Call Sign: N1RUQ
Wade B Rogers
86 Transit St
Providence RI 02906

Call Sign: WR1R
Frank Almeida Iii
104 West Clifford St
Providence RI 02907

Call Sign: AB1CY
James L Tourigny
197 Wyndham Ave
Providence RI 029082831

Call Sign: KA1UXX
Christian T Reimer
130 Transit St
Providence RI 02906

Call Sign: KA1ZBM
Efrain Nieves
44 Whipple St
Providence RI 02908

Call Sign: KB1TB
James L Tourigny
197 Wyndham Ave
Providence RI 029082831

Call Sign: KE1IG
Alexander J Cimini
20 Trinidad St
Providence RI 029082329

Call Sign: N1HDZ
Robert A Andriole Sr
118 Winchester St
Providence RI 02904

Call Sign: KB1I
James L Tourigny
197 Wyndham Ave
Providence RI 029082831

Call Sign: KB1SLP
Rena Swartz
66 Tucker Ave
Providence RI 02905

Call Sign: K1VSJ
Howard M Bromberg
21 Wingate Rd
Providence RI 02906

Call Sign: W1VDI
Peter De Quattro
60 Zella St
Providence RI 02908

Call Sign: KA1FFH
David Yashar
Providence RI 029409023

Call Sign: KA1VAQ
Carlos R Thillet
Providence RI 02905

Call Sign: KA1YYQ
Raymond P Aldoyn Jr
Providence RI 02907

Call Sign: KB1AKC
Joseph L Haddock
Providence RI 02909

Call Sign: N1APW
Paul S Gonicberg
Providence RI 029400820

Call Sign: N1BEE
Michael S Bilow
Providence RI 02940

Call Sign: N1BUA
Vincent A Blas
Providence RI 029080271

Call Sign: N1JDA
Neville J Bedford
Providence RI 02908

Call Sign: N1JNI
Matthew J Ventura
Providence RI 02940

Call Sign: N1LDB
Anthony E Bendigo
Providence RI 02907

Call Sign: N1RGQ
Ramon A Cardenes
Providence RI 02907

Call Sign: W1BSN
Barry S Noel
Providence RI 029080091

Call Sign: WD1R
Frederick Escobar
Providence RI 02907

Call Sign: KB1FBE
Robert C Soares
Providence RI 02901

Call Sign: KB1FNM
Uss Saratoga Arc
Providence RI 02909

Call Sign: AA1YO
Matthew J Ventura
Providence RI 02940

Call Sign: N1YO
Matthew J Ventura
Providence RI 029401031

Call Sign: AB1AO
Vincent A Blas
Providence RI 02908

Call Sign: KB1NCI
Damaris Lopez
Providence RI 02906

Call Sign: WA1DH
Douglas M Harrington
Providence RI 02940

FCC Amateur Radio Licenses in Prudence Island

Call Sign: K1MFZ
Andrew R Allard
200 Daniel Ave
Prudence Island RI 02872

Call Sign: KB1KMZ
Albert C Bielitz Jr
Prudence Island RI 02872

FCC Amateur Radio Licenses in Richmond

Call Sign: KA1NKF
Georgia A Torrisi
3 Morning Road
Richamond RI 02892

Call Sign: KB1QWX
Brian Smith
35 Beaver River Rd
Richmond RI 02892

Call Sign: KB1BPS
Brian Smith
35 Beaver River Rd
Richmond RI 02892

Call Sign: KB1QZN
Richmond Eoc
Communications Team
35 Beaver River Road
Richmond RI 02892

Call Sign: KA1RCX
Brian W Hart
465 Gardner Rd Lot 59
Richmond RI 02892

Call Sign: KA1JNP
William C Torrisi Jr
3 Morning Road
Richmond RI 02892

Call Sign: KA1NXS
James B Pacheco
3 Morning Road
Richmond RI 02892

Call Sign: KA1SOO
Christopher A Pacheco

3 Morning Road
Richmond RI 02892

Call Sign: KB1AUU
James P Mc Nally
Wood River Jct
Richmond RI 02894

FCC Amateur Radio Licenses in Riverside

Call Sign: KA1IOO
Michael W Martin
82 Anson Dr
Riverside RI 02915

Call Sign: KB1FWI
Eugene Silva
38 Armington Ave
Riverside RI 02915

Call Sign: KA1OSW
Adolph T Littlefield
15 Bergin St
Riverside RI 02915

Call Sign: W1JAC
Richard R Bushnell
133 Brookfield Rd
Riverside RI 029153800

Call Sign: N1QBH
Harold S Hillman
876 Bullocks Point Ave
Riverside RI 02915

Call Sign: KD7CKI
John P Clancy
680 Bullocks Pt Ave
Riverside RI 02915

Call Sign: N1SGH
Paul J Mercier
43 Bullocks Pt Ave 8c
Riverside RI 02915

Call Sign: W1ICQ
Alfred A Perry
4 Carousel Dr W Apt 203
Riverside RI 02915

Call Sign: N2VCB
Casey J O Donnell
49 Carousel Drive
Riverside RI 02915

Call Sign: KB1HWA
David C Pearson
93 Cedar Ave
Riverside RI 02915

Call Sign: KB1OYR
Robert E Boulay
83 Circuit Dr
Riverside RI 02915

Call Sign: KB1ADR
Thomas R Galligan
9 Dartmouth Ave
Riverside RI 02915

Call Sign: N1QQX
Shaun P Murphy
64 Dyer Ave
Riverside RI 02915

Call Sign: KB1RYX
Mark D Mueller
106 Elder Ave
Riverside RI 02915

Call Sign: KB1UAV
Stephen D Fortner
46 Euclid Ave
Riverside RI 02915

Call Sign: KV7SDF
Stephen D Fortner
46 Euclid Ave
Riverside RI 02915

Call Sign: KB1OVN
Russell C Pimental
37 Ferncrest Dr
Riverside RI 02915

Call Sign: N1PZD
Michael K Clark
55 Floyd Ave
Riverside RI 02915

Call Sign: KO1M
Michael K Clark
55 Floyd Ave
Riverside RI 02915

Call Sign: W1DK
Eugene B Petit
66 Garden Dr
Riverside RI 02915

Call Sign: N1HHT
Kurt Hofmann
61 Gerald St
Riverside RI 02915

Call Sign: K1URT
Kurt Hofmann
61 Gerald St
Riverside RI 02915

Call Sign: W1UIA
Robert W Greenlaw
82 Indian Rd
Riverside RI 029153102

Call Sign: K1EBC
Manuel M Vincent
11 Jackson Ave
Riverside RI 02915

Call Sign: KB1TUE
Jillian A Berg
34 Lakeside St
Riverside RI 02915

Call Sign: N1BBM
Gilbert F Brown
49 Lakeside St
Riverside RI 029153133

Call Sign: KB1DFY
Matthew W Robinson
34 Lakeside Street
Riverside RI 029153135

Call Sign: W1MWR
Matthew W Robinson
34 Lakeside Street
Riverside RI 029153135

Call Sign: KA1STS
Robert W Sherman
29 Legion Way
Riverside RI 02915

Call Sign: K1FER
Deborah R Williams
58 Locust St
Riverside RI 02915

Call Sign: W1VWR
Howard E Walker
58 Locust St
Riverside RI 02915

Call Sign: W1ZOK
Norma R Walker
58 Locust St
Riverside RI 029154644

Call Sign: KB1LLR
Nancy L Macdonald
53 Maple Ave
Riverside RI 02915

Call Sign: KB1LLS
Craig R Macdonald
53 Maple Ave
Riverside RI 02915

Call Sign: WB1ALC
Robert S Osborne
77 Metropolitan Park Dr
Riverside RI 02915

Call Sign: KA1QHD
Diane E Letourneau
19 North St
Riverside RI 02915

Call Sign: KA1QHF
David J Letourneau
19 North St
Riverside RI 02915

Call Sign: K1NEF
Jeffrey M Rockwell
64 Padelford Ave
Riverside RI 02915

Call Sign: WA1ROJ
Robert H Rockwell
2924 Pawtucket Ave
Riverside RI 029154942

Call Sign: N1XGJ
David Viveiros
3044 Pawtucket Ave
Riverside RI 02915

Call Sign: N1GED
Ronald R Testa
2936 Pawtucket Ave Apt
310
Riverside RI 02915

Call Sign: N1GPS
Dorothy P Sheldon
2936 Pawtucket Ave Apt
310
Riverside RI 02915

Call Sign: KB1DKY
Michael J Conley

124 Prescott Ave
Riverside RI 02915

Call Sign: KO1E
David Viveiros
2 Ravena Dr
Riverside RI 02915

Call Sign: N1CFQ
John F Wilhelm
41 Rogers Ave
Riverside RI 02915

Call Sign: WA1RNC
Dobbs E Boomer
141 Rounds Ave
Riverside RI 02915

Call Sign: N1XHU
Luis M Araujo
10 Spinnaker Drive
Riverside RI 02915

Call Sign: WA1KSN
Michael J Skorvanek Iii
21 Sunnyside Ave
Riverside RI 02915

Call Sign: WA1NSI
Joseph R Antaya
78 Turner Ave
Riverside RI 02915

Call Sign: KB1HWH
Michael P Fitzpatrick Jr
Village Green North
Riverside RI 02915

Call Sign: KA2WHG
Henry T Valliere
1430 Wampanoag Tr
Riverside RI 02915

Call Sign: KB1AZU
Lawrence Bilida

Riverside RI 02915

Call Sign: KB1JUC
Rhode Island State React
Riverside RI 02915

Call Sign: W1KNE
Michael P Fitzpatrick Jr
Riverside RI 02915

FCC Amateur Radio Licenses in Rockville

Call Sign: N1LQE
John E Lindberg
Spring St
Rockville RI 02873

FCC Amateur Radio Licenses in Rumford

Call Sign: KB1KHX
Daniel J Roberts
50 Agawam Park Rd
Rumford RI 02916

Call Sign: KA1PKV
Eleanor L Tavares
25 Albert Ave
Rumford RI 02916

Call Sign: KY1G
Frank L Tavares
25 Albert Ave
Rumford RI 02916

Call Sign: K1PEL
Charles E Plante
80 Barney St
Rumford RI 029161212

Call Sign: KA1FWK
Arthur Rose
43 Bellevue Blvd
Rumford RI 02916

Call Sign: KA1TNV
Clifford H Mc Gowan Jr
11 Bowen St
Rumford RI 02916

Call Sign: W1DLZ
Joseph Cilcius
34 Brentwood Dr
Rumford RI 02916

Call Sign: W1PRO
William H O Brien Iii
37 Centre Street
Rumford RI 02916

Call Sign: KB1ATY
Louis D Mester
4 David St
Rumford RI 02916

Call Sign: KB1CVE
M Nazare Aguiar Mester
4 David St
Rumford RI 02916

Call Sign: K1LII
Chester P Tammany
14 Deer St
Rumford RI 029162102

Call Sign: KA1JKV
Elizabeth M Tammany
14 Deer St
Rumford RI 029162102

Call Sign: KA1OCC
Kyle S Andrade
252 Don Ave
Rumford RI 02916

Call Sign: KB1LLT
Fred F Broun
12 Glenwood Ave
Rumford RI 02916

Call Sign: W1MQF
Edward A Farrell
115 Greenwood Ave
Rumford RI 02916

Call Sign: KB1PGP
William Litchman
51 Magnolia St
Rumford RI 02916

Call Sign: KB1UO
W Charles Doherty
261 Newman Ave
Rumford RI 02916

Call Sign: KB1BFU
Lisa E Blais
51 Pavilion Ave
Rumford RI 02916

Call Sign: KB1XF
Felix C Blais Jr
51 Pavilion Ave
Rumford RI 029161216

Call Sign: KB1OHH
Claude H Duckworth
52 Pavilion Ave
Rumford RI 02916

Call Sign: N1IVB
David E Czerwonka
2 Pawtucket Ave
Rumford RI 02916

Call Sign: N1BMK
David F Shaw
180 Redland Ave
Rumford RI 02916

Call Sign: N1BRG
Manuel S Larangeira
27 Riverwood Ct
Rumford RI 02916

Call Sign: WB1CRR
Nelson G Hayward
55 Vermont Ave
Rumford RI 02916

Call Sign: W1OGT
Robert L Burkett
Rumford RI 02916

Call Sign: W1CH
Louis D Mester
Rumford RI 02916

FCC Amateur Radio Licenses in Sauderstown

Call Sign: K1OYC
Russell E Taylor
2099 Boston Neck Rd
Saunderstown RI 02874

Call Sign: KB1PTE
Adam B Hobgood
9 Bow Run
Saunderstown RI 02874

Call Sign: K1OCD
Adam B Hobgood
9 Bow Run
Saunderstown RI 02874

Call Sign: KB1TXT
Hayden N Radke
521 Carpenter Ln
Saunderstown RI 02874

Call Sign: WA1QMV
Daniel M Powers
80 Congdon Hill Rd
Saunderstown RI 02874

Call Sign: KA1ZZQ
Barbara M Swanson
519 Congdon Hill Rd

Saunderstown RI 02874

Call Sign: N3VHI
Stephen Day
110 Cottrell Road
Saunderstown RI 02874

Call Sign: W1WQY
Douglass F Arnold
54 Ferry Rd
Saunderstown RI 02874

Call Sign: AA2DW
David M Rogovitz
13 Finch Ln
Saunderstown RI 02874

Call Sign: W2DW
Radio Society Of Southern
Rhode Island
13 Finch Ln
Saunderstown RI 02874

Call Sign: KA1UZ
Robert G Cox
21 Fleetwood Dr
Saunderstown RI
028743112

Call Sign: W1JMT
Francis W Jenard Sr
9 Horizon Dr Box 55
Saunderstown RI 02874

Call Sign: KA1QAP
John F Kenney Jr
30 Mac Intosh Ln
Saunderstown RI 02874

Call Sign: KB1RAR
Andrew E Flesia
15 Meadowrue Trail
Saunderstown RI 02879

Call Sign: W1ICR

Thomas W Birch
70 Pierce Rd
Saunderstown RI
028743418

Call Sign: K1NQG
Fidelity Amateur Radio
Club
490 Shermantown Rd
Saunderstown RI 02874

Call Sign: KB1EJB
Jeffrey M Egan
490 Shermantown Rd
Saunderstown RI
028742005

Call Sign: N1WWA
Judith A Mc Guire
460 Shermantown Road
Saunderstown RI 02874

Call Sign: N1WWB
James A Mc Guire Jr
460 Shermantown Road
Saunderstown RI 02874

Call Sign: KB1LQP
Noah P Forden
905 Slocum Rd
Saunderstown RI 02874

Call Sign: N1VDJ
Norman L Gould Iii
965 Slocum Rd
Saunderstown RI 02874

Call Sign: KQ6SL
A Davis Whittaker Jr
8 Sweet Birch Trail
Saunderstown RI 02874

Call Sign: KA2KKN
Roland P Kurz
164 Willet Rd

Saunderstown RI 02874

Call Sign: KA2KKO
Elizabeth N Shamer
164 Willet Rd
Saunderstown RI 02874

Call Sign: KA1UZE
Richard Z Zimmermann Jr
54 Willett Rd
Saunderstown RI 02874

Call Sign: KB1RWW
James W Taylor
110 Winterberry Rd
Saunderstown RI 02874

Call Sign: K1GS
George M Schwartze
Saunderstown RI 02874

Call Sign: N1VAY
Thomas E Hynes
Saunderstown RI
028740203

Call Sign: KB1NLY
Amy J Paulsen
Saunderstown RI 02874

**FCC Amateur Radio
Licenses in Scituate**

Call Sign: N1YKF
Jonathan W Delmonico
110 Pine Hill Rd
Scituate RI 02857

Call Sign: K1RAM
Robert A Moio Sr
70 Regina Drive
Scituate RI 02857

**FCC Amateur Radio
Licenses in Shannock**

Call Sign: N1ZJE
Charles A Caswell
Shannock RI 02875

Call Sign: WA1ZEQ
Stephen A Wheeler
Shannock RI 02875

Call Sign: WB1CEP
David I Smith
Shannock RI 028750036

Call Sign: WB1CEQ
Lucille E Wheeler
Shannock RI 02875

**FCC Amateur Radio
Licenses in Slatersville**

Call Sign: KE1KO
Daniel B Middleton Sr
73 N Main St
Slatersville RI 028760893

Call Sign: W1EAS
Lucien A Desquenne
Slatersville RI 02876

Call Sign: KB1ELW
Sean D Spicer
Slatersville RI 028760582

Call Sign: KC1MRC
Michael R Cote
Slatersville RI 028760700

Call Sign: N1MRC
Michael R Cote
Slatersville RI 028760700

**FCC Amateur Radio
Licenses in Slocum**

Call Sign: N1LYT

Gabriel A Mooradjian
257 S County Tr
Slocum RI 02877

**FCC Amateur Radio
Licenses in Smithfield**

Call Sign: KA1ONF
Robert R Van
Nieuwenhuyze
8 A Overlook Cir
Smithfield RI 02917

Call Sign: W1WMW
William M Ward
77 And One Half Farnum
Pike
Smithfield RI 02917

Call Sign: N1OSI
Steven J Serapiglia
2 Arnold Ave
Smithfield RI 029173802

Call Sign: N1VVS
Christine A Serapiglia
2 Arnold Ave
Smithfield RI 02917

Call Sign: KB1PGR
Todd S Manni
7 Arnold Ave Apt 3
Smithfield RI 02917

Call Sign: KB1SAB
Christopher J Foti
7 Blue Feather Trl
Smithfield RI 02917

Call Sign: KB1EU
John F Verduchi
124 Burlingame Rd
Smithfield RI 02917

Call Sign: KF1T

James W Archer
10 Crestview Dr
Smithfield RI 02828

Call Sign: WB1GMI
Christopher M Ambrose
30 Deer Run Trail
Smithfield RI 02917

Call Sign: N1QMF
Anthony J Veltri
56 Esmond St
Smithfield RI 02917

Call Sign: N1AHJ
William T Garriepy
209 Farnum Pike
Smithfield RI 029170701

Call Sign: KB1RYR
Paul T Lagreca
39 Forestwood Dr
Smithfield RI 02917

Call Sign: K1PTL
Paul T Lagreca
39 Forestwood Dr
Smithfield RI 02917

Call Sign: N1UIE
Siegfried E Szurley
111 Harris Rd
Smithfield RI 02917

Call Sign: KB1MUQ
Michael R Quigley
193 Harris Road
Smithfield RI 02917

Call Sign: KA1YYT
E Ann Blandin
20 Higgins St Apt 208
Smithfield RI 02917

Call Sign: W1GSD

Dorothea M Nutini
47 Indian Run Trail
Smithfield RI 02917

Call Sign: W1CDH
Milton L Nutini
129 Indian Run Trl
Smithfield RI 02917

Call Sign: N1ZCT
Ronald Turner
38 John Mowry Rd
Smithfield RI 02917

Call Sign: N1PRR
Gary Blandino
38 Meadow View Dr
Smithfield RI 02917

Call Sign: KD1LJ
William P Dowd
Pheasant Run
Smithfield RI 02917

Call Sign: N1KJV
Romeo P Gervais Sr
171 Pleasant View Ave Apt
320
Smithfield RI 02917

Call Sign: N1JAY
Richard Cabral
135 Pleasant View Ave Apt
8
Smithfield RI 02917

Call Sign: K4FVV
Anthony W Ziemnisky
715 Putnam Pike Apt 129
Smithfield RI 02828

Call Sign: KA1RYN
James W Bell
168 Ridge Rd
Smithfield RI 029172517

Call Sign: KB1ISZ
William J Carlson
186 Ridge Rd
Smithfield RI 02917

Call Sign: N1VVY
David Branca
180 Ridge Rd.
Smithfield RI 02917

Call Sign: KA1YOJ
Guilherme V Silva
110 Rocky Hill Rd
Smithfield RI 02917

Call Sign: KA1RSH
Daniel Muto
16 Scenic View Dr
Smithfield RI 02917

Call Sign: KB1OKY
Lance D Drew
24 Scenic View Dr
Smithfield RI 02917

Call Sign: W1LDD
Lance D Drew
24 Scenic View Dr
Smithfield RI 02917

Call Sign: WA1TAQ
Joseph J Varin
4 Varin Dr
Smithfield RI 02917

Call Sign: K1AHQ
Charles E Lebeau
15 Whipple Rd
Smithfield RI 02917

Call Sign: KB1HAQ
Henry J Cibor
60 Whipple Rd
Smithfield RI 029172513

Call Sign: KB1RLQ
Carl A Passarelli
143 Whipple Rd
Smithfield RI 02917

Call Sign: KB1WBX
James T Isherwood Jr
71 Wolf Hill Rd
Smithfield RI 02917

FCC Amateur Radio Licenses in South Kingstown

Call Sign: N1WWE
James V Wyman
44 Starflower Ct
South Kingstown RI 02879

Call Sign: KW2G
Donald V Watson
860 J Curtis Corner Rd.
South Kingstown RI 02879

Call Sign: AC7HG
Wolfgang Decker
Mooresfield Rd.
South Kingstown RI
028792087

Call Sign: AA1YL
Wolfgang Decker
Mooresfield Rd.
South Kingstown RI
028792087

Call Sign: W1XX
John F Lindholm
48 Shannock Rd
South Kingstown RI 02879

FCC Amateur Radio Licenses in Tiverton

Call Sign: KA1LH
Wayne A Souza
128 Beardsworth Rd
Tiverton RI 02878

Call Sign: WA1GXH
Robert M Rousseau
128 Beardsworth Rd
Tiverton RI 02878

Call Sign: WA1DGW
Bristol County Repeater
Association Inc
128 Beardworth Rd
Tiverton RI 02878

Call Sign: W2DAN
David A Neal
45 Beth Rd
Tiverton RI 028783701

Call Sign: KB1MAG
Sharon L Neal
45 Beth Rd
Tiverton RI 02878

Call Sign: KB1KWH
Tanya M Beaulieu
71 Blueberry Ln
Tiverton RI 02878

Call Sign: N1XOY
Thomas B Haley
55 Bonniefield Dr
Tiverton RI 02878

Call Sign: NF1X
Robert Mugnai
235 Brackett Ave
Tiverton RI 028781834

Call Sign: KB1VYD
Steven A Rys
201 Bridle Way
Tiverton RI 02878

Call Sign: WB1CPO
August F Reis
254 Bulgarmarsh Rd
Tiverton RI 02878

Call Sign: KB1SDQ
Alfred F Almeida Jr
434 Bulgarmarsh Road
Tiverton RI 02878

Call Sign: KA1JF
Vincent J Tarricone
520 Bulgarmarsh Road
Tiverton RI 028783853

Call Sign: KA1ZGF
Kelly A Murphy
8 Colonial Ave
Tiverton RI 02878

Call Sign: KA1DMV
Paul J Otis
61 Colonial Ave
Tiverton RI 02878

Call Sign: K1ICM
Kenneth Smith
94 Colonial Ave
Tiverton RI 02878

Call Sign: K1JEA
Charlotte A Smith
94 Colonial Ave
Tiverton RI 02878

Call Sign: KB1CUB
Tiverton Middle School Arc
29 Cottage Ave
Tiverton RI 028784332

Call Sign: WA1VQY
Jeffrey P Lynch
29 Cottage Ave
Tiverton RI 028784332

Call Sign: KB1OAL
Bradford S Lynch
29 Cottage Ave
Tiverton RI 02878

Call Sign: K1CI
Ronald K Moniz
579 Crandall Rd
Tiverton RI 02878

Call Sign: N1QLZ
Ronald P Rego
1401 Crandall Rd
Tiverton RI 02878

Call Sign: KB1HRI
Southeastern Massachusetts
Amateur Radio Group
1401 Crandall Rd
Tiverton RI 02878

Call Sign: WJ1J
George R Ethier
114 Cypress Ave
Tiverton RI 02878

Call Sign: W1UPA
William F Csisar Sr
1680 Eagleville Rd
Tiverton RI 02878

Call Sign: WA1LBE
Arthur J Deschenes
1735 Eagleville Rd
Tiverton RI 02878

Call Sign: KB1SAC
Brent T Fisher
564 East Road
Tiverton RI 02878

Call Sign: KB1LNH
Dane A Swanson
25 Edwards Ave

Tiverton RI 02878

Call Sign: N1NMI
David E Sagamang
37 Emma James Way
Tiverton RI 02878

Call Sign: N1RQT
Marianne Lamb
475 Fish Rd
Tiverton RI 02878

Call Sign: K1KXT
Evelyn A Lizotte
27 Furey Ave
Tiverton RI 02878

Call Sign: K1PDE
Robert B Delisle
7 Gatsby Ln
Tiverton RI 02878

Call Sign: W1SFX
Charles J O Gara
67 Grinnell Ave
Tiverton RI 02878

Call Sign: W1YV
Thomas F Mc Donald
98 Haskins Ave
Tiverton RI 02878

Call Sign: K1HND
Joseph F Camara
84 Hayden Ave
Tiverton RI 02878

Call Sign: KB1KWK
Anne M Lantz
191 Hayden Ave
Tiverton RI 02878

Call Sign: KB1KWL
Russell A Lantz
191 Hayden Ave

Tiverton RI 02878

Call Sign: W1HIQ
John J Majkut
13 Holly Cir
Tiverton RI 02878

Call Sign: W1PAG
Philip E Combellack
44 Holly Cir
Tiverton RI 02878

Call Sign: KA1UIC
Elizabeth A Lapre
320 Hurst Ln
Tiverton RI 02878

Call Sign: K1TPK
Manly C Beebe
86 Island View Dr
Tiverton RI 02878

Call Sign: KD6ROM
John R Nickerson
125 John Duggan Rd
Tiverton RI 02878

Call Sign: W1UHE
Norman H Patenaude
43 Kaufman Rd
Tiverton RI 02878

Call Sign: N1GOV
James Reid
725 Lafayette Rd
Tiverton RI 028783403

Call Sign: K1TL
Thomas F Lizak
948 Lake Rd
Tiverton RI 028783417

Call Sign: KB1NYU
Harold B Cole
145 Lawrence Court

Tiverton RI 02878

Call Sign: KB1NLK
Harold B Cole Iv
145 Lawrence Ct
Tiverton RI 02878

Call Sign: KB1WCE
Dylan T Rodriguez
53 Lawton Ave
Tiverton RI 02878

Call Sign: KB1KOC
Jeffrey B Wenzel
150 Lazywood Ln
Tiverton RI 02878

Call Sign: KB1UZA
Jeremy T Giguere
169 Lazywood Ln
Tiverton RI 028783870

Call Sign: KB1UZG
George J Giguere Iii
169 Lazywood Ln
Tiverton RI 02878

Call Sign: KB1EL
Owen M Hartnett
98 Long Pasture Way
Tiverton RI 02878

Call Sign: KB1KWG
Kelley Carton
19 Main Rd
Tiverton RI 02878

Call Sign: WA1UHR
David B Collins
4001 Main Rd
Tiverton RI 02878

Call Sign: W1LNK
William H Burke
1215 Main Road Apt 309

Tiverton RI 02878

Call Sign: K1RAF
Ronald A Franklin
1 Mill St. - Unit 1415
Tiverton RI 02878

Call Sign: KB0VTV
Lisa M Aldrich
136 N Christopher Ave
Tiverton RI 02878

Call Sign: K1JSM
John S Mills
139 Nanaquaket Road
Tiverton RI 02878

Call Sign: WA1CXF
Charles L Sheehan
35 Narragansett Ave
Tiverton RI 02878

Call Sign: N1XFU
Charles E Rosenthal
37 Nonquit Ln
Tiverton RI 02878

Call Sign: WA1FFL
James D Hagerty
64 Nonquit Ln
Tiverton RI 02878

Call Sign: K1WEW
Sub Sig Amateur Radio
Club
60 Norman Dr
Tiverton RI 02878

Call Sign: KB1HAT
Lynn M Jamieson
60 Norman Dr
Tiverton RI 02878

Call Sign: KB1HAU
Scott P Jamieson

60 Norman Dr
Tiverton RI 02878

Call Sign: AA1ZI
Scott P Jamieson
60 Norman Dr
Tiverton RI 02878

Call Sign: KO1W
Scott P Jamieson
60 Norman Dr
Tiverton RI 02878

Call Sign: KB1IPO
Heather L Jamieson
60 Norman Dr
Tiverton RI 02878

Call Sign: W1LUV
Lynn M Jamieson
60 Norman Dr
Tiverton RI 02878

Call Sign: K0EKJ
Eric K Jamieson
60 Norman Drive
Tiverton RI 02878

Call Sign: KO1K
Eric K Jamieson
60 Norman Drive
Tiverton RI 02878

Call Sign: KB1SDO
Dustin A Foley
11 North Brayton Rd
Tiverton RI 02878

Call Sign: KA1DGX
Elaine C Glowacki
63 Paul James Dr
Tiverton RI 02878

Call Sign: WA1BYE
Norman A Glowacki

63 Paul James Dr
Tiverton RI 02878

Call Sign: KB1NLJ
Donald A Rosinha Ii
12 Paul Terrace
Tiverton RI 02878

Call Sign: N1VDY
Henry Beckman
124 Poinsetta Way
Tiverton RI 02878

Call Sign: KB1XN
Frank L Ungvary Jr
64 Pools Ln
Tiverton RI 02878

Call Sign: N1ZFO
Arthur S Massie
27 Poplar St
Tiverton RI 02878

Call Sign: KB1KWI
Gretchen A Dauphin
12 Presidential Dr
Tiverton RI 02878

Call Sign: KB1LIZ
David A Mccarthy
2 Redwood Rd
Tiverton RI 028781423

Call Sign: N1MCP
David A Mccarthy
2 Redwood Rd
Tiverton RI 028781423

Call Sign: N1YG
David A Mccarthy
2 Redwood Rd
Tiverton RI 028781423

Call Sign: KB1SDM
William Tavares

62 Richard Dr
Tiverton RI 02878

Call Sign: N1YCK
Carl C Gallagher
484 Riverside Dr
Tiverton RI 02878

Call Sign: N1YCL
Robert A Gallagher
484 Riverside Dr
Tiverton RI 02878

Call Sign: N1XXV
Russell P Cambra
37 Rockland Terr
Tiverton RI 02878

Call Sign: K1JOA
Gladys A Wilde
82 Russell Dr
Tiverton RI 02878

Call Sign: KA1SUF
Steven Lopes
71 Shove St
Tiverton RI 02878

Call Sign: WA1ESO
John C Nery
3 Springer Ave
Tiverton RI 02878

Call Sign: K1MQE
Lester W Cory
45 Summit Ave
Tiverton RI 02878

Call Sign: N1TVV
Patricia L Cory
45 Summit Ave
Tiverton RI 02878

Call Sign: W1MC
James P Amarantes

3 Sunset View Dr
Tiverton RI 02878

Call Sign: AA1QB
Albert C Labossiere
121 Thibault Ln
Tiverton RI 028783124

Call Sign: AA1BB
Thomas W Molinski
122 Thomas St
Tiverton RI 02878

Call Sign: AB1PI
David R Dion
146 Tower Hill Rd
Tiverton RI 02878

Call Sign: WA1BXY
Albert F Boivin
24 Vale St
Tiverton RI 02878

Call Sign: N1NK
James L Spears Jr
494 W Demello Dr
Tiverton RI 028782771

Call Sign: N1OHQ
Kevin J Ratcliffe
30 Warren Ave
Tiverton RI 02878

Call Sign: KA1BWB
Maurice L Crotteau
Tiverton RI 02878

Call Sign: N1MFU
Charles R Lapre
Tiverton RI 02878

FCC Amateur Radio Licenses in Wakefield

Call Sign: KB1DMM

Joseph R Kirkwood
53 Alcides Dr
Wakefield RI 02879

Call Sign: N1HGO
Charles Rostrup
378 Allen Ave
Wakefield RI 02879

Call Sign: KB1EBK
Steven M Pinch
445 Allen Ave
Wakefield RI 02879

Call Sign: W1PXI
William H Mowbray
25 Arrowhead Trl
Wakefield RI 028792039

Call Sign: W1FO
Normand E Tetreault
114 Breakwater Rd
Wakefield RI 028796552

Call Sign: N1YFY
Dawn Marie Fernstrom
169 Briarwood Dr
Wakefield RI 02879

Call Sign: N1AVC
Howard M Raitano Sr
51 Canterbury Rd
Wakefield RI 02879

Call Sign: KB1JZR
Walter W Pike
210 Columbia St
Wakefield RI 02879

Call Sign: N1NNZ
Steven D Brown
2581 Commodore Perry
Hwy
Wakefield RI 02879

Call Sign: KA1WSL
Richard A Soderberg
37 Fire Ln 4
Wakefield RI 02879

Call Sign: N1CIA
Earl C Sparks Jr
111 Gale Dr
Wakefield RI 02879

Call Sign: K1SSO
Paul B Williams
12 Hartford Avenue
Wakefield RI 02879

Call Sign: WB1FDJ
Clifford E Thresher Jr
80 Hillcrest Rd
Wakefield RI 028794204

Call Sign: WB1FDK
John C Thresher
80 Hillcrest Rd
Wakefield RI 028794204

Call Sign: KB1EDG
Nicholas E Hill
221 Indigo Pt
Wakefield RI 02879

Call Sign: KB1UZF
Gregory J Rosa
70 Kings Ridge Rd
Wakefield RI 02879

Call Sign: W2OJC
Boris Dzula
1959 Kingstown Rd Apt
333
Wakefield RI 028791611

Call Sign: KB1URK
Kenneth F White
205 Kogoli Way
Wakefield RI 02879

Call Sign: W1ROS
Kenneth F White
205 Kogoli Way
Wakefield RI 02879

Call Sign: WA1QFP
Larry A Simoneau
169 Legend Rock Rd
Wakefield RI 02879

Call Sign: N1WWD
Benjamin F Potter
149 Little Pond Rd
Wakefield RI 028794490

Call Sign: K1NW
Brian K Maynard
99 North Road
Wakefield RI 02879

Call Sign: WA1IKU
Guy W Badger
45 Oak Rd
Wakefield RI 02879

Call Sign: KA1RCM
Gabriel T Brunelli
110 Oak St
Wakefield RI 028790602

Call Sign: W3PDK
Ellis H Maris Jr
One Post Rd
Wakefield RI 02879

Call Sign: KB1ISX
Matthew P Pallini
201 Peaked Rock Rd
Wakefield RI 02879

Call Sign: W1PAH
Matthew P Pallini
201 Peaked Rock Rd
Wakefield RI 02879

Call Sign: KB1UQV
John W Wedlock Jr
136 Pond St
Wakefield RI 02879

Call Sign: KA1WRD
Arnold J Adams
34 Potter Rd
Wakefield RI 02879

Call Sign: KA1WRE
Linda B Lupo Adams
34 Potter Rd
Wakefield RI 02879

Call Sign: K1JAH
Joseph J Dean Jr
68 Potter Rd
Wakefield RI 02879

Call Sign: KB1FCD
Paul M Mello
22 Red Feather Tr South
Wakefield RI 02879

Call Sign: W1PMM
Paul M Mello
22 Red Feather Tr South
Wakefield RI 02879

Call Sign: KB1UZD
Timothy S Cashman
61 River St
Wakefield RI 02879

Call Sign: KA1REO
Mark F Rippe
57 Rockland Dr
Wakefield RI 028793152

Call Sign: KB1LLF
Bert F Hess
59 Rosebriar Ave
Wakefield RI 02879

Call Sign: KB1SJS
Daniel D Traficante
36 Sandy Bottom Shores Dr
Wakefield RI 02879

Call Sign: WA1KRD
William L Ferrigno Jr
140 Seaview Ave
Wakefield RI 02879

Call Sign: KB1QIR
South Kingstown Eoc Ares
48 Shannock Rd
Wakefield RI 02879

Call Sign: KA1RI
South Kingstown Eoc Ares
48 Shannock Rd
Wakefield RI 02879

Call Sign: KA1MSQ
John K Nelson
212 Shannock Rd
Wakefield RI 02879

Call Sign: KB1HCM
Earl A Juday
68 Silver Lake Ave
Wakefield RI 02879

Call Sign: KB1RPV
Robert M Gilbert
111 Straw Lane
Wakefield RI 02879

Call Sign: WA1ZPC
Phyllis A Jordan
430 Tuckertown Rd
Wakefield RI 02879

Call Sign: WA1YLN
Harold T Curry
5 W Side Rd
Wakefield RI 02879

Call Sign: KA1RL
Karl E Mortensen
97 Wendy Ln
Wakefield RI 02879

Call Sign: WA1MKS
Walter L Lototski Jr
34 West View Dr
Wakefield RI 02879

Call Sign: WA1YLO
Charlotte M Curry
5 Westside Rd
Wakefield RI 02879

Call Sign: KB1RFJ
Michael Visich
31 White Falls Trail
Wakefield RI 02879

Call Sign: KE1BO
Thomas E Tamayo
84 Whitewood Dr
Wakefield RI 02879

Call Sign: N1FGJ
Stephen E Brunelli
Wakefield RI 02880

Call Sign: WA1QXV
Albert J Musto Sr
Wakefield RI 028805487

**FCC Amateur Radio
Licenses in Warren**

Call Sign: AB1EJ
Stephen P Capizzano
66 Almy Ave
Warren RI 02885

Call Sign: WB2IYF
William C Goltsos
53 Asylum Road

Warren RI 02885   Warren RI 028851729   Warren RI 02885

Call Sign: AG1K
James A Di Sarro
9 Aubin Ave
Warren RI 02885

Call Sign: N1KJO
Timothy L Avila
32 George St
Warren RI 02885

Call Sign: N2FQU
John C Conley
634 Main St
Warren RI 02885

Call Sign: KB1UVL
Hugh A Morrison Iv
28 Barney St Apt 2
Warren RI 02885

Call Sign: N1MHX
Fabyan R Saxe
5 Hanley Farm
Warren RI 02885

Call Sign: AB1BX
Andrew Ferranti
785 Main St
Warren RI 02885

Call Sign: N1PVV
Orlando E Vitullo
44 Bridge St
Warren RI 02885

Call Sign: KA1ETT
Stephen A Asselin
1 Hanley Lane
Warren RI 02885

Call Sign: KB1WHW
Apostoli Zafiriadis
464 Main Street
Warren RI 02885

Call Sign: N1RI
George H Simmons
46 Broad St
Warren RI 02885

Call Sign: N1ZSR
Richard A Travers
63 Harris Ave
Warren RI 02885

Call Sign: N1GQC
Bradley J Olson
26 Maple Road
Warren RI 02885

Call Sign: N1TNR
Frank E Garrity
3 Charity Dr
Warren RI 02885

Call Sign: N1VVT
Patricia A O Donnell
20 Libby Lane Apt H111
Warren RI 02885

Call Sign: K1LNL
Carl E Berg
4 Maple Street
Warren RI 02885

Call Sign: N1GVE
Paul S Oliveira
550 Child St
Warren RI 02885

Call Sign: N1SXK
Waldon J Bonevelle
20 Libby Lane C-31
Warren RI 02885

Call Sign: AA1QM
Gabriel F Luis
1 Overhill Rd
Warren RI 02885

Call Sign: KB1JIY
Robert A Sevin
510 Child St Apt 302a
Warren RI 02885

Call Sign: W1WJB
Waldon J Bonevelle
20 Libby Lane C-31
Warren RI 02885

Call Sign: KA1JRQ
Howard F Perrone
55 Overhill Rd
Warren RI 02885

Call Sign: N1SXN
Matthew Panarello
2 Church Street
Warren RI 02885

Call Sign: N1VDL
Donald J O Donnell
20 Libby Lane H-111
Warren RI 028852008

Call Sign: KB1GQC
Henry Keefe Jr
59 Overhill Rd
Warren RI 02885

Call Sign: KB1HEG
Matthew D Sarasin
35 Fern Dr

Call Sign: N1RAJ
Ralph P Russo
20 Libby Ln D20

Call Sign: N1ERW
Henry E Sippen
19 Prudence Ln

Warren RI 02885

Call Sign: KA1RWP
Diane E Mendes
8 S Cornell Ave
Warren RI 02885

Call Sign: WB1DXQ
Ferdinand Mendes Jr
8 S Cornell Ave
Warren RI 02885

Call Sign: N1QPA
Thomas D Gordon
175 Touisset Rd
Warren RI 02885

Call Sign: KB1ZE
William E Brailey
15 Wilbur Ave
Warren RI 02885

Call Sign: KK1MP
Moises F Pereira
21 Wilbur Ave
Warren RI 02885

Call Sign: NN1K
Forrest L Avila
Warren RI 02885

**FCC Amateur Radio
Licenses in Warwick**

Call Sign: K1FTA
Carol L Perry
27 15th Ave
Warwick RI 02886

Call Sign: KB1VPQ
John D Allenson Jr
43 Aberdeen Ave
Warwick RI 02888

Call Sign: K1DFT

Robert J Vincent
71 Adams St
Warwick RI 02888

Call Sign: KA1DKL
Donna L Varin
131 Adelaide Ave
Warwick RI 02886

Call Sign: KB1IFB
Michael W Demaio
178 Airport Rd
Warwick RI 02889

Call Sign: KB1HEO
Timothy L Bergeron
55 Alabama Ave 1a
Warwick RI 02888

Call Sign: KB1KJW
Dean Famiano
251 Algonquin Dr
Warwick RI 02888

Call Sign: W1JUE
Egidio A Catri
65 Almy St
Warwick RI 02886

Call Sign: KB1ISD
Wayne E Labanca
140 Almy St
Warwick RI 02886

Call Sign: K1COI
Pasquale Mancini
11 Amherst Rd
Warwick RI 02889

Call Sign: NM1Y
Aram N Farmanian
14 Amsterdam Ave
Warwick RI 02889

Call Sign: KB1EFR

Lawrence W Basile
23 Amsterdam Ave
Warwick RI 02889

Call Sign: KA1URW
Maureen Leneker O
Gorman
88 Anderson Ave
Warwick RI 028884820

Call Sign: N1IFT
Peter F Campbell
258 Armstrong Ave
Warwick RI 02889

Call Sign: WQ1Q
Charles W Mac Kinnon
146 Arnolds Neck Dr
Warwick RI 02886

Call Sign: W1KDA
Ronald P Brodeur
240 Arnolds Neck Dr
Warwick RI 02886

Call Sign: KB1MQU
Ronald P Brodeur
279 Arnolds Neck Dr
Warwick RI 02886

Call Sign: KB1JEE
John S Knowles
94 Asylum Rd
Warwick RI 02886

Call Sign: KB1JEG
Joseph E Hackman
97 Asylum Rd
Warwick RI 02886

Call Sign: KB1FUP
Matthew E Hackman
97 Asylum Road
Warwick RI 028868001

Call Sign: KA1KWU
Randolph M Govey
203 Atlantic Ave Apt 1
Warwick RI 028882021

Call Sign: K1NBO
Paul Bogosian
72 Audubon Rd
Warwick RI 02888

Call Sign: KA1MXL
Kevin T Halton
158 Audubon Road
Warwick RI 02888

Call Sign: W1JJM
John J Mc Manus
50 Austin Rd
Warwick RI 02818

Call Sign: W1JJ
John J Mc Manus
50 Austin Rd
Warwick RI 02818

Call Sign: AB1CZ
Enrico Vittorio Colombo
50 Austin Rd
Warwick RI 02818

Call Sign: K2GSO
Enrico Vittorio Colombo
50 Austin Rd
Warwick RI 02818

Call Sign: KB1RLD
Peter P Clark
55 Balcom Ave
Warwick RI 02889

Call Sign: KA1NO
Anthony W Castillo
153 Baldwin Rd
Warwick RI 02886

Call Sign: KA1JNO
Arthur W Mannette Jr
232 Baldwin Rd
Warwick RI 02886

Call Sign: WA1WET
Judith G Cameron
5 Barre Ct
Warwick RI 02886

Call Sign: K1AZH
Edwin C Peabody
93 Baywood St
Warwick RI 028862349

Call Sign: KA1BT
Rudi Metz
258 Beach Avenue
Warwick RI 02889

Call Sign: N1HSF
Paul H Brookes
239 Bedford Ave
Warwick RI 02886

Call Sign: W3OLF
Randolph M Govey
59 Belfort Avenue
Warwick RI 02889

Call Sign: KA1ESO
Sylvia L Kennedy
108 Bend St
Warwick RI 02889

Call Sign: KB1UNI
Elizabeth V Eddy
23 Benefit St Apt 18
Warwick RI 02886

Call Sign: K1EQX
James P Hughes
239 Betsy Williams Dr
Warwick RI 02889

Call Sign: N1ERC
James F Hughes
239 Betsy Williams Dr
Warwick RI 02889

Call Sign: KB1KHZ
Richard J Andreano
141 Bingham St
Warwick RI 02886

Call Sign: K3OQH
Richard J Andreano
141 Bingham St
Warwick RI 02886

Call Sign: KA1OJM
Edith V Von Weltin
75 Birch St
Warwick RI 02888

Call Sign: WA1RXV
Arnold E Butziger
44 Bowen Briggs Ave
Warwick RI 02886

Call Sign: WA1RYD
Rosalind G Butziger
44 Bowen Briggs Ave
Warwick RI 02886

Call Sign: KB1BBH
Susan A Maguire
33 Brewster Dr
Warwick RI 02889

Call Sign: KB1IVM
Joseph M Rossi
17 Brianwood Ct
Warwick RI 02886

Call Sign: W1JMR
Joseph M Rossi
17 Brianwood Ct
Warwick RI 02886

Call Sign: KB1MHC
George W Horsley
118 Brinton Ave
Warwick RI 02889

Call Sign: N1OLF
Ronald L Bouthillier Jr
41 Broad St
Warwick RI 02888

Call Sign: K1PHO
Richard P Davenport
54 Brunswick Dr
Warwick RI 02886

Call Sign: N1IRY
Nancy J Bonnell
410 Buttonwoods Ave
Warwick RI 02886

Call Sign: KA1QJE
Richard J Mancini
586 Buttonwoods Ave
Warwick RI 028868309

Call Sign: KD1BE
Bruce B Hecker
614 Buttonwoods Ave
Warwick RI 02886

Call Sign: N1GRT
Anne M Hecker
614 Buttonwoods Ave
Warwick RI 02886

Call Sign: K1DYA
Bruce F Cushman
61 Calderwood Dr
Warwick RI 02886

Call Sign: W1GLF
Bruce F Cushman
61 Calderwood Dr
Warwick RI 02886

Call Sign: KB1FFP
Joseph M Graves
176 Calderwood Drive
Warwick RI 02886

Call Sign: N1XCV
Robert D Hutchins Jr
163 Canfield Avenue
Warwick RI 02889

Call Sign: KB1KOJ
Shawn J Masse
11 Carnation Dr
Warwick RI 02886

Call Sign: KB1KOL
William D Masse
11 Carnation Dr
Warwick RI 02886

Call Sign: WA1WDH
Paul M Finstein
70 Carnation Dr
Warwick RI 02886

Call Sign: N1WGI
Giro R Russo
32 Carpenter Ave
Warwick RI 02886

Call Sign: W7JHG
Donald B Miller
27 Cedar Pond Dr
Warwick RI 02886

Call Sign: KB1NWK
Cherienne D Peterson
19 Cedar Pond Dr Suite 3
Warwick RI 02886

Call Sign: N3VMH
Jeffrey W Ryan
15 Cedar Pond Dr. # 3
Warwick RI 02886

Call Sign: KA1PBG
Walter R Tucker Jr
925 Cedar Swamp Rd
Warwick RI 02886

Call Sign: KB1ISL
Thomas L Depetrillo
988 Centerville Rd
Warwick RI 02886

Call Sign: W1IUP
Thomas L Depetrillo
988 Centerville Rd
Warwick RI 02886

Call Sign: KE1JF
Thomas M Anderson
1195 Centerville Rd
Warwick RI 028864208

Call Sign: KB1UPJ
Centerville Amateur Radio
Club
1195 Centerville Rd
Warwick RI 02886

Call Sign: WA1FCE
Centerville Amateur Radio
Club
1195 Centerville Rd
Warwick RI 02886

Call Sign: N1ZPM
John Sutton
331 Centerville Rd Apt 103
Warwick RI 028864327

Call Sign: N1RCO
Frederick G Harrison
19 Channel View Dr #2
Warwick RI 028896522

Call Sign: KA1ZVY
Gennaro Pagnozzi
101 Chapmans Ave

Warwick RI 02909

Warwick RI 02886

Warwick RI 02886

Call Sign: WA1CYN
Arthur C Eddy
112 Chapmans Ave
Warwick RI 02886

Call Sign: WI1T
Merton L Whatley Jr
239 Cole Ave
Warwick RI 02886

Call Sign: KA1HTW
Edward J Martins Mr.
64 Crowfield Dr
Warwick RI 02888

Call Sign: WA1LZH
Nedra G Johnson
292 Chatham Cir
Warwick RI 02886

Call Sign: KB1SJQ
Matthew S Mccalligett
600 Colefarm Rd 13-20
Warwick RI 02889

Call Sign: KB1KPY
Patrick E Maloney Jr
11 Dawson Ave
Warwick RI 02888

Call Sign: W1PTM
Paul T Mc Donald
619 Church Ave
Warwick RI 028893249

Call Sign: K1RLE
Norman H Guillette
1 Colesonian Dr
Warwick RI 02888

Call Sign: K1TBK
William M Floskis
68 Deborah Rd
Warwick RI 02888

Call Sign: KA1WMZ
George H Campbell
33 Cleveland Ave
Warwick RI 02888

Call Sign: K1ZRU
James E Collins
67 Community Rd
Warwick RI 028892205

Call Sign: N1MAC
Frank P Di Rissio Iii
5 Dedham Rd
Warwick RI 02888

Call Sign: N1NFG
Michael S Wingert
121 Clinton Ave
Warwick RI 02886

Call Sign: KA1VDE
Karla Carroll
14 Cooke Pl
Warwick RI 02888

Call Sign: WV1Y
Kenneth F Magee
17 Deirdra Ct
Warwick RI 02889

Call Sign: K1SDV
Michael T Owen
175 Coburn St
Warwick RI 02886

Call Sign: N1NRF
Donald G Scott
117 Country Club Dr
Warwick RI 02888

Call Sign: N1XNJ
Daniel T Drake
105 Delwood Rd
Warwick RI 02889

Call Sign: N4EJC
Francis J Henry
155 Coldbrook Rd
Warwick RI 02888

Call Sign: KA1MHA
Stephen M Cote
208 Cove Ave
Warwick RI 02889

Call Sign: KB1COZ
Shirley A Farias Mrs
226 Dodge St
Warwick RI 02886

Call Sign: KA1OTO
Martha A Whatley
239 Cole Ave
Warwick RI 02886

Call Sign: KA1QIH
Laurel M Cote
208 Cove Ave
Warwick RI 02889

Call Sign: N1ZXG
Peter J Farias Mr
226 Dodge St
Warwick RI 02886

Call Sign: KA1OTP
Merton L Whatley Jr
239 Cole Ave

Call Sign: W1LDX
Richard H Nelson
64 Craig Rd

Call Sign: K1ABZ
Austin M Kairnes Jr
19 Dory Rd

Warwick RI 02886   Warwick RI 02889   Warwick RI 02888

Call Sign: WA1AGZ   Call Sign: KA1VKL   Call Sign: KE4OZK
Nils A F Anderson   Peter D Pendergast Jr   Christopher D Nowak
157 Douglas Rd   5 Edmond Cir   20 Farmland Rd
Warwick RI 02886   Warwick RI 02886   Warwick RI 02889

Call Sign: KA1NTU   Call Sign: KA1WWW   Call Sign: N1GRQ
Lynn M Hawkins   Paul S Houldsworth   Robert E Paolozzi
238 Draper Ave   28 Edmond Dr   63 Farmland Rd
Warwick RI 02889   Warwick RI 02886   Warwick RI 02889

Call Sign: K1TVM   Call Sign: W1KZP   Call Sign: WA1WEE
Edward J Hawkins   Clinton F Shaw Jr   John R Butler
99 Dryden Blvd   440 Elm St   102 Fern St
Warwick RI 02888   Warwick RI 02888   Warwick RI 02889

Call Sign: N1FRC   Call Sign: WX1M   Call Sign: KB1SEY
Walter Bilida   Steven D Rayhill   Jon J Ash
170 Dryden Blvd   81 Endicott Dr   40 Flamingo Dr
Warwick RI 02888   Warwick RI 02886   Warwick RI 02886

Call Sign: KB1QZQ   Call Sign: KA1ABE   Call Sign: N1YTG
Kenneth F Page Jr   Herbert E Anthony   Juan C De Leon
319 Easton Ave   85 Ethan Street   89 Frawley St
Warwick RI 02888   Warwick RI 02888   Warwick RI 02889

Call Sign: N1BSD   Call Sign: KB1OAK   Call Sign: KE1AB
William N Place   Michael L Osborne   Sean O Brennan
12 Ebony Dr   83 Eton Ave   94 Freeman St
Warwick RI 02818   Warwick RI 02889   Warwick RI 02886

Call Sign: WA1DQO   Call Sign: N1KRP   Call Sign: KB1MYT
Reginald B Palmer   Wayne G Michaels   Elizabeth Nelson
182 Edgewater Dr   5 Euclid Ave   11 Frontier Rd
Warwick RI 02886   Warwick RI 02886   Warwick RI 02889

Call Sign: KB1VQ   Call Sign: N1JMD   Call Sign: KB1RCD
Walter S Renfree   Carl F Koch   Michael L Basile
67 Edison St   136 Everleth Ave   37 General Hawkins Dr
Warwick RI 02889   Warwick RI 02888   Warwick RI 02888

Call Sign: KB1VDF   Call Sign: KA1WNA   Call Sign: WA1JUR
Walter S Renfree   David C Clark   Donald J Koly
67 Edison St   39 Fair St Front   347 George Arden Ave

Warwick RI 02886

Call Sign: KB1RTL
Robert A Federico
109 George St
Warwick RI 02888

Call Sign: K1TAX
Robert A Federico
109 George St
Warwick RI 02888

Call Sign: K1FRA
Robert A Federico
109 George St
Warwick RI 02888

Call Sign: N1UIB
Kevin W Nurse
149 George St
Warwick RI 02888

Call Sign: KA1PCF
James F Caruolo
237 Gertrude Ave
Warwick RI 02886

Call Sign: KB1TUG
Geoffrey C Rainville
321 Gertrude Ave
Warwick RI 02886

Call Sign: N1TUD
David P Killian
51 Gillooly Dr
Warwick RI 02888

Call Sign: KA1WWX
Thomas P Zeppa
135 Gillooly Dr
Warwick RI 028884646

Call Sign: KB1KHY
Chris M Hager
35 Glenbrook Rd

Warwick RI 02889

Call Sign: W1LDL
Anton E Langhammer
77 Glenbrook Rd
Warwick RI 028891805

Call Sign: N1RQU
John G Shaheen
77 Glendale Ave
Warwick RI 02889

Call Sign: KA1VNJ
Richard A Perreault
112 Gould Ave
Warwick RI 02888

Call Sign: KB1RGS
Lisa M Perreault
112 Gould Ave
Warwick RI 02858

Call Sign: N1SEF
Jeremy M Kubica
132 Governors Dr
Warwick RI 02818

Call Sign: N1PGL
Carol L Carraturo
18 Granger Ct
Warwick RI 02889

Call Sign: N1AJS
David G Underwood
1040 Greenwich Ave
Warwick RI 02886

Call Sign: N1YZL
Dennis C Guertin
309 Greenwich Ave C133
Warwick RI 02886

Call Sign: N1PRF
Deanna M Perry
339 Grove Ave

Warwick RI 02889

Call Sign: KA1WOT
Barbara L Arnold
31 Hackman Pl
Warwick RI 02889

Call Sign: W1KMA
Christopher Kilpert
38 Hagerstown Road
Warwick RI 028868014

Call Sign: KB1SYB
Joseph G Swift
28 Hallmark Dr
Warwick RI 02886

Call Sign: N1IFO
Joseph E Palmieri
355 Hardig Rd Bldg 3 Apt
A303
Warwick RI 02886

Call Sign: WA1RAT
Louis G Biancucci
11 Harmony Ct
Warwick RI 02889

Call Sign: KA1WWV
Michael J Daniels
305 Harrington Ave
Warwick RI 02888

Call Sign: N1QDK
Gayle A Daniels
305 Harrington Ave
Warwick RI 02888

Call Sign: KB1HHT
James M Boucher
25 Haverhill Ave
Warwick RI 02886

Call Sign: N1WOJ
Mary L Pescatore

34 Hawley Ave
Warwick RI 02889

31 Horseneck Rd.
Warwick RI 02889

100 June Avenue
Warwick RI 02889

Call Sign: KA1CTX
Laurence P Bouthillier
86 Hawthorne Ave
Warwick RI 028868230

Call Sign: KB1HZA
Peter S Tranchida
33 Houston Drive
Warwick RI 028868112

Call Sign: N1PVU
Donald I Thornton
64 Kalmer Rd
Warwick RI 02886

Call Sign: KB1GIB
Paul R Macomber
31 Hazard Ave
Warwick RI 02889

Call Sign: WA1QEF
Bernard C Brennan Sr
17 Hoyle Ave
Warwick RI 02888

Call Sign: WA1RCV
Robert J Coffey Sr
11 Keeley Ave
Warwick RI 02886

Call Sign: N1AMN
Robert L Le Blanc
89 Herbert St
Warwick RI 02818

Call Sign: N1XCW
Stephen A Hammerschmidt
261 Hoysie Ave
Warwick RI 02889

Call Sign: K1HGC
Robert C Mancini
54 Keeley Ave
Warwick RI 02886

Call Sign: KA1CNY
Frederick J Mc Carthy Sr
28 Hillside Dr
Warwick RI 028895811

Call Sign: N1VDF
Raymond A Cotoia
89 Huron St
Warwick RI 02889

Call Sign: KA1ELB
William E Montella Jr
151 Keeley Ave
Warwick RI 02886

Call Sign: KA1TFZ
Frederick J Mc Carthy Jr
28 Hillside Dr
Warwick RI 02889

Call Sign: N1VVX
Mark A Cotoia
89 Huron St
Warwick RI 02889

Call Sign: KB1MJH
David J Applegate
48 Kenneth Ave
Warwick RI 02889

Call Sign: K1RFS
Richie E King
119 Holmes Rd
Warwick RI 02888

Call Sign: N8PZS
Bette Rivera
89 Huron St
Warwick RI 02889

Call Sign: W1DJA
David J Applegate
48 Kenneth Ave
Warwick RI 02889

Call Sign: N1SW
Ernest E Piche Jr
9 Hornet Rd
Warwick RI 02886

Call Sign: KB1BHQ
David G Ashworth
77 Inman Ave
Warwick RI 02886

Call Sign: N1MJF
Mathew J Ferreira
27 Kentucky Ave
Warwick RI 028885911

Call Sign: N1LLX
Christopher S Lamarsh
19 Horse Neck Rd
Warwick RI 02886

Call Sign: KB1FUS
Joseph E Drury
55 Irene Street
Warwick RI 02886

Call Sign: W1SNT
Joseph E St Germain
231 Killey Ave
Warwick RI 02889

Call Sign: KB1PVM
Robert J Sawler

Call Sign: N1BKM
Mark C Mc Millen

Call Sign: KA1SQV
Willard B Gould

30 King St
Warwick RI 02886

319 Lansdowne Rd
Warwick RI 028885741

153 Longfellow Dr
Warwick RI 02818

Call Sign: N1REN
John S Martucci
72 Kiwanee Rd
Warwick RI 02888

Call Sign: KB1ADO
Kenneth L Cambio
33 Larchmont Rd
Warwick RI 02886

Call Sign: K1NOU
Donald A Ciolfi
187 Lucas Rd
Warwick RI 02818

Call Sign: KC1JR
John A Parente
159 Kiwanee Rd
Warwick RI 02888

Call Sign: K1DFY
William Y Parker
22 Laura St
Warwick RI 028881324

Call Sign: KB1IKA
Francis M Sullivan
77 Madison St
Warwick RI 02888

Call Sign: N1FVS
Wendy S Parente
159 Kiwanee Rd
Warwick RI 02888

Call Sign: KA1RAM
Laurent Fortin Jr
38 Law St
Warwick RI 02889

Call Sign: W1CSL
Christopher S Lamarsh
153 Madison St.
Warwick RI 02888

Call Sign: KB1WBD
Alexander N Parente
159 Kiwanee Rd
Warwick RI 02888

Call Sign: KB1PMO
Shannon J Tillman
7 Lawn Ave
Warwick RI 02888

Call Sign: K1AST
Arlindo S Torres
180 Manolla Ave
Warwick RI 02888

Call Sign: K1ZRS
Chester V Foster Jr
31 Lakecrest Dr
Warwick RI 02889

Call Sign: N1PZW
James A Cole
107 Lawndale Dr
Warwick RI 02818

Call Sign: KB1BNP
Royal M Disley
285 Maple St
Warwick RI 02888

Call Sign: KC8ULN
Yangwook Choi
157 Lancaster Avenue
Warwick RI 02886

Call Sign: WA1GCX
Stephen J Carroll
32 Leslie Rd
Warwick RI 02888

Call Sign: K1GTI
Arthur P Daniels
48 Maplehurst Ave
Warwick RI 028895011

Call Sign: W1UIV
Albert E Becker Sr
134 Landon Rd
Warwick RI 028884621

Call Sign: KB8YHD
Allan H Reed
27 Lillian Ct
Warwick RI 02886

Call Sign: KA1UKB
David E Perreault
45 Marine Ave
Warwick RI 02888

Call Sign: KB1OAN
Matthew E Last
319 Lansdowne Rd
Warwick RI 028885741

Call Sign: KB1MYY
Ann C St Pierre
132 Long Meadow Ave
Warwick RI 02889

Call Sign: KA1UKE
Sheila E Perreault
45 Marine Ave
Warwick RI 02888

Call Sign: K9MEL
Matthew E Last

Call Sign: N1NTP
Terry P Brennan

Call Sign: KB1ANX
David W Perreault

45 Marine Ave
Warwick RI 02888

Call Sign: KB1EGM
Helen M Herrick
55 Masthead Dr 28
Warwick RI 02886

Call Sign: N1SMK
Bruce F Herrick
55 Masthead Dr 28
Warwick RI 02886

Call Sign: KR1Z
Bruce F Herrick
55 Masthead Dr 28
Warwick RI 02886

Call Sign: N1HDE
Adam T Hecker
97 Mc Kinley St
Warwick RI 02886

Call Sign: KA1BJC
Kenneth R Lundstrom
52 Merle St
Warwick RI 02889

Call Sign: KB1JZS
Jeffrey J Defelice
69 Metropolitan Dr
Warwick RI 02886

Call Sign: KB1MYR
Christopher J Defelice
69 Metropolitan Dr
Warwick RI 02886

Call Sign: KB1MYX
Karen L Defelice
69 Metropolitan Dr
Warwick RI 02886

Call Sign: KB1TXZ
William E Holmes

76 Mia Ct
Warwick RI 02886

Call Sign: N1ISA
John C Jarvie
94 Miantonomo Dr
Warwick RI 02888

Call Sign: N1JMB
John S Jarvie
94 Miantonomo Dr
Warwick RI 02888

Call Sign: KB1VEZ
Steven P Sorel
12 Middlefield Dr
Warwick RI 02889

Call Sign: KB1AVU
Charles D Kernan
43 Midway Dr
Warwick RI 028868133

Call Sign: N1DWR
Philip J Mc Cafferty Jr
32 Montcalm Rd
Warwick RI 028894312

Call Sign: WB1EFL
Raymond J Turbitt
36 Namquid Drive
Warwick RI 02888

Call Sign: K1EGM
Frederic S Mc Kay
75 Naples Ave
Warwick RI 028861948

Call Sign: N1AZD
Carlo E Pisaturo Jr
181 Narragansett Bay Ave
Warwick RI 028896725

Call Sign: K1JAI
Joseph J Dean

400 Narragansett Pkwy
Warwick RI 02888

Call Sign: WA1NGP
James A Gershman
750 Narragansett Pky
Warwick RI 028884905

Call Sign: K1JJJ
James A Gershman
750 Narragansett Pky
Warwick RI 028884905

Call Sign: N1EAJ
Michael E Carley
291 Nausauket Rd
Warwick RI 02886

Call Sign: W1GSE
Warren T Woodbine
344 Nausauket Rd
Warwick RI 02886

Call Sign: N1KLH
Michael A Imbornone
40 Nekick Road
Warwick RI 02818

Call Sign: N1GUX
Ralph P Mello
423 New London Ave Unit
605
Warwick RI 02893

Call Sign: N1GTF
Robert C Mancini Jr
55 Normandy Dr
Warwick RI 028865151

Call Sign: K1NER
Paul A Feeney
36 North Fair St
Warwick RI 02888

Call Sign: KB1BJY

Ernest S Bertrand
122 North St
Warwick RI 02886

Call Sign: KA1PBP
Patricia A Maher
184 Norwood Ave
Warwick RI 02888

Call Sign: KB1AKJ
David A White
229 Norwood Ave
Warwick RI 02888

Call Sign: KB1NCZ
David W Wyman Sr
57 Ocean Ave
Warwick RI 02889

Call Sign: N1IUH
William C Naughton
100 Old Homestead Rd
Warwick RI 02889

Call Sign: WA1QQX
Clarence M Carey
124 Old Homestead Rd
Warwick RI 02889

Call Sign: KB1ARN
Terry L Ketchel
133 Overbrook Ave
Warwick RI 02889

Call Sign: K1KT
Kenneth A Tata
90 Park View Ave
Warwick RI 02888

Call Sign: KB1PNO
Fidelity Amateur Radio
Club
90 Park View Ave
Warwick RI 02888

Call Sign: W1MB
Fidelity Amateur Radio
Club
90 Park View Ave
Warwick RI 02888

Call Sign: KB1OQT
Patricia Day
368 Parkside Dr
Warwick RI 02888

Call Sign: N1ATU
Lincoln W Hubbard
52 Parkview Ave
Warwick RI 02888

Call Sign: N1LVT
David A Vigneau
204 Pawtuxet Ave
Warwick RI 02888

Call Sign: N1PSN
Kenneth R Kershaw
297 Pawtuxet Ave
Warwick RI 02888

Call Sign: KB1NCV
Paul Montella
49 Peace St
Warwick RI 02888

Call Sign: KB1KON
Cory M Cotoia
35 Penguin Ave
Warwick RI 02818

Call Sign: KB1MYW
Janis M Dufresne
7 Petansett Ct
Warwick RI 02888

Call Sign: WA1LPW
Henry N Petit
21 Peter St
Warwick RI 02886

Call Sign: NN1T
Alfred Kondvar
51 Pettaconsett Ave
Warwick RI 02888

Call Sign: KA1YXC
John H Anglin
2 Pilgrim Dr
Warwick RI 02888

Call Sign: KA1YXD
Thomas H Anglin Iii
2 Pilgrim Dr
Warwick RI 02888

Call Sign: KB1CXN
Robert L Swinehart
191 Pinegrove Ave
Warwick RI 028898711

Call Sign: KA1SNR
Peter P Ruggieri
75 Pond View Dr
Warwick RI 02886

Call Sign: KB1EZH
Lawrence R Gallo
957 Post Rd
Warwick RI 028883368

Call Sign: N1TDQ
Sean M Carroll
3987 Post Rd
Warwick RI 02886

Call Sign: N1WDM
James P Mc Guire
4042 Post Rd 10
Warwick RI 02886

Call Sign: KA1GSM
Peter J Kmiec
200 Post Road   Unit 616
Warwick RI 02888

Call Sign: K1RCI
William G Hill
4591 Post Road Apt: A2
Warwick RI 02818

Call Sign: KA1PBS
Michael J Lill
84 Potowomut Rd
Warwick RI 02818

Call Sign: NN1E
Patricia A Lill
84 Potowomut Rd
Warwick RI 02887

Call Sign: KA1GIR
Gardiner M Williams
190 Potters Ave
Warwick RI 02886

Call Sign: N1PIJ
Eugene W Zommer Sr
76 Powhatan St
Warwick RI 02889

Call Sign: N1TVQ
Kenneth S Wilde Sr
18 Prince St
Warwick RI 02888

Call Sign: K1DT
David Tessitore
79 Priscilla Avenue
Warwick RI 028895718

Call Sign: KB1VLG
William J Porter Iii
257 Promenade Ave
Warwick RI 02886

Call Sign: KA1TOT
William F Lantz
341 Providence St
Warwick RI 028860671

Call Sign: N1EEU
James D Ray
479 Providence St - A3
Warwick RI 02886

Call Sign: KB1VZF
Timothy W Quilty
579 Providence St Apt 3
Warwick RI 02886

Call Sign: KB1LN
Bobby V Rogers
40 Quail Ridge Lane
Warwick RI 028864262

Call Sign: KB1KMS
Russian Sub Radio Club
40 Quail Ridge Lane
Warwick RI 02886

Call Sign: N1THE
John R Mc Kenna
300 Quaker Ln Pmb 244
Warwick RI 02886

Call Sign: KA1WTE
Albert R Cambio
232 Red Chimney Dr
Warwick RI 02886

Call Sign: WA1GNB
Stephen R Williams
27 River Vue Ave
Warwick RI 028894717

Call Sign: KA1OEH
William A Dalgliesh Jr
92 Rivervue Ave
Warwick RI 02889

Call Sign: KJ4SIV
Shirley M Brooke
10 Rutherford Court
Warwick RI 02886

Call Sign: W1YHH
George P Wells Jr
26 Rutland St
Warwick RI 02888

Call Sign: WL7Z
Patrick F Atwood
197 Sand Pond Road
Warwick RI 02888

Call Sign: NG1G
Patrick F Atwood
197 Sand Pond Road
Warwick RI 02888

Call Sign: KB1PS
Robert E Chapman
105 Sandy Ln
Warwick RI 02889

Call Sign: WA1ANT
Eric P Ewart
329 Sargent St
Warwick RI 02888

Call Sign: K1MD
Richard P San Antonio
60 Seacrest Ln
Warwick RI 028895451

Call Sign: WA1NQH
Ellery F Martin
5 Senior City
Warwick RI 02893

Call Sign: K1KEM
Rose M Murray
1 Shalom Dr
Warwick RI 02886

Call Sign: WB1EQL
John S Coppolino
88 Shamrock Dr
Warwick RI 02886

Call Sign: KB1MYU
Laurie A Collins
140 Shamrock Dr
Warwick RI 02886

Call Sign: N1UQM
C Scott Giglio
22 Silver Lake Ave
Warwick RI 02888

Call Sign: K1HJS
Frank J Mullins
139 Spencer Woods Dr
Warwick RI 028185055

Call Sign: KA1YQL
Frank J Robbins
79 Spofford Ave
Warwick RI 02888

Call Sign: KA1SML
Robert E Evans
222 Sprague Ave
Warwick RI 02889

Call Sign: N1VSU
Michael B Melancon
80 Spring Grove Ave
Warwick RI 02889

Call Sign: KB1BZG
George Grayson
221 Squantum Dr
Warwick RI 02888

Call Sign: KB3BZH
Ted Strike
221 Squantum Dr
Warwick RI 02888

Call Sign: N3ZWT
John Holden
221 Squantum Dr
Warwick RI 02888

Call Sign: WA1PTY
George Mitchell
80 Stanfield St
Warwick RI 02886

Call Sign: WA1AJE
Ira J Bates
19 Staples Ave
Warwick RI 02886

Call Sign: N1SXA
Robert W Darigan
146 Staples Ave
Warwick RI 02886

Call Sign: N1EFX
Joseph E Couie
100 Strawberry Field Rd
Warwick RI 02886

Call Sign: WA1OZF
John G Laramee
333 Strawberry Field Rd
Warwick RI 02886

Call Sign: N1GVI
Henry E Longo
253 Sumner Ave
Warwick RI 028881926

Call Sign: KB1JFE
Robert D Heon
270 Sumner Ave
Warwick RI 02888

Call Sign: KB1JFF
Matthew R Heon
270 Sumner Ave
Warwick RI 02888

Call Sign: KA1QHI
Jane M Gemma
149 Tennyson Rd
Warwick RI 02888

Call Sign: W1RVO
Peter B Gemma
149 Tennyson Rd
Warwick RI 02888

Call Sign: K1YUV
Anthony J Conca
11 Terrace Ave
Warwick RI 02889

Call Sign: W1CZD
John S Krikorian Jr
5 Thayer Pl
Warwick RI 02888

Call Sign: KE1AF
Abel M Da Silva
107 Tiernan Ave
Warwick RI 02886

Call Sign: KB1TFE
Charles E Lewis Iii
122 Tiernan Ave
Warwick RI 02886

Call Sign: K1CEL
Charles E Lewis Iii
122 Tiernan Ave
Warwick RI 02886

Call Sign: N1XVY
John A Daneau
88 Timberline Rd
Warwick RI 02886

Call Sign: KB1HUD
John M Walsh
19 Timberline Road
Warwick RI 02886

Call Sign: WO1P
James D Mc Elroy Sr
979 Toll Gate Rd #42
Warwick RI 02886

Call Sign: N1PSM
Mark A Fondi
8 Tomahawk Ct
Warwick RI 02886

Call Sign: KB1QZO
Alexander J Potts
20 Tomahawk Ct
Warwick RI 02886

Call Sign: KC1DF
Charles R Benson
54 Tourtelott Ave
Warwick RI 02886

Call Sign: WO1D
Edward J Scallon
39 Transit St
Warwick RI 028892018

Call Sign: WA1ZGG
David M Mossberg
94 Underwood Ave
Warwick RI 028881224

Call Sign: K1CU
Louis J Dichiaro
80 Union Ave
Warwick RI 028898529

Call Sign: KB1OCU
Paul T Berry
73 Van Zandt Av
Warwick RI 02889

Call Sign: K1EZN
Livingston B Reuter
40 Vaughn Ave
Warwick RI 02886

Call Sign: W1PPV
Nicholas S Mochary
205 Vaughn Ave
Warwick RI 02886

Call Sign: KB1AXB
Gregory R Santos
142 Vera St
Warwick RI 02886

Call Sign: N1FTH
William A Bonnick
8 Viceroy Rd
Warwick RI 02886

Call Sign: WA1RVH
Michael J Ferrante
552 W Shore Rd
Warwick RI 02889

Call Sign: WB1AJX
Howard P Rowland
3073 W Shore Rd
Warwick RI 02886

Call Sign: WA1FOS
Ronald D Cameron
3495 W Shore Rd
Warwick RI 02886

Call Sign: KB1NGD
Glenn S Jackson
169 Wampanoag Rd
Warwick RI 02818

Call Sign: KB1VZG
Potowomut Radio Club
169 Wampanoag Rd
Warwick RI 02818

Call Sign: AD1RI
Potowomut Radio Club
169 Wampanoag Rd
Warwick RI 02818

Call Sign: KA1WTD
Michael E Thomas
839 Warwick Ave
Warwick RI 02888

Call Sign: KB1VLF
Jeff L Howard
103 Warwick Neck Ave
Warwick RI 02889

Call Sign: KB1KFB
Jason L Salzsieder
1090 Warwick Neck Ave
Warwick RI 02889

Call Sign: W1KCS
Albert N Fraser
63 Warwick Nk Ave
Warwick RI 02889

Call Sign: KA1ZLE
Dorothy B Burdick
157 Weeden Dr
Warwick RI 02818

Call Sign: KL0RV
Christine R Atwood
124 Welfare Ave
Warwick RI 02888

Call Sign: KB1LOQ
Erin C Atwood
124 Welfare Ave
Warwick RI 02888

Call Sign: K1PG
Giuseppe Pirri
204 Wellspring Dr
Warwick RI 02886

Call Sign: KB1WCM
Mark J Leinhauser
58 Westfield Rd
Warwick RI 02888

Call Sign: KB1MYV
Andrea J Zito
248 Wethersfield Dr
Warwick RI 02886

Call Sign: KA1TMG
Royden A Alexander
45 White Acorn Cir
Warwick RI 02886

Call Sign: KA1ZPO
Scott C Farrar
105 Wilde Field Dr
Warwick RI 02886

Call Sign: WA1DQU
Douglas W Palmer
2 Winston Ct
Warwick RI 02886

Call Sign: KB1HAS
Horace P Houtchens
43 Winter Ave
Warwick RI 02889

Call Sign: K1PYO
Gregory C Chase
Warwick RI 02887

Call Sign: KB1EBM
Jodi A Souza
Warwick RI 028880931

Call Sign: N1OTB
Roland J Enos
Warwick RI 02888

Call Sign: N1WEM
Jon J Ash
Warwick RI 02887

Call Sign: N1WQH
Carmine D Olivieri
Warwick RI 02887

Call Sign: N2EEN
Robert E Swanberg
Warwick RI 02887

Call Sign: W1VHF
Intouch Radio Society
Warwick RI 02888

FCC Amateur Radio Licenses in West Glocester

Call Sign: KA1WFP
Marcel A Govin
447 Durfee Hill Rd
West Glocester RI 02814

FCC Amateur Radio Licenses in West Greenwich

Call Sign: WA1RJP
Rodger P Booth Iii
25 Bates Tr
West Greenwich RI 02817

Call Sign: N1EMN
Robert A Thompson
20 Blueberry Heights
West Greenwich RI 02817

Call Sign: KA1OFB
Linda E Thompson
20 Blueberry Hts
West Greenwich RI 02817

Call Sign: N1LDG
John G Daneau
34 Catherine Wight Ct.
West Greenwich RI 02817

Call Sign: N1MIW
Laurence W Zielinski
28 Cherokee Trail
West Greenwich RI 02817

Call Sign: NB1U
Mark A Johnsen
64 Clubhouse Rd

West Greenwich RI
028171882

Call Sign: KB1BQE
Christopher S Eastman
20 Division Rd
West Greenwich RI 02817

Call Sign: N1VDG
Milton F Eastman
20 Division Rd
West Greenwich RI 02817

Call Sign: N1VDH
Linda I Eastman
20 Division Rd
West Greenwich RI 02817

Call Sign: N1JWY
Jacqueline M Albro
70 Fish Hill Rd
West Greenwich RI 02816

Call Sign: KA1THY
Kathleen A Swann
306 Fry Pond Rd.
West Greenwich RI 02817

Call Sign: N1BS
Brian R Swann
306 Fry Pond Rd.
West Greenwich RI 02817

Call Sign: KB1EAP
Robert P Frazier Jr
27 Greenridge Ct
West Greenwich RI 02817

Call Sign: N1MKN
Richard S Parkinson
86 Hazard Rd
West Greenwich RI 02817

Call Sign: KB1TXV
William H Clay

605 Hazard Rd
West Greenwich RI 02817

Call Sign: K1SC
William H Clay
605 Hazard Rd
West Greenwich RI 02817

Call Sign: N1NCX
Robert N Cioci
661 Hazard Rd
West Greenwich RI 02917

Call Sign: WB1FIA
Harris Hammersmith Iii
16 Julie Ct
West Greenwich RI 02917

Call Sign: KB1RON
Daniel E Hass
64 Kimberly Dr
West Greenwich RI 02817

Call Sign: KB1FFN
Donald S Abrahams
312 Mischnock Road
West Greenwich RI 02817

Call Sign: KA1HAP
James J Cross
241 Nooseneck Hill Rd
West Greenwich RI 02817

Call Sign: KA1KXW
Phebe A Cross
241 Nooseneck Hill Rd
West Greenwich RI 02817

Call Sign: N1KHM
Kenneth J Brayman
420 Nooseneck Hill Rd
West Greenwich RI 02817

Call Sign: KB1ADN
Ronald B Gauthier

Nooseneck Hill Rd
West Greenwich RI 02817

Call Sign: N1OZJ
Terrence M Lee
76 Parkside Dr
West Greenwich RI
028172024

Call Sign: W1PHD
Kenneth B Gilleo
16334 Patriot Way
West Greenwich RI 02817

Call Sign: W1TKO
Thomas K Olsson
110 Plain Meetinghouse Rd
West Greenwich RI
028172044

Call Sign: KA1PBN
Cameron M Hubbard
393 Plain Rd
West Greenwich RI 02817

Call Sign: N1LVS
Peter V Yates Sr
54 Racoon Hill Rd
West Greenwich RI 02817

Call Sign: WB1AHH
Robert G Leonard
140 Sharpe St
West Greenwich RI 02817

Call Sign: KB1VDC
Steven A Boufford
150 Stubble Brook Rd
West Greenwich RI 02817

Call Sign: KZ1E
Edwin M Bellamy Ii
30 Tanglewood Drive
West Greenwich RI 02817

Call Sign: K1DAM
David A Mc Manus
1 Victory Hwy
West Greenwich RI 02817

Call Sign: K1KX
Karl D Wherry
267 Victory Hwy
West Greenwich RI 02817

Call Sign: W1ZHV
Wilbur E Jordan
228 Weaver Hill Rd
West Greenwich RI 02817

Call Sign: W1AAB
Allen A Baton Jr
126 Carrs Pond Rd
West Grennwich RI 02817

FCC Amateur Radio Licenses in West Kingston

Call Sign: N1KDE
Keith J Storti
242 A Laurel Lane
West Kingston RI 02892

Call Sign: K1PNX
John M Sieburth
408 Barber Pond Rd
West Kingston RI 02892

Call Sign: KB1CDS
Jeanne B Patric
241 C Dug Way Bridge Rd
West Kingston RI 02892

Call Sign: N1ZHM
Earl F Patric
241 C Dug Way Bridge Rd
West Kingston RI 02892

Call Sign: W1HNT
William E O Neel

23 D Heaton Orchard Rd
West Kingston RI
028921141

Call Sign: KB1JZQ
Ken St Amour
336 Dugway Bridge Rd
West Kingston RI 02892

Call Sign: KB1JZP
Iris Dewhurst
376 Dugway Bridge Rd
West Kingston RI 02892

Call Sign: WA1GXC
Harris R Pitnof
37 Estelle Dr
West Kingston RI 02892

Call Sign: N1VDW
Jeremy S Thayer
452 Gardiner Rd
West Kingston RI 02892

Call Sign: N1LPW
Daniel J Dorson
550 Gardner Rd
West Kingston RI
028921083

Call Sign: W1CFT
Mary E Cline
Gardner Rd
West Kingston RI 02892

Call Sign: W1GBO
Donald L Dorson
Gardner Rd
West Kingston RI 02892

Call Sign: KA1YXE
Clarence B Donath Iii
345 Hillsdale Rd.
West Kingston RI 02892

Call Sign: K1PNI
Anthony W Cline
13 Hoxsie Rd
West Kingston RI 02892

Call Sign: N1LWO
Paul R Whelan
245 Hundred Acre Pond Rd
West Kingston RI 02892

Call Sign: KB1WUM
Anthony M Sweet
217 James Trail
West Kingston RI 02892

Call Sign: KB1WUN
Marc W Barrington
262 James Trail
West Kingston RI 02892

Call Sign: KB1UEN
Jesse T Ellis
393 Waites Corner Rd
West Kingston RI 02892

Call Sign: KA1HAC
Linda A Steere
West Kingston RI 02892

FCC Amateur Radio Licenses in West Warwick

Call Sign: N1VSW
Michelle M Krocka
10 Tiffany Ave
West Warnick RI 02893

Call Sign: KB1EBL
Edward C Porter Jr
92 Harris Ave
West Warrick RI 02893

Call Sign: KC1AS
David E Tretton
7 Huckleberry Ln

West Warwich RI 02893

Call Sign: KB1HKM
Ken Franklin
93 Aberdeen St
West Warwick RI 02893

Call Sign: N1KJF
Ken Franklin
93 Aberdeen St
West Warwick RI 02893

Call Sign: KF1O
Ken Franklin
93 Aberdeen St
West Warwick RI 02893

Call Sign: W1KCG
Inc The Kent County
Amateur Radio Group
93 Aberdenn St
West Warwick RI 02893

Call Sign: KB1LED
Charles E Sczuroski Jr
22 Alden Dr
West Warwick RI 02893

Call Sign: N1BQW
Chester A Browning
46 Alden Dr
West Warwick RI 02893

Call Sign: K1EW
John Ambrose
28 Bayberry Dr
West Warwick RI 02893

Call Sign: AA1PE
Frank A Jarvis
8 Bratt Ln
West Warwick RI 02893

Call Sign: N1VJL
Kathy E Jarvis

8 Bratt Ln
West Warwick RI 02893

Call Sign: K1IIT
George J Varatta
1 Bryant Pl
West Warwick RI 02893

Call Sign: K1MLU
Olivia I Varatta
1 Bryant Pl
West Warwick RI 02893

Call Sign: NZ1T
Anselmo T Araujo
50 Centraccio Ct
West Warwick RI 02893

Call Sign: N1YGA
Eileen F Jacques
116 Cleveland St
West Warwick RI 02893

Call Sign: N1ZBA
Gerald E Jacques
116 Cleveland St
West Warwick RI 02893

Call Sign: K1WPH
Peter Certo
136 Cleveland St
West Warwick RI 02893

Call Sign: KA1NN
Edward H Hackney
135 Cochran St
West Warwick RI 02893

Call Sign: KB1AUV
John F Hozlock Jr
142 Cochran St
West Warwick RI 02893

Call Sign: KB1GBT
George E Antaya

25 Colvin St
West Warwick RI 02893

Call Sign: N1HYO
Ronald R Schlag
57 Cowessett Ave Apt 65
West Warwick RI 02893

Call Sign: KB1WUL
Darren M Wigley
60 Crestwood Dr
West Warwick RI 02893

Call Sign: KB1FDJ
John J Clarke Jr
53 Crossland Rd
West Warwick RI 02893

Call Sign: AA1CE
David W Reid
27 Drawbridge Drive
West Warwick RI
028935575

Call Sign: N1LYA
Barbara A Reid
27 Drawbridge Drive
West Warwick RI 02893

Call Sign: KB1PXH
Jairo R Arce
267 E Greenwich Ave
West Warwick RI 02893

Call Sign: KB4ZLY
Jairo R Arce
267 E Greenwich Ave
West Warwick RI 02893

Call Sign: KD4ZLY
Jairo R Arce
267 E Greenwich Ave
West Warwick RI 02893

Call Sign: N1RJW

Richard A Corley
650 East Greenwich Ave.
#6-211
West Warwick RI 02893

Call Sign: N1PIH
Anthony L Fisher Sr
50 Eddy St Apt 13
West Warwick RI 02893

Call Sign: N1ZJI
James G Ferranti
1 Edge Street
West Warwick RI 02893

Call Sign: WA1RAU
Jean C Blanchard
23 Enfield Dr
West Warwick RI 02893

Call Sign: KA1VNK
Sherri L Burton
39 Ethle St
West Warwick RI 02893

Call Sign: N1JXV
Joseph L Geoffroy
9 Fairgreen Dr
West Warwick RI 02893

Call Sign: KB1JLO
Dwain E Denoncour
73 First St.
West Warwick RI
028932701

Call Sign: KB1AWX
Denis E Belanger
32 Gardner Ave
West Warwick RI 02893

Call Sign: KB1LAJ
Ri Wire Antenna Club
68 Garnet St
West Warwick RI 02893

Call Sign: W1WIR
Ri Wire Antenna Club
68 Garnet St
West Warwick RI 02893

Call Sign: KD1IA
John G Sexton
68 Garnet Street
West Warwick RI 02893

Call Sign: KO1H
John G Sexton
68 Garnet Street
West Warwick RI 02893

Call Sign: N1FJE
Francis P Gleason
11 Harding St
West Warwick RI 02893

Call Sign: WA1AJB
William D Armitage
66 Harding St
West Warwick RI 02893

Call Sign: N1WSH
Merideth A Woodside
30 Hilltop Ave
West Warwick RI 02893

Call Sign: WA1LAD
Gilbert D Woodside Iii
30 Hilltop Ave
West Warwick RI 02893

Call Sign: KB1FWG
Pawtuxet Valley Amateur
Radio Club
30 Hilltop Ave
West Warwick RI 02893

Call Sign: WA1USA
Inc Pawtuxet Valley
Amateur Radio Club

30 Hilltop Avenue
West Warwick RI 02893

Call Sign: KB1PGW
Jubilee Amateur Radio Club
Of Rhode Island
153 James P Murphy Hwy -
Ste D
West Warwick RI 02893

Call Sign: W1RI
Jubilee Amateur Radio Club
Of Rhode Island
153 James P Murphy Hwy -
Ste D
West Warwick RI 02893

Call Sign: W1JW
Joseph A Accetta
153 James P. Murphy Hwy
Suite C
West Warwick RI 02893

Call Sign: KB1RWP
Anthony Ferrara
56 Kimberly Lane
West Warwick RI 02893

Call Sign: KB1RWR
Nancy M Ferrara
56 Kimberly Ln
West Warwick RI 02893

Call Sign: K1VFM
James R Hopkins
1 Kristee Cir
West Warwick RI
028937507

Call Sign: N1TIK
Brian A Mattias
9 Kulas Rd
West Warwick RI
028933321

Call Sign: KA1LWA
Samuel G Volpe
14 Lawrence
West Warwick RI 02893

Call Sign: N1JDI
Jason M Ventura
3 Leo St
West Warwick RI 02893

Call Sign: WA1YVV
Cyrille W Cote
22 Lexington Ave
West Warwick RI 02893

Call Sign: WA1CSM
Cyrille W Cote
22 Lexington Ave
West Warwick RI 02893

Call Sign: KB1TYD
Janice E Mathews
167 Lockwood St
West Warwick RI 02893

Call Sign: WA1IIN
Alfred Pacheco
33 Maple Ave
West Warwick RI
028934413

Call Sign: KB0IMO
Richard E Waterhouse Iii
26 Matteson Ave
West Warwick RI 02893

Call Sign: W1JUN
Alfred A Lautieri
1 Mc Teers Ct
West Warwick RI 02893

Call Sign: N1KSG
Robert A Paolantonio
51 Morris Street
West Warwick RI 02893

Call Sign: W1PDV
Frederick A Gilchrist
8 Myron St
West Warwick RI 02893

Call Sign: W1HKE
Eugene W Zarr Jr
134 New London Ave
West Warwick RI 02893

Call Sign: K1EYD
Joseph E Hoffman Jr
304 New London Ave
West Warwick RI 00

Call Sign: N1HNW
Angelo A San Giovanni
117 Newell St
West Warwick RI 02893

Call Sign: K1DVY
Roland J Verrier
17 Nolan St
West Warwick RI 02893

Call Sign: K1YJO
Waneta M Verrier
17 Nolan St
West Warwick RI 02893

Call Sign: KB1AAQ
Sokkong Mey
14 Payan Street
West Warwick RI 02893

Call Sign: N1XZW
Charles P Anctil
6 Pearson St
West Warwick RI 02893

Call Sign: KB1UNV
David A Fabrizio
44 Pepin St
West Warwick RI 02893

Call Sign: K1WYC
Robert V Di Pippo
80 Pepin St
West Warwick RI 02893

Call Sign: K1VET
Ronald P Bertrand
25 Petti Dr
West Warwick RI 02893

Call Sign: KB1HCK
Paul R Bertrand
25 Petti Drive
West Warwick RI 02893

Call Sign: N1YNR
Johanne M Cornell
Po Box 1238
West Warwick RI 02893

Call Sign: KA1LXJ
George M Voit
564 Providence St
West Warwick RI 02893

Call Sign: KB1VZZ
Georgia E Weidman
185 Providence St A422
West Warwick RI 02893

Call Sign: KB1ISW
John C Flynn
319 Providence St Apt 803
West Warwick RI 02893

Call Sign: N1RGR
Robert C Jackman Iii
11 Reveve Avenue
West Warwick RI 02893

Call Sign: N1CVD
Jay E Kaufman
53 River Farms Dr
West Warwick RI 02893

Call Sign: W1DBR
John J Clarke Jr
83 River Farms Dr
West Warwick RI 02893

Call Sign: KB1AV
Frank S Lane
34 Scenic Dr
West Warwick RI
028935492

Call Sign: KB1ADS
Nicole L Roch
138 Setian Ln
West Warwick RI 02893

Call Sign: N1FTS
Cynthia G Roch
138 Setian Ln
West Warwick RI 02893

Call Sign: NR1H
Norman E Roch
138 Setian Ln
West Warwick RI 02893

Call Sign: N1JMC
Glenn M Butterfield
47 Sheffield Avenue
West Warwick RI
028936021

Call Sign: N1LEC
Carol A Butterfield
47 Sheffield Avenue
West Warwick RI
028936021

Call Sign: K1JBP
Glenn M Butterfield
47 Sheffield Avenue
West Warwick RI
028936021

Call Sign: K1SPJ
Carol A Butterfield
47 Sheffield Avenue
West Warwick RI
028936021

Call Sign: KA1RWD
Joseph L Laurent Sr
66 Shippee Ave
West Warwick RI 02893

Call Sign: KA1VKJ
Donald M Robertson
14 Sisson St
West Warwick RI 02893

Call Sign: N1XBU
Simon Korowitz
14 Starling Way
West Warwick RI 02893

Call Sign: KA1BNO
Daniel A Roy
23 Stevens Dr
West Warwick RI
028931324

Call Sign: KA1SJJ
Elizabeth D Roy
23 Stevens Dr
West Warwick RI
028931324

Call Sign: N1QBG
Mark J Amaral
65 Summit Ave
West Warwick RI 02893

Call Sign: N1RPV
Anthony L Andrea Jr
5 Terrace Avenue
West Warwick RI 02893

Call Sign: KA5KQY
Linda M Krocka

10 Tiffany Ave
West Warwick RI 02893

Call Sign: N1ZPU
Steven E Gobin
10 Tobin St
West Warwick RI 02893

Call Sign: KB1ERN
Barbara A Chilton
10 Tobin St
West Warwick RI 02893

Call Sign: KA1URK
Christopher J Senerchia
16 Tobin St
West Warwick RI 02893

Call Sign: KA1VAY
Thomas F Senerchia
16 Tobin St
West Warwick RI 02893

Call Sign: KB1JEB
Scott T Senerchia
16 Tobin St
West Warwick RI 02893

Call Sign: K1NAP
Albert D Desmarais
105 Tower Rd
West Warwick RI 02893

Call Sign: KA1RDB
Jerremy J Pezza
105 Tower Rd
West Warwick RI 02893

Call Sign: N1WFR
Jonathan C Waugh
24 Valley View Dr
West Warwick RI 02893

Call Sign: N2YQA
James G Atchison

46 Vincenzo Drive
West Warwick RI 02893

Call Sign: KB1IYG
Raymond A Taylor
205 Wakefield St
West Warwick RI 02893

Call Sign: W1PCW
Raymond A Taylor
205 Wakefield St
West Warwick RI 02893

Call Sign: KB1SXG
West Warwick Emergency
Management Agency
145 Washington St
West Warwick RI 02893

Call Sign: WW1EMA
West Warwick Emergency
Management Agency
145 Washington St
West Warwick RI 02893

Call Sign: KD1VM
Robert N Turner
26 Wells St
West Warwick RI 02893

Call Sign: N1DRM
William M Ward
93 West Warwick Ave. 3
West Warwick RI 02893

Call Sign: N1DMS
David M Smith
51 Youngs Ave
West Warwick RI
028934615

Call Sign: N1LAA
August J Gomes
West Warwick RI 02893

Call Sign: KB1OGW
Inc The Kent County
Amateur Radio Group
West Warwick RI 02893

Call Sign: KB1TSK
Andrew A Cooke
West Warwick RI 02893

Call Sign: KB1UHD
Christina A Cooke
West Warwick RI 02893

FCC Amateur Radio Licenses in Westerly

Call Sign: KB1LCQ
Jayson M Laferriere
69 - A Cross St
Westerly RI 02891

Call Sign: N1PVE
Lora J Vaughan
392c Oak St
Westerly RI 02891

Call Sign: KB1TZV
Eric E Schell
54 A Westminster St
Westerly RI 02891

Call Sign: KA1ZZR
William H Hays Ii
90 Ashaway Rd
Westerly RI 028911400

Call Sign: KA1ZZW
Marcia M Hays
90 Ashaway Rd
Westerly RI 02891

Call Sign: N1JMK
Greg Hangac
6 Ashel St
Westerly RI 02891

Call Sign: KA1AWO
Marie J Booth
50 Avondale Rd
Westerly RI 02891

Call Sign: KA1BAX
Robert A Booth
50 Avondale Rd
Westerly RI 02891

Call Sign: KB1CTP
John P Chupka
9 B Apache Dr
Westerly RI 02891

Call Sign: N1VWK
Stephen L Crawford
36 Babcock Rd
Westerly RI 028913327

Call Sign: WT1X
Richard J Capezzano
61 Boom Bridge Rd
Westerly RI 02891

Call Sign: W1AH
Albert B Hodson
37 Boombridge Road
Westerly RI 02891

Call Sign: KB1QWY
Paul R Perrone
1 Branch St
Westerly RI 02891

Call Sign: KB1QBS
Dawn E Smith
2 Brookview Ct
Westerly RI 02891

Call Sign: KB1PSZ
Anne M Garvey
17 Champion St
Westerly RI 02891

Call Sign: WA1AMS
Anne M Garvey
17 Champion St
Westerly RI 02891

Call Sign: KB1PVY
Lucy L Garvey
17 Champion St
Westerly RI 02891

Call Sign: KB1QVB
Kyran J Horne
17 Champion St
Westerly RI 02891

Call Sign: KB1RPL
Sarah I Garvey
17 Champion St
Westerly RI 02891

Call Sign: WA1SAR
Sarah I Garvey
17 Champion St
Westerly RI 02891

Call Sign: KB1RYK
Caeles M Garvey
17 Champion St
Westerly RI 02891

Call Sign: KA1ZZV
Richard A Muller
5 Champlin Dr Avondale
Westerly RI 02891

Call Sign: AA1KM
Walter F Neugent
6 Charles Ave
Westerly RI 02891

Call Sign: KD1GN
Robert J Pucci Sr
7 Chickadee Ln
Westerly RI 02891

Call Sign: N1NNR
Michael A Crowley
5 Cottage Ct
Westerly RI 02891

Call Sign: WM1X
Robert B Scott
45 Cove Rd
Westerly RI 02891

Call Sign: AB1OI
Theodore L Rice
22 Cross St
Westerly RI 02891

Call Sign: N1FPH
Thomas B Christiansen Sr
106 Cross St - Apt 13
Westerly RI 02891

Call Sign: KB1AUR
Adrian J Tourgee
122 Cross St Ext Apt D107
Westerly RI 02891

Call Sign: KB1MAO
Francis J Creamer Jr
2 David Ave
Westerly RI 02891

Call Sign: KB1VFI
Westerly Amateur Radio
Team
2 David Ave
Westerly RI 02891

Call Sign: W1WRI
Westerly Amateur Radio
Team
2 David Ave
Westerly RI 02891

Call Sign: N1ODO
John J Gencarella Jr

16 Dayton St Apt2
Westerly RI 02891

Call Sign: KA1SOG
Tobias M Goodman
41 East Ave
Westerly RI 02891

Call Sign: KA1TWI
Burleigh E Nickerson
41 East Ave
Westerly RI 028913113

Call Sign: N1LAB
James L Steadman
115 East Ave
Westerly RI 028913014

Call Sign: W1DAR
Ralph R Mele
2 Egret Ln
Westerly RI 028914418

Call Sign: N1IBA
Jonathan S Schreier
8 Fletcher Dr
Westerly RI 02891

Call Sign: KB1VPP
John D Merkel
10 Fletcher Dr
Westerly RI 02891

Call Sign: AJ1DM
John D Merkel
10 Fletcher Dr
Westerly RI 02891

Call Sign: WA1ZXZ
Robert W Crooks Jr.
2 Frontage Rd Unit 2
Westerly RI 02891

Call Sign: KB1OYN
Roy A Harley Jr

19 Gallop St
Westerly RI 02891

Call Sign: N1EOJ
Frederick A Weiss
7 Gallup St
Westerly RI 02891

Call Sign: N1FAA
Dorothy R Weiss
7 Gallup St
Westerly RI 028912552

Call Sign: W1DOT
Dorothy R Weiss
7 Gallup St
Westerly RI 028912552

Call Sign: W1ESK
Anton Obermann
45 George Street
Westerly RI 02891

Call Sign: AC5GI
Christopher Williamson
153 High St Unit 8
Westerly RI 028911782

Call Sign: KB1QBP
Michael Brancato
15 Holly Dr
Westerly RI 02891

Call Sign: WD1EMA
Michael T Brancato
15 Holly Dr
Westerly RI 02891

Call Sign: KB1ONJ
Peter M Deperry Jr
7 Horne Dr
Westerly RI 02891

Call Sign: KB1PMD
Peter M Deperry Jr

7 Horne Dr
Westerly RI 02891

Call Sign: N1LMA
Charles P Recchia
27 Horne Drive
Westerly RI 02891

Call Sign: WB1GTK
Frank X Pellicano
14 Jolly Ln
Westerly RI 02891

Call Sign: WA2LRL
Charles J Godberson
10 Laurel Hill Dr
Westerly RI 02891

Call Sign: KA1ZJF
Paul R Bishop
6 Ledward Ave
Westerly RI 02891

Call Sign: K1SHK
Raymond G Marra
3 Lofty Heights Rd
Westerly RI 02891

Call Sign: K1SQZ
Harvey L Dugas
19 Lorraine Rd
Westerly RI 02891

Call Sign: NP2AN
Geoffrey G Curtin
65 Margin St
Westerly RI 02891

Call Sign: KA1ZZP
Robert B Stadelmann
13 Marylou Ave
Westerly RI 02891

Call Sign: AA1XF
Carl W Reiner

8 Mountain Ave
Westerly RI 02891

Call Sign: K1RGF
Rosario V Miceli
2 Narragansett Ave
Westerly RI 02891

Call Sign: K1RLB
Nicholas W Ferrigno Sr
9 Nichols Ln
Westerly RI 02891

Call Sign: K1GOX
Raymond L Highland
17 North Dr
Westerly RI 028912916

Call Sign: N1KEG
Leslie S Goodman
69 Noyes Neck Rd
Weekapaug
Westerly RI 02891

Call Sign: K1MFJ
Joseph N Ballata
6 Old Woody Hill Rd
Westerly RI 02891

Call Sign: K1QN
Albert P Gerheim
1 Osprey Lane
Westerly RI 02891

Call Sign: N1VKK
Bryan E Pedersen
51 Pierce St Apt 3
Westerly RI 02891

Call Sign: KD4UVI
Charles H Dudley
81 Pierce St. #3
Westerly RI 02891

Call Sign: K1DAB

Dean A Bailey
43 Potter Hill Rd
Westerly RI 02891

Call Sign: KB1FXS
Dean A Bailey
43 Potter Hill Road
Westerly RI 02891

Call Sign: KB1ONH
Robert V Russell
51 Quannacut Rd
Westerly RI 02891

Call Sign: WD4OYF
Ronald D Ghen
4 Richard Cir
Westerly RI 02891

Call Sign: N1KZT
Robert T Gionet
2 Rock St
Westerly RI 02891

Call Sign: KB1SVD
Gary J Wright
24 Saratoga Ave
Westerly RI 02891

Call Sign: KB1IOW
Abba's House Amateur
Radio Club
57 Spruce St
Westerly RI 02891

Call Sign: W9OLY
Carroll D De Groff
8 Spruce Street Apt.1
Westerly RI 028911966

Call Sign: N1SRB
Harold J Rocketto
18 Stenton Ave
Westerly RI 02891

Call Sign: KA1JIB
Craig H Moody
34 Stuart St
Westerly RI 02891

Call Sign: KA1JIF
Lincoln D Moody
34 Stuart St
Westerly RI 02891

Call Sign: K1CHM
Craig H Moody
34 Stuart St
Westerly RI 02891

Call Sign: KB1QWW
Lynn M Moody
34 Stuart St
Westerly RI 02891

Call Sign: KA1BDM
Samuel J P Grills
7 Summer St
Westerly RI 028912242

Call Sign: KB1NKX
John T Ouderkirk Jr
60 Summer St
Westerly RI 028911961

Call Sign: N1ELK
John T Ouderkirk Jr
60 Summer St
Westerly RI 028911961

Call Sign: KB1RHD
Sally Hanson
60 Summer St
Westerly RI 02891

Call Sign: WY1M
Christopher P Tate
5 Sunrise Dr
Westerly RI 028912030

Call Sign: KB1LBB
David A Struzik
33 Terrace Ave
Westerly RI 02891

Call Sign: W1SLC
Walter R Hollis Jr
6 Timothy Dr
Westerly RI 02891

Call Sign: WY1E
John R Rudert Jr
14 Verdi Rd
Westerly RI 02891

Call Sign: W1GSH
Lawrence T Albert
15 Verdi Rd
Westerly RI 02891

Call Sign: KB1ONG
Elaine M Chicoria
25 West Beach Street
Westerly RI 02891

Call Sign: N1AEL
Wayne J Booker
29 Wicklow Road
Westerly RI 02891

Call Sign: KI4FAD
Mason B Merchant
13 Williams Avenue
Westerly RI 02891

Call Sign: W1MBM
Mason B Merchant
13 Williams Avenue
Westerly RI 02891

Call Sign: N1FRA
Douglas C Gent
139 Woodline Dr
Westerly RI 02891

Call Sign: N1OKU
Richard W Morrone Sr
Westerly RI 02891

Call Sign: KB1ONK
Joyce S Babbin
Westerly RI 02891

FCC Amateur Radio Licenses in Wickford

Call Sign: KB1HEU
Jean-Pierre Sauvain
146 Main St
Wickford RI 02852

Call Sign: KB1CCZ
Gary E Miller
181 W Main St
Wickford RI 02852

Call Sign: KB1DVK
Gordon W Fletcher
252 Wickford Point Rd
Wickford RI 02852

FCC Amateur Radio Licenses in Wood River Junction

Call Sign: W1DRL
Dewey R Lawing Jr
328 B Church St
Wood River Junction RI 02894

Call Sign: KA1VKC
Jack A Norris
863 Kings Factory Rd
Wood River Junction RI 02894

Call Sign: N1JAN
Jack A Norris
863 Kings Factory Rd.

Wood River Junction RI
02894

FCC Amateur Radio Licenses in Woodsocket

Call Sign: WP4EZF
Wilson D Marin
88 Bourdon Blvd
Woodsocket RI 02895

Call Sign: N1RWV
David A Eastwood
520 2nd Ave; Apt. #B-115
Woonsocket RI 028954181

Call Sign: KB1ASL
Shirley A Hodgkins
520 2nd Avenue Apt 209
Woonsocket RI 02895

Call Sign: KB1AOK
Phillip E Hodgkins
520 2nd Avenue Apt. 209
Woonsocket RI 02895

Call Sign: N1ZJK
Remo A Picchioni
531 Aylsworth Ave
Woonsocket RI 02895

Call Sign: N1OBM
Eliud Ortiz Jr
235 B Sixth Ave
Woonsocket RI 02895

Call Sign: N1JQG
Wilfrid R Niquette
81 Bayberry Rd
Woonsocket RI 02895

Call Sign: K1KEG
Kevin R Marshall
590 Bernon St
Woonsocket RI 02895

Call Sign: KU1P
Richard P Gagnon
749 Bernon St
Woonsocket RI 02895

Call Sign: KE4RBR
Mark C Jewell
148 Bernon St. -2
Woonsocket RI 02895

Call Sign: N1ZHO
August S Dellacona
301 Blackstone
Woonsocket RI 028951907

Call Sign: KB1KBH
Stephen Teper
20 Boyden
Woonsocket RI 028953002

Call Sign: N1NMX
Donald A Riendeau
110 Burnside Ave
Woonsocket RI 02895

Call Sign: N1XAE
Raymond E St Pierre
197 Capwell Ave
Woonsocket RI 028955905

Call Sign: KB2YPQ
Luke M Dusterhus
70 Cass Avenue Apt 1f
Woonsocket RI 02895

Call Sign: KA1CGL
Richard O Berard Sr
19 Circle St
Woonsocket RI 02895

Call Sign: KA1JIJ
Richard O Berard Jr
19 Circle St
Woonsocket RI 02895

Call Sign: KN1L
Jeanne M Berard
19 Circle St
Woonsocket RI 02895

Call Sign: K1ORM
Joseph A Beaudoin
177 Circle St
Woonsocket RI 028955547

Call Sign: K1PRY
Ernest E Guilbault
547 Clinton St Apt 907
Woonsocket RI 028953230

Call Sign: AA1OW
George Therien
547 Clinton St Apt 922
Woonsocket RI 02895

Call Sign: K1HFZ
Rene A Lamoureux
547 Clinton St Kennedy
Manor Apt217
Woonsocket RI 02895

Call Sign: W1DOR
Warren P Greene
547 Clinton St. Apt 803
Woonsocket RI 028953234

Call Sign: N1QAI
John G Glennon
460 Coe St
Woonsocket RI 02895

Call Sign: KD1QH
Lucien A Desrosiers
196 Congress St
Woonsocket RI 02895

Call Sign: KB1CSZ
Stephen W Dowling
48 Cooper Ave.

Woonsocket RI 02895

Call Sign: N1GQD
Roger A Guilbault
76 Cranston St
Woonsocket RI 02895

Call Sign: N1PSD
Nathan P Guilbault
76 Cranston St
Woonsocket RI 02895

Call Sign: KD1CD
Edward C Hamilton
2055 Diamond Hill Rd Apt
G
Woonsocket RI 028951521

Call Sign: N1UFS
David A Hetu
346 Dulude Ave
Woonsocket RI 02895

Call Sign: N1KRO
Dennis A Latini
429 East School St Apt 310
Woonsocket RI 02895

Call Sign: K1JEN
Jennifer A Galipeau
70 Ella Ave
Woonsocket RI 02895

Call Sign: K1OLB
Robert G Sacs I
310 Elm St
Woonsocket RI 028953472

Call Sign: AA1FE
Donald Lacroix
100 Front St Apt 205
Woonsocket RI 02895

Call Sign: N1WVY
Normand M Aubin

26 Garden St
Woonsocket RI 02895

Call Sign: W1ZFV
David Pascal
617 Gaskill St
Woonsocket RI 02895

Call Sign: N1NAW
Edwin M Warren
153 Grand St
Woonsocket RI 02895

Call Sign: N1ZFA
Thomas W Gingras
101 Grand St.
Woonsocket RI 02895

Call Sign: W1UZE
Laurent R Rheaume
130 Grove St
Woonsocket RI 02895

Call Sign: N1ZTH
Joseph A Brown Sr
473 Grove St Apt 5
Woonsocket RI 02895

Call Sign: N1FQD
Samuel J Adams
32 Hanton Rd Ns
Woonsocket RI 02895

Call Sign: KB1IEX
David R King
24 Hillview St
Woonsocket RI 02895

Call Sign: WA1VFP
Jules L Pignolet
103 Linden Ave
Woonsocket RI 02895

Call Sign: WV1VHF
Jules L Pignolet

103 Linden Ave
Woonsocket RI 02895

Call Sign: KB1ADK
James R Russell
139 Maple St
Woonsocket RI 02895

Call Sign: KA1EIU
George R Berard
314 Olo St
Woonsocket RI 02895

Call Sign: KB1EBJ
Philippe J Jacques
367 Orchard St
Woonsocket RI 02895

Call Sign: N1YWV
Richard F Balboni
37 Paradis Ave
Woonsocket RI 02895

Call Sign: KB1KKF
Bruce E Wood
877 Park Ave
Woonsocket RI 02895

Call Sign: W1BRU
Bruce E Wood
877 Park Ave
Woonsocket RI 02895

Call Sign: W1DDD
Blackstone Valley Amateur
Radio Club
154 Patton Rd
Woonsocket RI 02895

Call Sign: W1HW
David A St Onge
154 Patton Rd
Woonsocket RI 02895

Call Sign: KB1NQI

Lee M Lemoine
138 Piedmont St
Woonsocket RI 028956270

Call Sign: KB1OCV
W J Lemoine
138 Piedmont St
Woonsocket RI 028956270

Call Sign: K1LLL
W J Lemoine
138 Piedmont St
Woonsocket RI 028956270

Call Sign: KB1SXU
Tri State Repeater
Association
138 Piedmont St
Woonsocket RI 02895

Call Sign: K1TSR
Tri State Repeater
Association
138 Piedmont St
Woonsocket RI 02895

Call Sign: KB1ASK
Martha J Lauzon
68 Pine Street
Woonsocket RI 02895

Call Sign: KD1CA
Dennis A Lauzon
68 Pine Street
Woonsocket RI 02895

Call Sign: K1PRU
Joseph F Mahoney
262 Poplar St
Woonsocket RI 02895

Call Sign: KA1JHB
Gordon R Bouchard
8 Priscilla Rd
Woonsocket RI 02895

Call Sign: N1CRF
Nancy C Bouchard
8 Priscilla Rd
Woonsocket RI 028953826

Call Sign: W1HQV
Richard A Bouchard
8 Priscilla Rd
Woonsocket RI 02895

Call Sign: N1JIL
Edmund L Fox
660 Providence St
Woonsocket RI 02895

Call Sign: N1SEH
Richard A Tessier
301 Rathbun St
Woonsocket RI 02895

Call Sign: K1SWC
Leonidas A Gagne
242 Rhodes Ave
Woonsocket RI 02895

Call Sign: N1UFQ
Harold D Evers
31 Rutland St
Woonsocket RI 02895

Call Sign: W1SQM
George E Wilcox
463 S Main
Woonsocket RI 028955163

Call Sign: KB1BIG
Lucille F Rock
463 S Main St
Woonsocket RI 02895

Call Sign: KA1HIV
Michael A Mancuso
174 St Cecile Ave
Woonsocket RI 02895

Call Sign: W1GJN
Jean P Guilbault
4 St Joseph Street
Woonsocket RI 02895

Call Sign: K1YQZ
William T Kilcline Jr
1 Star Ave
Woonsocket RI 028951619

Call Sign: W1QUG
Charles R Masi
179 Star Ave
Woonsocket RI 02895

Call Sign: N1QPW
Alfred Tarvis Jr
123 Stoneham Dr
Woonsocket RI 02895

Call Sign: K1FLD
Armand E Lambert
144 Summer St
Woonsocket RI 02895

Call Sign: N1QCP
Maurice E Desrosiers
27 Summit Street
Woonsocket RI 02895

Call Sign: KB1SCF
John M Guilbault
41 Thomas St Apt 2
Woonsocket RI 02895

Call Sign: KB1QVE
Albert D Stadalski
350 Village Rd Apt 14
Woonsocket RI 02895

Call Sign: K1ETY
Albert D Stadalski
350 Village Rd Apt 14
Woonsocket RI 02895

Call Sign: KB1PLO
Norman E Blais
350 Village Rd Apt 15
Woonsocket RI 02895

Call Sign: KE1BZ
William J Gervais
136 Ward St
Woonsocket RI 02895

Call Sign: KA1INL
Andre N Genereux
31 Wilson Avenue
Woonsocket RI 02895

Call Sign: N1NDH
Steven N Dextraze
447 Winter St
Woonsocket RI 02895

Call Sign: N1NDI
Chris J Dancause
467 Wood Ave
Woonsocket RI 02895

Call Sign: N1FUY
Alfred F Gibau
527 Wood Ave
Woonsocket RI 02895

Call Sign: KB1RQJ
John W Bacon
66 Wood Ave Apt 2
Woonsocket RI 02895

Call Sign: KC1ZZ
Michael Carter
Woonsocket RI 02895

FCC Amateur Radio Licenses in Wyoming

Call Sign: W2CFW
Charles T Peterson

64 Baker Pine Rd
Wyoming RI 02898

Call Sign: N1WVZ
Timothy A Thayer
186 Carolina Nooseneck Rd
Wyoming RI 02898

Call Sign: N1VEZ
Everett J Lovenbury Jr
232 Carolinanooseneck Rd
Wyoming RI 02898

Call Sign: KB1QWV
Justina J Victorino
10 Chelsea Farm Dr
Wyoming RI 02898

Call Sign: KA1EVA
Michael H Grotzke
Meadowbrook W
Wyoming RI 02898

Call Sign: K1GSE
George S Edwards Jr
6 Whispering Pines Rd
Wyoming RI 028981217